D0554121

Aldous Huxley

and the Way to Reality

Aldous Huxley

and the Way to Reality

CHARLES M. HOLMES

Indiana University Press

BLOOMINGTON/LONDON

Published in Canada by Fitzhenry & Whiteside Limited, Don Mills, Ontario

Library of Congress catalog card number: 70-126211
ISBN: 253-10070-4

Manufactured in the United States of America

T O

Harold Denison Holmes

(1893-1959)

THE SIGNIFICANCE OF [MAN'S] . . . *outlook*
varies according as he sunders
himself into spirit and flesh,
into understanding and sensuality,
into soul and body,
into duty and inclination. . . .
There is no human existence without cleavage.

The mental situation today compels man,
compels every individual, to fight wittingly
on behalf of his true essence.

KARL JASPERS, Man in the Modern Age

We are all well on the way to
an existential religion of mysticism.

ALDOUS HUXLEY, "Shakespeare and Religion"

CONTENTS

Aldous Huxley about 1932 (*UCLA Library photo*).

On the reverse of this page, Huxley about 1960 (*George Kramer, UCLA photo*), and, with Swami Prabhavananda and Christopher Isherwood about 1947 (*Black Star Photo*).

PREFACE

Two years after Aldous Huxley's death in 1963, on the same day as President Kennedy's, Huxley's brother Julian published a collection of tributes and reminiscences.[1] *Aldous Huxley: A Memorial Volume* is richly rewarding, not so much for the critical comments on Huxley's work as for the vivid memories of Huxley the living man. Sybille Bedford describes the life of the Huxleys at their villa near Toulon, where picnics with such guests as Edith Wharton and the Paul Valérys followed periods of work on *Eyeless in Gaza* and *Beyond the Mexique Bay*. Humphry Osmond tells how, years later at a conference of psychiatrists, Huxley kept crossing himself every time a speaker referred to Sigmund Freud. Gervas a younger cousin, recalls the days at Hillside school; Julian's wife concentrates on Garsington, the setting of *Crome Yellow,* locale of the famous gatherings of Lady Ottoline Morrell; Anita Loos tells a riotous tale involving Bertrand Russell, Charlie Chaplin, a group of Indians, and Greta Garbo disguised as a tramp. More serious recollections are offered by Robert Hutchins, Leonard Woolf, Gerald Heard, and Isaiah Berlin. Surprisingly, these distinguished people seem almost to parrot each other in expressing their attitude toward Aldous Huxley the man. Again and again they refer to Huxley's gentleness, to his kindness, sweetness, and benevolence. To those who knew him best Huxley's friendship was a most meaningful part of their lives because, as even his Italian servants felt, he was not merely a learned and fascinating man, but a truly good one. Perhaps the most eloquent tribute came from Igor Stravinsky, who at the time was still too shocked by the loss of his "guiding spirit" to write more than a few brief lines.

The kind, sensitive, humble Huxley honored in these essays is the man of more recent memory, the Huxley of the nineteen-forties and fifties rather than of the years between the wars. A far more complicated person is revealed in Huxley's letters, a man who could see himself as "by nature extremely malicious"[2] and find in himself "great capacity for not being human,"[3] yet elsewhere claim that "friendship, love, whatever you like to call it is the only reality."[4] He could write to one correspondent with the detachment of the scientist he had wished to be, to another with indignant intensity, when faced with the proposed mutilation of one of his plays. He appears as the solicitous father indicting himself for earlier unconcern, as the admiring yet not uncritical friend of D. H. Lawrence, as a lover of Beethoven, a widower confident of his late wife's continuing existence, a descendant conscious of T. H. Huxley's attitude toward fools, a concerned observer of all the major problems facing the world. Most frequently, perhaps, he appears as a hurried professional writer who, forced to write sometimes avidly for money, had the next book in mind before the present one was finished; one who struggled in some of his books to meet high literary standards, yet became increasingly aware of the limitations of his gift.

The letters, with their new and varied images of Huxley, provide an extended and invaluable autobiography. The recent memoir by his second wife[5] focuses on the warmly affectionate husband, the courageous victim of cancer, the advocate of

mescaline and LSD. Ronald Clark's study of the whole family
helps to explain Aldous as the pacifist, the expatriate and the
human being who was "close to being a saint."[6] Yet the most
interesting and important Huxley remains the man who appears in his books. For the friends writing in the *Memorial
Volume* Huxley's *oeuvre* contains at best a part of the truth,
but for the reading public, for the literary tradition, for modern
culture his books are almost all that is available of it. In a special
sense, not merely the obvious one, all of Huxley's comments
and proposals, along with his novels, stories, plays and poems,
were shaped and predetermined by the man: Huxley was a
far more introspective, autobiographical writer than is generally realized. We seem to find in his books, particularly his
fiction, more of him revealed than in even the frankest of his
letters. One letter would seem to contradict this claim: "I have
almost no ideas about myself and don't like having them. . . . If
one spent one's time knowing oneself. . . . , one wouldn't have
any self to know. . . ." Huxley is referring, however, to "having
ideas about oneself in letters or conversation," not to self-projection and analysis in books. To him introspection is "a kind
of suicide," but his "profession is to commit hara-kiri every
publishing season," to "wreathe" his "entrails in elegant festoons—le style c'est l'homme—all over the bookstalls."[7] Huxley's work can be provocative, shallow, maddening, witty, sometimes moving; but it is simultaneously almost always
confessional.

As a few of the *Memorial Volume* essayists hint, Huxley ex-
emplified the condition of modern men; he lived, and did not
merely pronounce upon, our problems. And because he was a
remarkable human being, he lived them in a heightened, un-
usually significant way. He was clearly a bigger person than
most—not only in the massive head which brought him the
nickname "Ogie" (for Ogre) in his youth—but in the intensity
of his responses, the range of his knowledge and interest, the

power he developed to amalgamate and synthesize. As one friend put it, he was "tremendously complex"; to another he was an "exceptionally sensitive human instrument."[8] He undertook, in an anxious age, a long, complicated and anguished mental journey, and recorded it, often unconsciously, in the kaleidoscopic patterns of his work. And when he seems to turn away from the world in disgust, he reflects our occasional desire to turn somewhere else ourselves. When he seizes upon mescaline and ESP as keys to the truth, he comments on our wish to be, or our fear of being, metaphysically new and brave. And when he proclaims that there is order in the apparent chaos of our world, his discovery is one we are eager to share.

The book that follows is an analytical study of Huxley's work, beginning with the early poems and ending with *Island* and *Literature and Science*. My concern is with Huxley's books as expressions of his mental life—his beliefs, his hopes, his often irrational loves and hates and fears, and particularly the inner conflicts and divisions which plagued him for forty or fifty years. There are only a few signs of this inner division in his letters—a late parenthesis that "so many intellectuals" are "divided against" themselves,[9] a long discussion of techniques for psychological help,[10] references to one of his novels as "jejune and shallow and off the point,"[11] to his "besetting sin," including "the dread and avoidance of emotion."[12] Huxley often dealt with "Personality and the Discontinuity of the Mind." as an essay title in *Proper Studies* puts it. But a close reading of his work reveals in *him* a related interplay of forces, a remarkably intricate pattern of self-projections, a struggle to find ways to express, to mask, eventually to unite the factions in himself even as he observed the divided condition of men. These are parts of the story that I have tried to tell. Yet because this approach helps to explain the failures and successes, I have also tried to evaluate Huxley's achievements—to show to what degree the confessional element in his work led to critical insight, logical soundness, and aesthetically pleasing form. If the theme of conflict seems to be exaggerated, it is the theme Huxley himself chose to emphasize. It is also the clue to a complex, elusive, yet fascinating coherence in the apparent heterogeneity of his work. Huxley is fooled—by the world or by himself; he is tempted—by sirens or gods—betrayed and tempted again. But by the end of his odyssey, no longer plagued by inner division, he has found the way to an intellectual and spiritual home. *Island* is a final vision of both practical and ultimate truth.

I should like to thank Grover Smith, who made available the typescript of his *Letters of Aldous Huxley* before the book was published; George Wickes, for sending me or informing me about various useful Huxley materials; Bradford Cook, for valuable comments on part of an earlier version of this book; Cass Canfield, for permission to examine the Huxley files at Harper and Row; Ian Parsons of Chatto & Windus, for sending me a proof copy of the *Letters*; Mrs. Laura Archera Huxley, for granting copying permissions; John MacQueen, Albert F. McLean, Jr., and John and Marjorie Harrison, for their suggestions; Huston Smith, for his ideas about Huxley and for information about Huxley and Trabuco College; William J. Woestendiek, for information related to *Brave New World Revisited;* and Brooke Whiting, for answering many inquiries about the UCLA Aldous Huxley Collection.

I am also grateful to several institutions whose assistance helped make this study possible: Transylvania University, for several research grants and a sabbatical leave; the University of Pittsburgh, for an Andrew Mellon Postdoctoral Fellowship; and the libraries of Harvard University, the University of Michigan, the University of California at Los Angeles, Transylvania University, the University of Kentucky, the University of Pittsburgh, and Washington University.

My greatest debt, however, is to my wife.

C. M. H.

ACKNOWLEDGEMENTS

To ROUTLEDGE AND KEGAN PAUL *Ltd.*, for permission to quote passages from *Man in the Modern Age,* by Karl Jaspers.

To THE UNIVERSITY OF TEXAS PRESS, for permission to use in Chapter I material which appeared originally as "The Early Poetry of Aldous Huxley," in *Texas Studies in Literature and Language,* Fall 1966.

To HARPER & ROW, PUBLISHERS, *Incorporated,* Mrs. Laura Huxley, and CHATTO & WINDUS *Ltd.* for permission to quote passages from *Time Must Have a Stop* and *Island,* by Aldous Huxley.

To THE LIBRARY OF THE UNIVERSITY OF CALIFORNIA, Los Angeles, for permission to quote from their copy of the Trabuco College Prospectus.

To HUGH R. TREVOR-ROPER for permission to quote from a letter about *Grey Eminence.*

Aldous Huxley

and the Way to Reality

CHAPTER ONE

STRUGGLES WITH STYLE AND FORM:

From the Early Verse to *Crome Yellow*

In Aldous Huxley's "Eupompus Gave Splendour to Art by Numbers,"[1] an intelligent, stable, normal man tells the story of his odd but brilliant friend named Emberlin. Emberlin, we learn, has been studying Eupompus, the fifth century B.C. painter mentioned by Ben Jonson, who actually did base his splendid canvases on numbers. One pictured a three-eyed, three-armed, three-naveled human being accompanied by thirty-three thousand "distinctly limned" black swans; others grouped people so as to imitate exactly the various constellations. Eupompus' final painting was designed to symbolize Pure Number, in the form of a "design of planes radiating out from a single point of light." Emberlin's interest in these works, however, has passed well beyond mere curiosity. He himself now counts whenever he has the chance—steps, stairs, and the number of tiles in a Holborn public lavatory. Eupompus killed himself before he finished his final masterpiece; Emberlin, we are told triumphantly, will also soon be mad.

There is no better introduction to the work of Aldous Huxley than "Eupompus," first published in an undergraduate review. It has the bizarre appeal of so much of the early work, the esoteric fecundity whereby Huxley could expand an obscure fragment of knowledge into a distinctive, sophisticated tragi-comedy of the mind. Its medium is the lucid urbanity of the early novels, which in a decade were to bring Huxley international fame. But most important and most surprising, like nearly everything he wrote, this weird tale is autobiographical. Under the zany surface of the story of Eupompus and Emberlin we can discern a portrait—or rather two portraits—of Aldous Huxley.

Huxley himself had the qualities his story attributes to Emberlin. He was "immensely erudite"; Arnold Bennett called his knowledge "inconceivable, incredible, and fantastic."[2] His books and essays were always strikingly, sometimes showily allusive, initially to figures (well known or unknown) in French literature, painting and Western philosophy, and ultimately to mysticism, ecology, and the Buddhist Tantra. Like Emberlin he was often "a mine of irrelevant information." Osbert Sitwell, speaking of Huxley's hospital visits, recalls the strange comments on Octopoi reading Ovid and making love,[3] doubtless gleaned from the *Britannica* Huxley rummaged in on his travels. For years, the record shows, Huxley also followed "Emberlin's way" of putting into practice "the ideas that he finds in books." He was (by his own admission) the Philip Quarles of *Point Counter Point*, whose "choice of moulds" depended largely on the author he happened to be reading: the "mould" for several years was D. H. Lawrence, later replaced by Meister Eckhart and Gerald Heard, before Huxley developed his own remarkable final synthesis. Finally, Huxley regularly succumbed to what he later called the "Higher Life," in "Eupompus" the "glassily perfect universe of ideas." The texture of the novels themselves suggests the degree of this surrender—the shimmering intellectual surface of *Crome Yellow* along with the tedious discourse in *After Many a Summer Dies the Swan*. Though Huxley worried publicly about this leaning in *Point Counter Point* and *Eyeless in Gaza,* he half consciously defended it in *The Perennial Philosophy* and illustrated it in composing his final statement, *Island*. Even Emberlin's love of Pure Number reappears, or at least Eupompus' attempt to capture it in paint. The radiating planes of Eupompus' final painting prefigure some of Huxley's later symbols: the twin cones that triumphantly end the novel *Eyeless in Gaza*, the pattern of telegraph poles and wheel tracks Sebastian sees in *Time Must Have a Stop*.

But Huxley also appears in Emberlin's friend, the narrator of the tale, who is not a caricature of the reality to be, but a kind of idealized, wished-for-self. He is a self-critical opposite, not odd like Emberlin but more conventional. He can recognize the danger of Emberlin's mental gyrations, see things in proportion, live in closer relationship to other human beings. He stands at the end of the tale as a champion of a sane humanity. He is the more spontaneous and balanced intellectual Huxley apparently often wished to be, perhaps the man his brother Julian had in mind as "the greatest humanist of our perplexed era."[4] His analog appears only rarely in Huxley's fiction, where shades of Emberlin are the ones we most frequently see; he sounds more like Huxley's hostile critics than like Huxley himself. Yet he too is both a Huxley creation and a Huxley self-projection. "Eupompus Gave Splendour to Art by Numbers" is not merely an amusing, exaggerated, and critical self-portrait, but one self-portrait observing and triumphing over another.

Such autobiographical dialectic is the most persistent pattern in Huxley's work, from the poetry of the Oxford youth to the *Island* of the courageous, distinguished, dying man. His large public, his friends and his opponents, usually envisioned a writer addressing the world in a changing series of tones and modes—in satirical fiction or conventional argument, in bitterness or exhortation, in the frustration or excitement of the quest which completed his life. But simultaneously, more than anyone seems to have suspected, Huxley projected, addressed, and debated with himself. The least public of men, until the last years of his career, he was in a curious but intriguing way among the most public of modern writers. He left no journals so frank as Gide's, few poems so obviously personal as those of Yeats. Instead Huxley's books are a kind of Rosetta stone, a complex but decipherable index to a lonely, anguished, but successful mental journey. Much of his work shows him plagued by inner conflict, struggling to explore his identity. In all the genres at which he tried his hand, a divided Huxley is likely to be present, by implication if not as a kind of Emberlin. In the early years the conflict is internal, and the dialectic involves attitudes and values Huxley seems to be testing for himself.[5] But eventually Huxley's dilemma reverberates with meanings and parallels of significance for other men. For a while his conflict provided material for a particular kind of brilliant art, for the fiction which made him the leading ironist of his age. As his struggle became a search for the answer to ultimate questions, he scorned brilliance, ignored the "rules" of form, irritated the critics and lost his popular appeal. But he left behind the record of a spiritual and intellectual odyssey which ended with a total view, a vision of reality both transcendental and pragmatic.

The conflict Huxley, at twenty-two, projected in "Eupompus" was doubtless intensified by certain events of adolescence. Huxley was born in Surrey in 1894, the son of Leonard and Julia Arnold Huxley, with the richest possible intellectual heritage. His father was a biographer, poet, and editor; his paternal grandfather, of course, was Thomas Henry Huxley; his great uncle was Matthew Arnold; his aunt was the novelist, Mrs. Humphrey Ward; his older brother was to become a famous biologist and a challenging writer on his own. But Aldous was jolted by one shock after another. He was devoted to his mother; she died of cancer when he was fourteen. A few years later his brother Trev (Noel Trevenen), to him "one that was among the noblest and best of men,"[6] committed suicide. Aldous himself, a scholarship boy at Eton after preparing at Hillside school, was violently afflicted at sixteen with *keratitis punctata*, a disease of the eyes.[7] He was tutored, he learned to read books and even music in Braille, he also typed out a novel—which, though he thought it was good, was lost before it was read by him or anyone else.[8] After two years, able to read with one eye and a magnifying glass, Huxley went down to Oxford and entered Balliol, no longer to become a doctor as he had planned, but to read English literature and philology. He took his degree in 1915, then finished out the war cutting wood at the Morrells' Garsington, working briefly for the Admiralty and the Air Board, and teaching at a school at Derby, and at Eton. At Garsington he met and fell in love with a Belgian girl, Maria Nys; in 1919, after almost two years of separation but with Huxley's literary career already begun, they married.[9] Though within a decade Huxley would know international fame, the period of blindness, even more than family deaths, had left deep marks. Since it "had the effect of isolating" him during adolescence, he once said, it was the single most important event of his life.[10] Years later he wrote to his son about "dust and aridity and a hard shell that makes communication . . . difficult," which raised problems during the early years of his marriage.[11] "Keratitis punctata shaped and shapes me," he told a friend; but he in his turn "made . . . use of it."[12]

"Eupompus Gave Splendour to Art by Numbers," an exhibit of two contrasting Huxley selves, is also almost a diagram of the first years of Huxley's career: Emberlin is a poet; so, at first, was Huxley—to one critic "among the most promising" of the younger poets of the time.[13] Emberlin has composed in various poetic styles; shifts in style are the distinguishing attribute of Huxley's verse. When the narrator prefers Emberlin's earlier "young ecstatic fashion" he has defined a style of Huxley's first collection, *The Burning Wheel*;[14] when Emberlin wants to destroy the volume he has produced, he suggests the Huxley who rejected (temporarily) his own romantic manner. The narrator regrets forgetting the poems of Emberlin in French, so well suited is the language to Emberlin's "peculiar" muse; four of Huxley's poems appear in French in *Jonah*.[15] And Emberlin's "curious" sonnet to the figure of a princess is, verbatim, the *Jonah* "Minoan Porcelain," by Huxley.

Though only a few Huxley poems have any permanent value, together they tell an interesting and indispensable story. They define even more clearly than the letters the unusual complexities with which Huxley's odyssey began, as his need to express himself became entangled with the problem of how to do so. They tell the story of their own inadequacy as an expressive medium even before Huxley discovered the "formidable and lovely freedom"[16] of the novel. But they also reveal much of the very structure of Huxley's mind, the traits that shaped almost all the work to follow.

I

As the early letters to his brother Julian show, Aldous was writing verses—amusing ones—by the time he was thirteen. A "most beautiful ode" celebrates Julian's coming of age;[17] a Noyesian imitation, two years later, pictures amoebae groping in the Balliol twilight, "Waiting for their enemy who wields the microscope."[18] In the published poetry, however, beginning after the period of shock and isolation, humor is less evident than another quality. Huxley's first desires, in "Home-Sickness . . . From the Town,"[19] are to "Feel goat hair growing thick and redolent," to watch his nymph girl's "moony floating flanks," to have us join him in drinking savagery and lust from mother nature's "wolfish teats." Yet a few months later, in *The Burning Wheel*, we find Arcadian wood-moths, flowers, and lutes; oxen "dewlap-deep" in the meadows; and a lady whose eyes hold all of the divine the poet has ever known. The most obvious trait of the earliest verse is inconsistency—inconsistency which strongly hints at inner division.

It would be foolish to identify the themes and attitudes of Huxley's verse with the whole mental life of the Oxford student, the Eton teacher, the young husband of Maria. The inconsistency of the poems has its parallels in the letters, and is obviously typical of almost any youth. It is the later work, the ultimate pattern of Huxley's career, that marks his poetic inconsistency as a most important symptom, not merely the sign of an inevitable but temporary stage. Though Huxley had not yet developed the intense seriousness of his later work, he saved something for his verse that his letters do not reveal, a way or ways of looking at himself that his intimates could probably know only momentarily, or in diluted form. Huxley himself saw "on every page" of *The Burning Wheel* "a deceased personality." Only a few months after publication, he found rereading "like going through my own private Morgue where every alcove is occupied by a corpse of myself. And that's only the corpses which could be shewed in public."[20]

"Escape," "Sentimental Summer," and their ilk, for all their banality, are a gesture toward the ideal; "Home-Sickness ... ", on the other hand, exaggerates but recognizes the earthly, the actual, the real. Like Shelley and other romantics a century before, Huxley saw a clash between the two. His poetry presents the ideal as beauty, as love, or as spirit and the real as the disappearance or transience of beauty, the loss of love, sometimes replaced by lust, or the ugly facts of the surrounding material world. Even more alarming than this disturbing clash is Huxley's feeling that his own soul is involved. Shelley could separate his unhappy personal life from his idealized visions of a reformed and better world; Huxley found both the ideal and the real within. Though he has been called a "frustrated romantic,"[21] he was inwardly split for most of his life even more than Keats or Byron or Coleridge. Only rarely could he even visualize an untarnished ideal, given such unpleasant realities as sexual lust, political power, spiritual emptiness, even —his own included—personality. The ideal had to become the ultimate truth of the mystics, the silence beyond all actuality. Though in Huxley's final years the cleavage disappeared, he began as the poem "Contrary to Nature and Aristotle" has it: his soul was an amphisbaena, a two-headed serpent looking in both directions at once.

Inconsistencies point to the inner split in Huxley; the split then produces further inconsistencies. One head of his soul's amphisbaena "Turns to the daytime's dust and sweat" while the other creeps toward solace in the ideal world of books. Sometimes books are not a true solution, for they can produce, in "Vision," the "black disease" of doubt. Their opposite, the bustling world, may even be the answer; were he to die, says Huxley in "The Choice," he would deliberately pick a noisy place to lie in where the world's activity would shake his "sluggish being." More surprising, however, than these contradictions is Huxley's own reaction to them; he is disturbed by what he finds in the world and in himself, but not by the inconsistencies in his own response. Whereas Yeats needed poetry for symbolically resolving conflict, Huxley merely found it a comfortable medium of self-expression. As a man he may have been searching for inner harmony; as a poet he obviously wanted a usable, original, pleasing style. The struggle for style, continuing throughout the early verse, helps to define the struggle for self, lasting most of Huxley's life.

Huxley's search for style has clearly begun in the symbolist experiment of "The Burning Wheel." The real-ideal conflict is symbolically generalized, as the opposition of life and death, the tension between activity and calm. Weary of turning, painfully spinning, the wheel of life agonizingly yearns to rest. A flame is begotten, somehow gains and then loses "bitterness," until death arrives to wake it and "once again" beget the yearning wheel, which again will search for "that vast oblivious peace." Important symbols appear occasionally in later works —the crystal of quiet Gumbril speaks of so urgently in *Antic Hay,* the twin cones, meeting at their tips, that embody all meaning at the end of *Eyeless in Gaza.* Yet neither in poetry nor in fiction was Huxley primarily a symbolist.

A kind of "romantic" style is far more common in Huxley's verse, a superannuated version of the manner perfected a century before. Surely Emberlin's earlier style, the one preferred by his narrator-friend, it is easily recognized by the direct, unguarded expression of emotion, by supposedly "poetic" phrases and words, by imprecise and worn-out metaphors. We find it, of course, when Huxley can believe in his ideal, when he can see "loveliness in a web of magic mesh," a "cross-weft harmony of soul and flesh." But just as frequently it expresses his disillusionment, his sense of the real, the unpleasant, victorious over the imagined, the ideal: " . . . all the heaven that one time dwelt in me/Has fled, leaving the body triumphing." Most of the poetry in this romantic style is buncombe, soon to be parodied by Huxley himself in *Crome Yellow,* when Denis Stone idealizes Anne as "The Woman who was a Tree."[22] Yet the romantic attitude continues to reappear, from the visions of Gumbril in the early novel, *Antic Hay,* to Huxley's final utopian dreams in *Island.*

Huxley also tried a simple dialectic, a style embodying versified argument or discussion, with no requirement that the argument be resolved. In "The Walk" He and She engage a conversational struggle over the significance of routine suburban life. They do not disagree about what they see on their stroll—meat and vegetables time and again, and mumblings of people engaged in weekly prayer—but rather over the nature and possible presence of God. To the man the pitiful old Infinite is dead; to the woman the divine, though in another dimension, still exists. Yeats in his dialectic poems usually awarded the victory, letting Homer and his Heart defeat von Hügel and his Soul. Huxley, on the other hand, merely argues with himself: in "The Walk" we do not learn what he finally concludes. Still without the will to believe that Yeats had never lacked, Huxley frequently seems to be nurturing his conflict, almost preserving it as a subject for his poems.

Huxley soon adapted his dialectic style into the sparkling conversations of *Crome Yellow* and *Those Barren Leaves*. But his fourth, "ironic" style—the one that Emberlin now prefers —was even more congenial, and the voice his public soon most eagerly wanted to hear. It became the trademark of his early fiction, the tone of *Point Counter Point*, even the very conception of *Brave New World*. Suggested as early as "Home-Sickness . . . From the Town," with its "debile" women and allusions to Rousseau and Keats, the style depends on the ironic contrast born of the unexpected, in the form of such learned allusions and esoteric words.[23] Its irony also involves setting the real against the ideal by collecting human specimens for a poetical zoo. The two-headed serpent of Huxley's soul lives there; so does the creature of "The Ideal Found Wanting," the unromantic, weird, wingless apteryx bird. "Mole" uses that smallish animal to allegorize the life of man, while "Two Realities" transforms the soul into the largest creature of the earth. When an idealist sees as "splendid" a blazing yellow-and-scarlet wagon, the realist supplies that adjective to a child kicking a turd. A grotesque, zoological pair of stanzas follows:

[10

Our souls are elephants, thought I,
  Remote behind a prisoning grill,
With trunks thrust out to peer and pry
And pounce upon reality;
  And each at his own sweet will

Seizes the bun that he likes best
And passes over all the rest.

In such verses does the family gene of biologist appear.

II

WHEN HUXLEY JUXTAPOSES "treasured things" and "golden memories" with turdkicking children and souls as elephants' snouts, he is obviously unsettled, perhaps thoroughly confused. Stylistic variety, however, led to further complications: Huxley's best verse demanded his ironic style, sincerity the more candid but less effective romantic or dialectic. In Huxley's first poetry for *Wheels*,[24] Edith Sitwell's animated, iconoclastic annual, the dialectic style seems to predominate. While the poet, in "The Life Theoretic," has been "fumbling over books/ And thinking about God and the Devil and all," others have been struggling in the world, or kissing the women with their "brazen faces like battering-rams." "God knows," he ends in inconclusive (and ineffective) fashion, "perhaps after all the battering-rams are right."[25] In "Retrospect," like the anti-heroes of the novels, the poet is plagued by "fears and jealousies and doubts" and tries to predict his attitude at forty. Again he ends in unresolved and formless fashion: "One will amuse oneself, decidedly . . . !" Yet even though his ironic style inhibited such candidness, Huxley seems to have recognized it led to better poetry. The result was a new element of conflict, the clash between sincerity and the desire to write good verse.

In a later essay, "Sincerity in Art," Huxley tried to avoid this new horn of his dilemma. Being sincere, he claimed, is not "a moral choice between honesty and dishonesty," but rather "mainly an affair of talent," a matter of "possessing the gifts of psychological understanding and expression."[26] It demands only a side step in logic to assume that talent is the result of sincerity, or at least that talent is the more important to show. The writer does not have to expose his feelings, to explore his deeper self, to heed the cries of his truest inner voice. He merely needs to use his talent, to compose the most skillful, the most carefully polished poems.

Hence in the dozen poems of the slim, rare volume *Jonah* (1917) the dialectic and the romantic styles have all but disappeared. Aided by the startling imagination of Arthur Rimbaud, Huxley began to add creatures to his weird, ironical zoo. In one Rimbaldien fantasy, "Behemoth," the huge beast sprawls asleep while "bold Ethiops," creeping up his flank, brew in his navel strength-imparting wine. In another, "Zoo Celeste," composed in Emberlin's French,[27] a familiar Huxley motif has been transformed. The "ideal" in this fantastic, supernatural garden is an ape who flaunts the "dazzling azure" of his rump. Other inhabitants of Huxley's zoo also appear. Elephants get drunk from the black milk they suck from a negress; whales dream on the flower-filled water, their crystal spray falling on lotus blossoms bathed in perfume; Behemoth this time walks on the golden shore, and whole new universes are produced from time to time, each equipped with a conceited little Almighty. The world of Rimbaud's famous "Après le Déluge," where a hare prays through a spider's web to the rainbow and "Madame*** sets up her piano in the Alps," is larger, more dazzling, more varied than Huxley's zoo, and his poem a more remarkable imaginative achievement. But "Zoo Celeste" is hardly less fantastic and less odd.

Rimbaud suggested, besides motifs and subjects, ways of

rendering ironically the imagined and the ideal. Jules Laforgue, to the young Huxley "one of the great poets of modern
times,"[28] helped him to find a congenial tone and to apply the
ironic style to himself. Laforguian, bored self-deprecation is
as evident in *Jonah* as Rimbaldien fantasy. Laforgue's Lord
Pierrot responds to a woman's love with a comment on the sum
of the angles of a triangle; the poet of Huxley's "The Betrothal
of Priapus," intrigued by the aroma of his lady's clothes and
hair, would like to swoon in languor yet responds with hideous
belching. "Sententious Song" ironically equates two kinds of
beauty: the "gorgeous buttocks of the ape" and "Autumn sun-
sets exquisitely dying." "Minoan Porcelain," the poem composed by Emberlin, combines a hint of Rimbaldien fantasy
with Laforgue's ironic attitude toward love—in a vocabulary
easily recognized as Huxley's. Rouge is "fard," overflow is
"spilth," and a small jar has become a "gallipot." In the title
poem, a similar poetic merger, Jonah from his seat on a kidney
can see "Many a pendulous stalactite/Of naked mucus," and
"whorls and wreaths/And huge festoons of mottled tripes."
To write such poems Huxley had to subjugate sincerity to his
talent. They do not represent the persistent attitudes of the
"romantic" poems, nor do they even hint at the continuing
struggle within.

Nevertheless, the *Jonah* poems involved or suggested a kind
of compromise whereby Huxley could write effectively yet
not totally stifle inner conflict: he could use his clever, ironic,
exaggerated style as an inverse kind of "sincere" poetic mask.
The poet, in a sense, is there for all to see. But his deeper concerns, his sensitivities are hidden; he is protected by his style
even in the act of self-expression. Wearing the mask he could
make gestures toward the sincere while composing his best
ironic poems. In doing homage to Laforgue, seen as also split
by a search for the ideal, Huxley may seem to write with un-
masked candor. Still living with two amphisbaenic heads,

again contrary "to Nature and to father Aristotle," he admits he has made himself rather ridiculous—but the "Hommage À Jules Laforgue" was published only in French. In a letter to his father he seems to want to reject the personal. Anticipating Eliot's theory of the objective correlative, he is "more and more . . . unsatisfied with what is merely personal in poetry" and wants to "re-objectify . . . thoughts and judgments" about the outer world "in a new world of fancy and imagination."[29] In the new world, however—under a mask—is Huxley himself. In "The Contemplative Soul," for example, he sees his soul as a fish. Since a danger awaits if she should try to swim upward, she steers her "fabulous gargoyle nef" many fathoms below the surface, or else merely sits still to contemplate. Perhaps Huxley is suggesting the appeal of mysticism, but his secret is hidden by the comical, self-deprecating mask.

III

THOUGH IN *Jonah* Huxley had forged a style for masked, partial self-expression, he employed it only briefly and still without consistency. For the 1918 cycle of *Wheels,* ignoring all of his previous styles, Huxley wrote prose poems imitating Rimbaud's *Illuminations.*[30] The zodiac beasts of "The Merry-Go-Round" briefly recall the Huxley zoo, yet the most important poem is the glowing, lyrically reflective "Beauty." In this search simultaneously for a way of living in the world with minimum conflict, and for a posture that will help him to create, Huxley speaks with the frankness we do not find in *Jonah.* He suggests that he is tempted to be a cynic, to flaunt his discovery that the ideal is mocked by the real and not to hide his idealism beneath a comic mask. When he finds not only Helen but Cressida in Troy, he admits knowing all about the "damning Theory of woman." The brotherly world to follow the successful quest for permanent beauty will include

eating and drinking, "Marrying and giving in marriage," but
also "taking and taken in adultery." The only true poets are
centaurs, he concludes, with their bellies close to the ground
and their heads up in the air. Huxley wears no mask, assumes
no ironical pose.

Yet even cynicism is but an alternative, a temporary phase.
In *The Defeat of Youth, and Other Poems,*[31] the opening son-
nets (the title poems) directly avow the cynical view. They
redescribe Huxley's earlier idyllic view of love; reaffirm his
idealized vision of true beauty; trace the change of love to lust
in consummation; and leave the weary poet disillusioned, now
in sight of a very different truth. Apparently stuck with his
earliest, least effective, romantic style, Huxley added other
trite and sentimental poems. More frequently, however, the
grotesque, ironic style is used—with esoteric words like "quotidian" and "crapulous," and a lady whose soul has "a slabby-
bellied sound" which rubs itself upon "the rind of things."
Again Huxley appears with his piscatorial mask, "remote and
happy, a great goggling fish." As if to reassert his need for
irony, he also reprinted "Minoan Porcelain," perhaps the best
ironic poem in *Jonah.* Not surprisingly, Aldous wrote Julian's
wife, it was "hard to judge" *The Defeat of Youth,* and he won-
dered whether one of his selves was "a sentimentalist . . . a
hero of romance . . . [or] a bon bourgeois."[32] Like the first, this
third book is bewildering in its contrasts and contradictions.

Nevertheless, *The Defeat of Youth* apparently served as a
kind of creative catharsis, an almost wholly successful purge
of all the less effective styles. In *Leda,*[33] Huxley's fourth collection, and in his final work for *Wheels,*[34] the ironic becomes the
characteristic voice. When the ragtime of "Frascati's" "swoons"
to a waltz, the poet sits blissfully with his lady, "quietly sweating palm to palm." When another heroine thrills to her lover's
supposedly "God-like" passion, he is really calculating the cost
of lunch, and the total expense she will put him to in a year.[35]

Huxley again appears exposed (yet hidden) under his mask, especially in the four self-deprecating "Philosopher's Songs." In the first, he is "a poor degenerate" inferior to the ape— except in his mind, which is itself

> . . . a nimbler beast
> Possessing a thousand sinewy tails,
> A thousand hands, with which it scales,
> Greedy of luscious truth, the greased
>
> Poles and the coco palms of thought . . .

In the fifth, he is the one sperm who happened to survive:

> And among that million minus one
> Might have chanced to be
> Shakespeare, another Newton, a new Donne—
> But the One was Me.

And in the second he tells his Lesbia that if he should ever take his life, his body "Would drift face upwards on the oily tide/ With the other garbage, till it putrified." Since hers would float face down modestly, exposing only its buttocks, it is obvious that this "best of worlds" has been carefully planned.

Such amusing grotesquerie masks the growing inner conflict more evident in other poems of love and lust. Desiring now to accept and now to reject the flesh, Huxley explored the problem in experiments with poetic narrative. The expansive, elegant blank verse of "Leda," a much admired poem,[36] offers in Leda herself another vision of "perfect loveliness," and in Jove not only superhuman power but a human restlessness and an irresistible sensual itch. Like the parade of women who soon will people Huxley's novels, Leda is unable and unwilling to resist. Even centuries ago, the implication is, the gross forces of life destroyed the virginal ideal. In "Soles Occidere et Redire Possunt," a Huxley projection (lying in bed) talks to himself

[16

in dialectic. An idealized dream battles with an approaching "quotidian" task; he reads a letter from a "heavenly vision" of his temple, who is also a "votary of the copulative cult"; and, after abandoning a poem about the difficulty of catching truth, he walks through the city and its "lumps of human meat," meditating about the cesspool in himself and the "mounds of flesh and harlotry" outside. Both poems were abortive efforts, however, in Huxley's struggle to find the proper mode for self-projection. The rhythms of "Soles" were cacophanous and jerky; the more pleasing blank verse of "Leda" was wedded to a distant past. Earlier, dialectic had made possible the frankest revelation of self, yet the self was what Huxley often most deeply wanted to mask. The ironic style provided the mask and produced effective poems, yet its economy and indirectness acted to inhibit full expression. Much of what he had written, Huxley told Edward Marsh in 1920, he found "strange and undesirable—the result of . . . following a spiral inwards, instead of outwards." Even this metaphor Huxley found "only partially comprehensible."[37] In trying to understand and express himself in verse, Huxley had found no poetic style or mode that really worked. Perhaps the answer could be found in drama or fiction.

IV

In 1918, while Huxley was still primarily a writer of verse, he thought of plays as the only literary form for making money, and he was "determined to make writing pay."[38] When he published *Limbo* (1920), the volume in which "Eupompus" was reprinted, he included "Happy Families," a miniature "symbolic farce." Though the play, dashed off hastily,[39] surely never made a shilling, it makes clearer than ever before Huxley's interest in masks and the problem of the divided self. The two families in the play are really only two maladjusted selves, each unhappily divided into four. Aston J. Tyrrell, capable only of learned discourse, has a black brother to express his sensuality, another brother to supply detached sarcastic comments, and a ventriloquist's dummy to be his social mask. Topsy Garrick, besides her dummy, has two sisters—one to write maudlin poems and represent her fear and virtue, the other to signify her unfulfilled desire. The families enter, to the strains of a waltz, a near-jungle of exotic, evil flowers; a dialogue showing and masking sexual inhibition follows; the climax occurs when, over Aston's shoulder, the Negro kisses Topsy. A virtually worthless play, "Happy Families" is yet an important autobiographical projection—the weirdest example of several important themes—sex, the divided self, even the problem of sentimental verse.

The only other play of the period Huxley bothered to collect treats the same themes, but with the selves back inside one body again. "Permutations Among the Nightingales"[40] explores the life of Sidney Dolphin—whose surname, a transmigration of Huxley's soul-as-a-fish, is but one of many echoes of the Huxley projected in verse. Shy, detached, yet sometimes maudlin and sometimes a "gargoyle," Sidney is wholly unable to judge his poems. "They may be merely the ingenious products of a very cultured and elaborate brain."

Not drama but fiction, however, made Huxley's writing pay, for the happy reason that it best satisfied his needs. Perhaps Huxley might have flourished in the theater of the absurd: "Happy Families" includes absurdist actions and "Permutations Among the Nightingales" has an Ionescan ring. Yet in drama self-expression must dissolve in dialogue, and a controlling theme takes precedence over the author's personal voice. During these early years the subjective, self-examining force was too strong for Huxley to find a proper outlet in drama. Fiction, he soon learned, was clearly the ideal mode. He could separate and embody a number of "selves" in fiction, combine and distribute them in any number of ways. But he could also, to a degree impossible in a play, invent a narrator to project himself, to shape his reader's attitude, to give himself the freedom to say what he wished to say. Having already explored these advantages in "Eupompus," he rapidly produced several collections of stories and tested the even more flexible form of the novel.

Of the five new stories in the first collection, *Limbo*, the most revealing is probably "The Farcical History of Richard Greenow." Whereas in "Happy Families" Aston J. Tyrrell is quartered, Richard Greenow is severed only in two. In the daytime Greenow attends first Aesop (probably Eton) College, then eventually Oxford; dislikes the masses but thinks highly of Fulke-Greville; and behaves as a serious, rational person of taste, intellect, and "powers of malicious irony." But when he has gone to bed and thinks he is asleep, he becomes his other personality, "Pearl Bellairs"—an ultra-romantic sentimentalist who spends the night writing highly marketable trash. The split is often amusing, yet also meaningful, since the activities of both can be traced to those of Huxley himself. But Huxley by the way he narrates the tale obscures the split: sometimes he seems to sympathize with Greenow, sometimes he treats Greenow as a convenient critical device. He uses Greenow's experience to take a crack at public schools; he shows Greenow personifying the "Life Theoretic" clash of thought and action; and in a scene where Greenow is "analyzed by a psychotherapist friend," he communicates his lifelong dislike of Sigmund Freud—unaware while he vents such fixations that the form of his tale is being destroyed. The "freedom" of fiction, we recall, Huxley found "formidable" as well as "lovely." He still was faced with the dilemma of the poems—the struggle between sincerity of self-expression on the one hand, and aesthetic control, or "style" on the other. His handling of point of view determined the result. In defining the narrator and the narrator's attitude toward others, Huxley could produce (as in "Richard Greenow") expressive, loosely structured failures or disciplined, less-than-sincere works of art.

The best stories in *Limbo* employ as narrators learned, urbane observers of life, much like the narrator-friend of Emberlin—idealized men rather than omniscient, mildly ironical projections. In "Cynthia," for example, one of the most intriguing stories, the narrator tells us a tale of his friend Lykeham. He captures the setting, this time at Oxford's "Swellfoot" College, by noting contrasting sounds, casually describing them with the technical jargon of music. The college bell was "shouting a deep E flat, with a spread of under-and-over-tones," while Lykeham's guitar "gibbered shrilly and hysterically in D-natural." The narrator learns that Lykeham has just held hands with a "frozenly virginal" goddess, a huntress Cynthia or Diana who has convinced him that he too is divine. Learnedly but unsuccessfully, the two men puzzle over the Olympian meaning of Lykeham's name. Two weeks later, appropriately during a moonlit walk, Lykeham spots his goddess on a distant hill. The narrator joins in the wild race to arrest her, turns away from the couple's "unequivocal" embraces, and checks his mythology again in Lemprière. By Lykeham's return he has the puzzle solved, and laughingly whispers "Goatfoot" (or satyr) in his ear.

Huxley projects himself in "Cynthia" as interested but un-involved, as a narrator who shows no sign of inner conflict or discontent. But though he is therefore an abstracted, false version of Huxley the man, he is nevertheless an appealing person, a man of both morality and taste. He is faced, of course, with a version of the problem of sex and lust: Lykeham is a lecher, Cynthia a pick-up. But he does not treat Lykeham as Huxley later treated Gerry Watchett, the vicious, heartless woman-hunter of *Eyeless in Gaza*. Sparing us the details of Lykeham's fornication, he regards the act instead with comic irony: "it is not for a mere mortal," he tells us, "to look on at the embracements of the gods," And though he borrows here Lykeham's mythological disguise, he will not allow Lykeham's trite lyricism to stand. He interrupts Lykeham's talk of "swooning away" and the meeting of eyes, of "rapturous" happiness while holding hands in the dark, with a comment on the "awful novelist's expression," and the image from the ironic poem "Frascati's" of the lovers sweating "quietly . . . palm to palm." From the beginning he wins our sympathy by some disarming remarks on himself, and a knowing reference to "our monstrous century." His early comments on music and, later, on letters, mark him as acute, sensitive, and civilized. The problem of sex and the love of erudition are brilliantly modulated through his sensibility into fully successful comic art.

v

SHORTLY AFTER *Limbo* was published, Huxley told his London friends about a Peacockian novel he was writing.[41] His choice of models was indeed a happy one. Combining the strategy of "Cynthia" with the greater expressiveness of earlier failures, Huxley escaped with the help of Peacock from his psycho-aesthetic dilemma. *Crome Yellow* (London: Chatto & Windus, 1921), the most delightful book of his career, was so popular that it loosed him from the social bonds of London to live and work largely in Italy.[42] His Peacockian oddities, gathered for a house-party at the country estate of Crome, owe their existence to the fantastic Ottoline Morrell, hostess sooner or later to Lawrence, Bertrand Russell, the Bloomsburies and others at her manor house near Oxford, the famous Garsington.[43] Huxley's sister-in-law has written sensitively of his visits to the house when she was "governess-companion" of the Morrells' son. With Maria Nys, his future wife, too far away to visit, Huxley "mooned about the place, silent and bottled-up" and inhabited a lonely, brooding private world.[44] However, when the time came to transform Garsington into *Crome Yellow*, the War was over and Maria had married him; he was able to synthesize old fragments of self and old concerns into a unified comedy of inimitable texture and tone.

Denis Stone, the novel's painfully self-conscious "younger poet," is an obvious projection of Aldous Huxley. Almost always a failure to himself, Denis thinks disdainfully of his first slim volume of poems, yet maintains the romantic manner of Huxley's *Defeat of Youth*. He complains of his own much too voracious reading, of the unhappy burden of "twenty tons of ratiocination." In the company of others he is constantly on the defensive. He has trouble getting his bicycle from the railroad-station guard; Priscilla won't listen to his report of life in London; he is even patronized by Barbecue-Smith, who tells him to "pipe the infinite" into the "turbines" of his mind. He can adore Anne Wimbush and idealize her in his verse but he cannot have any effect upon her life. Trying one evening to carry her, he drops her; when he tries to impress her, she sees him as merely "perfectly sweet." Like Emberlin, he is plagued by the clash between the "obscure," "embroiled" real world, and the relatively distinct and clear world of ideas.

Huxley the narrator, the older sophisticate presenting this younger self, is constantly alert to Denis' difficulties, yet he neither obscures them nor transforms them into something grotesque. He either identifies with Denis, as he explores his active mind, or is amused by its ironic implications: "Oh, he had had hundreds of hours, and what had he done with them? ... What right had he to sit in the sunshine, to occupy corner seats in third-class carriages, to be alive? None, none, none."[45] Huxley is similarly amused by the others at Crome: the ultra-serious Mary Bracegirdle, who tries to live according to the theories of Freud; Priscilla, with her "curiously improbable" coiffure, devoting herself to astrology, Annie Besant and Christian Science; her husband, roaming with quiet pleasure in the Crome of the distant past; Scogan, the rationalist, who talks by the paragraph to anyone he can find. Looking like "one of those extinct bird-lizards of the Tertiary," he is the only zoological grotesque. But his saurian appearance is rarely mentioned; the prominent animals are purely products of the farm—a family of ducks, another one of sixteen pigs, a few assorted cows and horses and geese.

Sex, once again predominant, is presented from a variety of angles and thereby also handled with mild irony. Gombauld extols procreation while thumping the side of a placid bull. Scogan visualizes an "Eros, beautifully and irresponsibly free, [that] will flit like a gay butterfly from flower to flower through a sunlit world."[46] Even when Mary manages to lose her repressions, she and Ivor appear during an especially beautiful sunrise and are praised without irony as "a young and charming couple." Only in the lecherous leers of two old men is there a hint of the sordidness that pervades the later novels. Though Mr. and Mrs. Bodiham find even bathing suits shocking, theirs is but one of many perspectives—all presented with a surprising gentleness—in the lightest, liveliest ironic contrast.

Such juxtaposition of approaches and attitudes to life forms the essential pattern of the novel. One Sunday breakfast has Priscilla applying her astrology to cricket, Barbecue-Smith discussing "h-piritual truth," Henry Wimbush announcing his departure for the local church, and Scogan his scheme for compelling the clergy to wear everything backward. Scogan is the most talkative and articulate one of the group, but almost all the others are highly verbal as well. They weave Huxley's often irrelevant erudition into the sparkling texture of a myriad of ideas. While Gombauld feverishly tries to emulate that "astonishing ruffian," Caravaggio,[47] Mary drones on annoy-

ingly over the theories of "Tschlupitski." Scogan, over the after-
dinner port, selects for himself and each of his fellow males the
most appropriate of the first six Caesars. Occasionally such fragments of learning provide coherence or transition. When Denis
answers "Blight, Mildew, and Smut" to Mary's question about
his favorite poets, she tries two chapters later to transform the
words to "Abercrombie, Drinkwater, and Rabindranath Tag-
ore." The pace and tension among this group of people varies:
Denis is mildly racked by fits of jealousy, Henry Wimbush so
placid that Mr. Bodiham would like to "shake him into life."

As the novel develops, its world becomes less a place of conflict and tension, more a creation like Emberlin's "glassily
perfect universe of ideas." Some reappear in different contexts
later, Priscilla's comical interest in communicating with spirits
as Huxley's avid interest in J. B. Rhine and ESP; Scogan's
predictions of class structure and bottled babies in only a decade
as elements of *Brave New World*. Ideas in this novel, like those
in Huxley's conversation,[48] seem to take on their own autonomous life—the indigenous appeal that Denis attributes to
words, and no greater degree of ultimate importance. Scogan's
claim that "we all know that there's no ultimate point" is not,
in this novel, at least, the metaphysic of Aldous Huxley; Scogan
after expressing it falls "innocently asleep." *Crome Yellow* is
something like the *Tales of Knockespotch* upholstering the
door of Henry's library: "All the ideas of the present and of the
past, on every possible subject, bob up . . . , smile gravely or
grimace a caricature of themselves, then disappear to make
place for something new."[49] Though the characters are stylized
people, limited and isolated in the way they live their lives,
their world is happy, not merely ironically amusing. It has no
particular symbolic significance; *Crome Yellow* is not a
"serious" modern novel. It is a sudden, happy creation of a
writer fated for renewed and greater anguish, of a man who
temporarily seems to have accepted the world—and himself.

[24

CHAPTER TWO

REPAINTINGS OF THE MASK:

From Gumbril to Archimedes

In THE DETACHED, happy atmosphere of Crome, where uncertainties and frustrations are too comical to last, one poignant, discordant note is heard. To a wrapt after-dinner audience one evening, Henry Wimbush reads the masterful story of Sir Hercules Lapith, the dwarf. Rejected by his father and scorned by a normal woman, yet brave, sensitive, and intelligent, Sir Hercules marries a three-foot Venetian girl and gradually constructs a totally dwarfish world. He and his wife lead a life of quiet happiness, hunting rabbits on Shetland ponies, playing duets with miniature harpsichord and flute—until their son proves to be of normal size. When the giant boy and his cronies make a mockery of his life, Sir Hercules nobly slays the dog who has mauled his wife, gives his wife an over-dose of opium, then with the help of a razor dies a "Roman death" himself.

Two years later, in rewriting the story for *Antic Hay* (London: Chatto & Windus, 1923), Huxley turned this fragile tragedy into a grotesque, appalling farce. In the cabaret drama observed by Gumbril and Myra, the dwarf has become "The Monster," again hated by his father and spurned by a woman, but also cursed with rickets and consumption. Though he is even more the besieged idealist than Sir Hercules, his death is no gallant exercise in self-destruction. Abandoned in an asylum he mounts a chair in a "quest," a search for the heights to which the human soul should aspire, but only manages to fall and break his neck. The transformation of the tale, along with Huxley's treatment of himself in *Antic Hay,* makes clear that the equilibrium of *Crome Yellow* has been lost. Immediately after that engaging first novel appeared, Huxley's inner ambivalence became even more complex. In his struggle for self-expression he tested new theories, yet continued to face the dilemma of the poems, the conflict between sincerity and art.

I

To EXPLORE RETROSPECTIVELY the Garsington past in *Crome Yellow,* Huxley wrote with restrained comic irony. To capture the spirit of postwar London in *Antic Hay,* he deliberately abandoned his restraint. Huxley and his contemporaries of the early 1920's believed, he later claimed, in a "philosophy of meaninglessness." To stage "a political and erotic revolt" for social justice and sexual freedom, they denied that the world "had any meaning whatsoever."[1] A literary treatment of the age could not possibly be tragic; the "social tragedy" had "gone too far" and was "too profoundly stupid to be represented tragically." Only a comic synthesis was possible in a world of chronic horror,[2] and comedy meant "wild gesticulations" essentially "extravagant" and "enormous." All the great comic artists, he felt—Aristophanes and Rabelais, Balzac and Dickens and Daumier—"have employed an extravagant, baroque, romantic style."[3] *Antic Hay,* the story of Gumbril and a group of his London friends, tries to be a comedy of meaninglessness, of extravagances like the Monster's suicidal quest. As he later wrote to his father, it would reflect the age "faithfully" by depicting it "fantastically."[4]

Yet wild extravagance is only one aspect of *Antic Hay*, we gather from Lypiatt, its most extravagant figure. This painter of self-proclaimed genius, author also of poems and even music, is a gesticulating parody of great artists of the past; his best paintings were worthless—except for advertising vermouth. Nevertheless, "magnificent" as well as "pathetic," Lypiatt at least has some notion of what nobility is. Moreover, he offers another theory to be repeated often in Huxley's work that "Everyone's a walking farce and a walking tragedy at the same time."[5] The Monster is the ridiculous complement of the tragic Sir Hercules; *Antic Hay* is a farce, a comic treatment of meaninglessness, but Lypiatt's theory suggests tragic meanings as well.

Both comedy-as-extravagance and farce-as-a-mask-for-tragedy are helpful in understanding Huxley's treatment of himself. He appears, of course, as Gumbril, the central figure of the novel—like Huxley a public-school teacher,[6] a romantic, an assimilator of often irrelevant information, a "chameleon" who changes his coloring with each new influence. Unlike Denis Stone he is a contemporary, not a retrospective creation. He lives in a curiously abstracted London of nightclubs, restaurants, and flats, peopled by writers and artists based on men Huxley probably knew.[7] There is much of the farcical in the way Gumbril can behave, and something potentially tragic, deeply serious. Such categories, however, are not adequate to describe him. Gumbril is a kind of reincarnated Richard Greenow, too plagued by ambivalence for *Antic Hay* successfully to contain.

The opening chapter is one of the best Huxley ever composed. As a master at Repton School he had attended chapel, he wrote, "with great pomp and piety," but could hardly check his "derisive laughter" when the Headmaster began to pray.[8] In the novel, Gumbril sits uncomfortably in a chapel while five hundred schoolboys listen to Deuteronomy. Speculating, free associating in his "rapid and rambling" fashion, Gumbril ponders the "existence and the nature of God." As Mr. Pelvey confidently reads about the Lord, Gumbril toys with the prefix theo- in a half-serious mental game: "Mr. Pelvey knew; he had studied theology. But if theology and theosophy, then why not theography and theometry . . . ? Why not theophysics and theochemistry? Why not that ingenious toy, the theotrope or wheel of gods?" The window opposite Gumbril is "all blue and jaundiced and bloody with nineteenth century glass"; the boys listen in "uneasy silence"; Pelvey's voice booms and the Book itself is "portentous." As Pelvey "foghorns away" and later "oboes" the words of the Bible "out of existence," he is supported by the "thick accompaniment" of Dr. Jolly, who blows "two sumptuous jets of reverence" from the organ. The attitude of comic extravagance has been established, Gumbril's milieu and its orthodoxy exposed as meaningless.

At the same time another Gumbril is evident, within the person for whom "theo-" is esoteric exercise for wit. This Gumbril wonders if "god as a rush of power or thought" can be reconciled with a God equivalent to truth. Echoing almost exactly one of Huxley's letters,[9] he recalls the old-fashioned goodness, the "active radiance" of his mother, her painful death, and her vision of his essential nature. He remembers the days when he used to pray; and his mother's admonition, when she read the Parable of the Sower, of the danger of sowing seeds in shallow ground.[10] Though Gumbril helps to establish the tone of comic extravagance, these thoughts are analytical, sentimental, even spiritually deep—a source of the tragic as the theory would have it, but possibly something different or something more. Recognizing the urgency of his spiritual dilemma, Gumbril checks the surge of feeling and frank self-recognition.

He joins the world of farce his thoughts have helped to create
—by mentally inventing buttock-comforting air-filled trousers.
The chapter closes with his comically wild visions of the future
—a house with Goyas, Maillols, and Chinese statues, conversations with Unamuno and Papini, and the laughter and adoring invitation of women.

The promise of chapter 1, however, is never fulfilled. We are
led to expect resolution or development in Gumbril, aesthetic
use of his deeper moments, of his talents or his obviously admirable traits. For another chapter the hope is well enough sus-
tained when he confronts the values of another character. Sick
of the farce of teaching boys who distort or parrot his remarks,
Gumbril bursts upon his father with his idea for padded trousers. Seen from without, Gumbril Senior is another comic
dramatis persona. He looks like "a strange and animated scare-
crow," he sounds like "the croaking of a very large and melod-
ious frog," his laughter shakes the hair into his eyes, and he is
given to "outbursts of Elizabethan fury." But he is also an
idealist nurtured by values from the past; he has built a model
of the magnificent London once visualized by Christopher
Wren. Even though the model has to be sold, idealism has
replaced meaningless absurdity. And though other gardens
are far more opulent, every evening a "faithful legion" of
birds settles in the plane-trees of his yard. Their ability to communicate in silence suggests a deeper truth, a metaphysical
hope. These sources of meaning offer outlets and alternatives
to Gumbril, Jr.; perhaps he can strive for what he has lost, or
never found.

But after Gumbril becomes immersed in the farcical world
of postwar London, he can only vacillate between active acceptance of the way of life he sees and introspective moments of
sensitivity. In the wild restaurant scene of chapter 4, with
Lypiatt shouting, Shearwater munching like a cow, and the
ferocious Zoe hurling bread at Coleman, Gumbril responds—

as he has earlier to Reverend Pelvey—by glorying "in the name of earwig" and vainly trying to describe his padded trousers. Yet when he hears a tale of misery after they leave the restaurant, he thinks of other sordid or heart-rending urban sights, like amputee veterans playing barrel-organs and an old woman with a disgusting disease in her eye. Once again he rejects these deeper feelings. They are only "melancholy emotions," which from time to time have "swelled windily within." He must join the others in the novel's "hay" or dance which, as Marlowe's phrase about satyrs hints, is sexual.[11] Myra Viveash glides languorously from one man to another, always with her comical, faint, expiring smile. Rosie Shearwater, an exhilarated contrast, dances to a faster pace, from her husband to Gumbril and Mercaptan, then to the unexpected bloody-bearded embraces of Coleman. Gumbril joins the dance by first donning a beard himself, becoming (as he puts it) a member of Coleman's "herd."

When Gumbril alternately dons and doffs the beard, his two vacillating tendencies are given something of a form. Bearded, he thinks of himself as a virile Complete Man, Rabelaisian, "a sort of jovial Henry the Eighth." Without the beard (and sometimes underneath it) he is Mild and Melancholy, a shy Huxley anti-hero. With it he pounds the table and vents his anger at Boldero, then seduces Rosie and almost lives his wild visions. Without it, in the company of the innocent Emily, his sensitivity is movingly re-evoked. In one of *Antic Hay's* most important passages Gumbril speaks to her of "quiet places ... in the mind." Such places form a beautiful, growing crystal, "terrifying as well as beautiful," embodying "something inexpressibly lovely and wonderful," alien to the bandstands and factories of the world. But because the crystal threatens the "regular, habitual, daily" self it has to be crushed to scattered fragments once again.[12] Gumbril, after thinking of Rosie's underclothes, leaves Emily, yields to Myra and the farcical, empty side of life and eventually joshes about the whole affair.

Though the beard motif makes Gumbril consistently inconsistent, the final impression of *Antic Hay* is one of an unhappy vacillation. As narrator of *Crome Yellow*, Huxley always maintains control. In *Antic Hay,* however, he can be distressingly uncertain. When the novel opens, his style and Gumbril's wit are one; Huxley and Gumbril seem identified. The identification becomes a drawback, however, when Huxley insists on Gumbril wearing his mask. Though Huxley is willing to remove it from time to time, before we learn what we want to he puts it on again. With Emily, for example, Gumbril wonders if he might have found the depths, might have "learned to await in quietness . . . that lovely terrible thing" from which so often he has "ignobly" fled. Except for the desert of sand which he faces, however, that is all we learn: as soon as the crystal of quiet appears it must be crushed.[13] Later Huxley is even more tantalizing and obscure. With Myra and Gumbril circling Piccadilly Circus in a taxi and Shearwater riding his bicycle to nowhere, the novel's end like its beginning is farcical. Yet before Gumbril enters the taxi he announces a trip to Europe where he will "really begin" to write his autobiography. People who know him, he says, will think it is "the sort of thing one ought to write," that he is pretending to "feel the emotions and have the great spiritual experiences." Though they may be right, so may his book be "genuine." The man who begins the novel making linguistic fun of God now has a premonition that he may "become a saint."[14] Huxley described *Antic Hay* as "a very serious book";[15] he clearly had something deeper on his mind than farce, tragedy, and the "meaningless" 1920's. He was unwilling, however, to give it full expression or unable to find a satisfactory focus or form.

The ambiguities increase when Huxley shifts the point of view away from Gumbril. Huxley's interest sometimes switches to Coleman, the satanist obsessed with sex and evil. He uses

Boldero to attack the ganglion mystique of D.H. Lawrence, Bojanus to talk Cockney about leisure time and political liberty. He is much more alert than Gumbril to the oddities of others; Mercaptan possesses a "gross, snouty" face which "ought to have been rather more exquisitely, rather more refinedly dix-huitième than it actually was." Mr. Albemarle, the art gallery director, moves with "a certain pomp" and "a butlerish gravity" that "are evidently meant to be ducal." Boldero is alternately a bull, a caterpillar, and a robin. Most important, even Gumbril himself is caricatured—as he "placidly ruminates" or gives them all "a piece of his father's mind." When Huxley thus refuses to identify with Gumbril, who has already proved to be a self-divided man, the meaning of Gumbril's life becomes even more obscure than before.

Antic Hay is almost a wonderful, engaging novel, even though it was written hurriedly at almost fifteen hundred words a day.[16] Huxley's reticence and uncertainty, however, keep his picture blurred. In projecting himself into the complexities of Gumbril, he could find neither the right attitude nor the right aesthetic distance. Too "farcical" to see his life as serious or tragic, he was also too serious to see his life as farce. He was far from ready to announce his new religion, yet Gumbril's remark about sainthood hinted that some day he would. Until the day arrived he still needed to find an appropriate form.

II

THE VACILLATIONS, the struggles with point of view in *Antic Hay* are a clear, though tacit sign of the sincerity-talent dilemma. Huxley's concern for sincerity is put somewhat more directly by Lypiatt, the spokesman-theorist of tragedy and farce. The raving painter, so frequently given to ridiculous dramatic posing, has one important moment of apparently complete candidness. He admits that he may have lied to himself, that he may be a charlatan, merely playing a role, insincere in boasting to others and deceiving himself. Though Lypiatt's life, his verses, his paintings are not Huxley's, his concern for the honesty of his attitude is. Lypiatt can accurately and sincerely understand Myra, though his painting of her is simply bluster and not art. Huxley, on the other hand, has the talent for what is called art, but may feel insincere or fraudulent in producing it. The short stories of *Mortal Coils* (1922), a year earlier than *Antic Hay,* highlight the dilemma in another way already familiar from the early poems. The more ironic (and self-suppressive) the story, the more brilliant; the more effectively Huxley wrote, the more popular he be-came—and the more his concern for sincerity appears to have increased.

Huxley's best-known story, "The Gioconda Smile," depends upon clever, sometimes dazzling ironies. The idea for the story, Huxley tells us, came from a poisoning case of the early 1920's, when a solicitor's wife was "carried off, very suddenly, after eating stewed gooseberries and drinking a glass of wine." The neighbors gossiped, an autopsy revealed the presence of arsenic, but the suspected husband was finally acquitted. Besides inventing new circumstances so that the mystery could be solved,[17] Huxley has transformed the ironic style of the most polished early poems into a fully disciplined, total ironic view. Janet Spence, the murderess, as ironically grotesque as the elephants and amphisbaenae, has a snoutish mouth like a penholder through which she talks like a cannon: "Bang! the charge in her soul was ignited, the words whizzed forth at the narrow barrel of her mouth." Mrs. Hutton thinks of herself as really "fond of French," yet she speaks "of the language of Racine as though it were a dish of green peas." Mr. Hutton, the major character, is sometimes another target, sometimes an ironist himself. He strokes his moustache in frank self-admiration but an instant later sees himself as a fool; he resolves one evening to work harder on his book, then succumbs in the morning to his recurrent sensual itch; he makes a graceful "Cinquecento" gesture to Janet, later runs with the "magnificent canter" of a horse. Hutton is almost as much of an enigma as Gumbril, but contributes to the irony by recognizing this fact himself. Almost all the characters have one justifiable identity to themselves, another ironically ridiculous one to us. Dr. Libbard, the only exception, understands the ironic way things work out. Though he knows of Janet's guilt, he is too fatigued by life's ironies to care. In the poems Huxley had shown a romantic tendency, mocked mildly in *Crome Yellow,* grown more complex in *Antic Hay.* In "The Gioconda Smile" the romantic is parodied, through Janet and through the cuddly, imperceptive Doris—whose name, Hutton recalls while kissing her, is "the scientific appellation of the sea-mouse." With the help of this protagonist so unlike yet like himself, Huxley maintained a focus, as he could not in *Antic Hay,* and established an unwaveringly consistent ironic view.

It is in "Nuns at Luncheon" that the struggle with irony, the cost of it, begin to be evident. The narrative line of this story is painful as well as bizarre: a young, virginal, recently converted nun, who has proved a wonder at converting others, is put in charge of a convalescent criminal. Unaware that he is an expert seducer and convinced she is acting on behalf of his salvation, she is led to steal clothes from her superior's wardrobe, is whisked by him away from the hospital, crudely seduced in a farmer's hut, then abandoned to return to a living death among the sisters—but not before he has robbed her of all of her teeth! So cruel are these ironies that Huxley, instead of narrating the story himself, turns it over to another writer, the less sensitive Miss Penny, an example of grotesque irony herself. Always wearing "massive and improbable jewellery," she has a pair of lengthy earrings which swing and rattle like "corpses hanging in chains," and she has the habit of laughing like a horse. Too obtuse to see her masculinity and too coarse to see any pathos in her tale, she provides an ironic framework for the irony of the virgin's life—the irony of an insensitive person describing pain.

The inhumanity of the story apparently left Huxley with misgivings. In "The Tillotson Banquet" he exposes the dangers of esoteric learning, one of the main supports for his ironic art. In "Green Tunnels" irony and its esoteric source are challenged again by the sentiments and fancies of a young, romantic girl sympathetically contrasted with her lifeless elders. Nevertheless, the greatest challenge to the irony of "Nuns at Luncheon" is, ironically, in "Nuns at Luncheon" itself. As Miss Penny gleefully reports the shocking facts, she raises questions about the very story in which she appears—and thereby very briefly exposes Aldous Huxley. She approves his vision of the nun before her conversion, "apocalyptically" perceiving that everything is "sex, sex, sex" and thus "disgusting." When she suggests that he "write pages about Destiny and its ironic quacking" because it is "impressive" and "there's money in every line," his reply is a terse "You may be sure I shall." And when she finally asks him if he seriously believes in literature, he finds the question "luckily . . . quite meaningless." When she reaches the point of the nun's actual seduction, with "the strangled crying, the movements . . . the emotions pulsing about," she sees it as "ready-made literature," good for many pages. With the absence of comment, the question of sincerity is closed, hidden under the mask almost as soon as it is posed. Nevertheless, while displaying his most sophisticated technique, Huxley has questioned the very value of literary art. Such misgivings, displayed while he plays the role of artist, help determine the very quality of most of his later novels and largely account for his fallen stature in the world of letters today.[18]

III

AFTER THE BRUTAL IRONY of "Nuns at Luncheon," it is a startling experience to read "Young Archimedes." Unlike the other stories in *Little Mexican* (London: Chatto & Windus, 1924), all of which are detached if not downright inhumane, this narrative of a peasant boy of potential genius is written with a deep, frank sensitivity. Not only are ironies less piercing, less rigorously imposed—again and again potential ironies are ignored. Instead, the occasional moments of genuine feeling shown by Gumbril have become the vital, integrating force. When Huxley dwells lovingly on the black cypresses and darkly rising Apennines, on the Italian landscape with its "humanness and domestication," he sets the tone for his attitude toward Guido. The obvious, spontaneous sincerity turns the story into the most moving piece that Huxley ever wrote.

The young Guido delights the narrator by sharing his—and Huxley's—musical taste. He is enraptured by the slow movement of Bach's D-Minor Concerto and soon prefers Mozart to Wagner, Debussy and Strauss; he likes "music," as he puts it, better than the human voice. But he shows where his prodigious talent really lies by suddenly proving the Pythagorean theorem, in an impromptu sketch drawn with the burnt end of a stick. By helping the boy to devour mathematics the narrator can watch Guido becoming an ideal human being. The watcher's emotions are stirred as the wonder of genius is revealed, his imagination filled with humility. The run of us, he realizes, could never have developed even our most familiar ideas alone,

[36

yet Archimedes had no successor for a thousand years or more, and there has been but one Michelangelo, one Buddha, one Jesus, and one Bach. Moved by the notion that men of genius are perhaps "the only true men," the narrator at one point sees himself as a teachable dog, a metaphor applied scornfully only to others in *Antic Hay*. As Guido shows him his crude but homemade dodecahedron, he feels he should have "gone down on all fours, wagged the spiritual outgrowth of his os coccyx, and barked his astonished admiration."

This appealing combination of the urbane and learned with the humble, absent in all the other early Huxley fiction, is developed effectively as the story moves to its close. When he walks to the grave of the young genius with the father, the narrator is wrapt in learned but irrelevant speculations; poised and impressive in his knowledge of art, he barely hints at his interest in "recognizably human things." When they reach the grave, after the explanation of Guido's suicidal fall, feeling colors the narrator's deep reflective mood. Tears come to his eyes as he thinks of the delighted expression which "illumined . . . [Guido's] face when he learned of some new idea that pleased him." His poise, though he retains it, does not serve to check his emotion; unlike the onlooker who narrates "Nuns at Luncheon," this Huxley projection clearly has a heart that can be moved. Though the father is furious at the Signora responsible for Guido's death, the narrator persuades him to "the harder path of grief." The final catharsis, however, is in his own humble mind and heart. The tragic beauty of Guido's life recalls the lyric beginning of the story, and it merges for the narrator into the wonders of Florence itself. In him we still find the sophisticated, cultured Huxley, but the split seems healed, the mask removed, and we seem to have another brief glimpse of Huxley's soul.

During an interview conducted later in the actual villa of the story, Huxley impressed his interrogator with his "great humanity." Told that his books did not really seem to express this quality, Huxley replied that they "express that part of my mind which is the product of a, perhaps, excessively intellectual upbringing. One generally finds that people who have tried to analyze the world in exclusively intellectual terms, end by discovering what everybody knows, almost by instinct, from the beginning."[19] Feeling, in other words, is inhibited by intellect; the active mind can very easily stifle the heart. In "Young Archimedes" the two are harmonized only because Guido is unique in his appeal. As a mathematical genius, Guido's potential is in the purest, least personal human endeavor. As a child he has had no chance to disillusion others—to become, for example, a brilliant but infantile adult like Maartens, the physicist, of *The Genius and the Goddess.* Guido is spared Huxley's irony, his satirizing intellect, his theory of tragedy and farce, not because he is a genius but because he has not lived to show his genius fulfilled He evokes feeling as no other Huxley character can because he personifies an uncontaminated vision, a worthy, unsullied cultural ideal. He is thus in a sense another—flawless—self-projection. We never look upon his like again.

CHAPTER THREE

THE PLIGHT OF DISCONTINUITY:

Toward *Point Counter Point*

THE LIVELIEST PASSAGES of *Those Barren Leaves,* the Italian novel following Huxley's great Italian story, are the dinner-table pronouncements of Tom Cardan, the aging materialist. Roaming intellectually over the present and the past, Cardan presents himself as an erudite immoralist commenting critically on Milton and Robert Browning, quoting Diderot and the poet-priest Parini, and loudly advocating Huxley's theories of the comic style and of tragedy and farce. He has the same wit, the same incisiveness, even more of the irrelevant knowledge of old Scogan. As a human being he represents a particular way of life, tested against and contrasting with certain others; as a conversationalist he is an important self of Aldous Huxley, a Huxley projection in yet another form. In 1919, needing a source of income to be able to marry Maria, Huxley had accepted Middleton Murry's offer to write for the *Athenaeum.*[1] In *Vanity Fair* and *House and Garden* he aired his views on "everything from decorative plaster to Persian rugs."[2] Cardan is obviously a character in a novel, yet he is also the voice of an essayist who paraded his ideas in reams of exposition.

Though Huxley claimed to find journalism increasingly

distasteful, "more and more difficult to combine with intelligent writing,"[3] he wrote for popular magazines off and on for his whole life. Sometimes he saved his important ideas for treatises and tracts, like *The Perennial Philosophy* and *Ends and Means*. Discourse on some level, however, he always found essential—surely in part because in it he could ignore the clash of inner conflict. He could shun the specific for the abstract, the facts of life for the facts of art, the personal dilemma for the problems of contemporary culture. More sincerely than in a fictional character like Cardan he could skirt the sensitive areas within. Yet he often makes revealingly clear, sometimes half-consciously, not only his philosophical or religious or social beliefs but his attitudes toward other human beings.

I

IN THE FIRST COLLECTION of essays—*On the Margin,* published the same year (1923) as *Antic Hay*—Huxley occasionally comments on himself. "I belong to that class of unhappy people who are not easily infected by crowd excitement," he admits, before demolishing a book on community singing.[4] "We were taught to believe that a Sunday walk ... was somehow equivalent to church-going," introduces a brief discussion of a new anthology of Wordsworth.[5] Usually, however, Huxley concentrates on literature. Chaucer, Ben Jonson, and Lytton Strachey are treated directly; "Accidie" is a well-known literary analysis of modern despair; even "Advertisement" turns out to be a kind of literature, spoofed as the "most pregnant" and "most arduous" of all. Ironies reminiscent of his fiction and verse sometimes appear: Dante is a bicycle rider "whizzing down the spirals of Hell,"[6] Strachey a "civilized Red Indian," tossing his "leisured degustations" over the walls of his private park.[7] Such hyper-cleverness, however, and Huxley's brief confessional remarks expose only the surface of his mind. One selection survived in the 1955 *Collected Essays*. In "The Subject Matter of Poetry" Huxley longs for a writer who doesn't yet exist—a poet who can deal with "the new ideas and astonishing facts" of science.[8]

Huxley was a far better travel writer, however, than literary critic; and the travel essays of *Along the Road* (1925) are more direct, perceptive, relaxed and personal. Fully aware of his growing public, conscious of its interest in him and in his remarks, Huxley sometimes flatters his reader or disarmingly criticizes himself. After first appealing to the man who may have to stay home,[9] then suggesting he could match the author's judgment had he but gone, Huxley alleges that travelling is not to him a way of improving his mind. Rather, it is a method of forgetting the mind exists—better than "betting, mah-jongg, drink, golf or fox-trots."[10] He brings along the half-size *Britannica,* whose very incoherence allows him to "wallow" in his other favorite vice.[11] He also appears as an aficionado of cars, envying the Alfa-Romeos, scorning the Fiats, and willing on matters of speed and mileage to utter "frigid and calculated lies."[12]

When the emphasis changes from himself to others, however, Huxley exhibits an important and distressing limitation. He practices, illustrates and tries to justify the snobbish reserve of "The Traveller's-Eye View." In a cafe or railway car, as a "pleasant diversion" to prevent the onset of ennui, he watches and listens to another human being. Like a Balzac or a Joyce he reconstructs imaginatively "the whole character, the complete life history" of the subject, yet his one vital rule forbids conversation, or any attempt to get to know the person he observes. At a distance, he tells us, people are "delightful, . . . queer and fantastic," doubtless potential inhabitants of his ironical zoo. Approached, they become "quite unworthy of any further interest"; to the travel-snob Huxley now seems to be, just dull.[13] In a 1920 *Athenaeum* article, seeing himself as a "secluded literary specialist," Huxley admitted acquaintance only with "journalists, poets, novelists, dons, editors, painters, upper middle-class families, a few domestic servants, peasants and gardeners," and a few of the idle rich. He was almost totally ignorant of commuters and business men; he had never even talked to an industrial worker.[14] Such an essay as "Montesenario," in this context, is a less surprising admission. As Huxley climbs to the monastery perched high above the city of Florence, a group of priestlings appears, "flapping along in their black skirts . . . with an unnatural decorum."[15] Speculating on the cloistered life they represent, Huxley closes with an image of "Mrs. Thingummy," emerging from her limousine on a Florentine street below. She is not only a person with whom he would never converse; as he sees her "waddling" into the jeweller's shop, he knows why the monastic life, with all its tyranny, has an appeal.[16]

The detachment Huxley expresses with such surprising frankness was hardly a secret to those who knew him best. Even at five he seemed to Julian to move "on a different level of being."[17] Raymond Mortimer remembers his difficulty in making contact,[18] a reaction even more vividly reported by Julian's wife.[19] Though the detachment of the novels has repelled a great many people, at times it lends Huxley's work a kind of purity, something like Guido's Pythagorean theorem or, once again, Emberlin's "glassily perfect universe of ideas." In parts of *Along the Road,* for example, people may not appear at all. "Sabbioneta," a treatment of the long-dead family of Gonzaga, transforms their absence into an effective central idea, as "faint ghostly oboes . . . play . . . among the Gonzaga ghosts."[20] In "Views of Holland," an even better essay, the human is replaced by the geometrical. The country itself is "the ideal plane surface"; the roads and canals are almost perfect straight lines; intersecting dykes and ditches criss-cross in "perfect parallels"; the meadowlands between the dykes make matching rectangles; and a farmhouse is a "tall pyramid," placed upon a cube, surrounded by a quincunx of trees. Though human beings are "deplorably out of place," they atone for their lack of geometry by riding bicycles.[21]

There is a connection between Huxley's love of geometry and his apparent scorn for most of the people he sees. Geometry eliminates the individual and insists upon the general.[22] Superimposed upon the plains of Holland, it leaves one "convinced that Euclid is absolute reality, that God is a mathematician, that the universe is a simple affair that can be explained in terms of physics and mechanics," and that, by extension, "all men are equally endowed with reason, . . . that it is only a question of putting the right arguments before them to make them see the error of their ways. . . ."[23] Eupompus, we remember, gave splendor to art by numbers; God, by cubes and rectangles, gives beauty to the earth.

Nevertheless, just as Eupompus' advocate was criticized by his friend, the Euclidean ideal must sooner or later yield to the real. Since "God thinks neither in terms of Euclid nor of Riemann," only what we invent is simple and rational. An honest look reveals actual imperfections in the landscape, for not all the canals are straight, nor "every house a wedded cube and pyramid." The real is "hopelessly diversified, complex and obscure." Similarly, people differ greatly in their ability to reason, and prejudice is far more powerful than argument. There is no human progress, hardly even evolution: the more we know, the more profound becomes the "surrounding darkness," and our contemporaries behave like prehistoric Altamirans.[24] Though such conclusions led Huxley eventually to his unorthodox religion, at this point (barely thirty) he can still manage an internalized escape. He can withdraw to the "rational simplicities" of his mind or observe "untempered reality" with the traveller's-eye view.[25]

Though Huxley sees Holland through the abstract forms of

Euclid, he much more often sees Europe in relation to its art. Fascinated by art and surprisingly knowledgeable, he is a far better critic of painting than of books. Even though his vision forced him to stand only inches away, he has been called "one of the most discerning lookers of our time."[26] His treatment in *Along the Road* of Pieter Breughel changed a general disdain to critical acceptance.[27] Praising Huxley as a "chief rediscoverer" of the years between the wars, Sir Kenneth Clark adds to the name of Breughel those of Callot, Piranesi, Caravaggio and Goya.[28] Huxley himself believed in an "incalculable" number of ways of painting well and rejected only "the incompetent, the mentally dishonest and the futile."[29] A travel-snob toward ordinary people, he maintained an eclectic view toward art. Hence in "Portoferraio," describing the Black Country ugliness of Elba, Huxley begins and ends his essay with the angels and palette of Tiepolo. His comment on the Flemish part of the Meuse depends upon paintings he imagines done by Joachim Patinir.[30] In a longer essay on "The Palio at Siena," Huxley is perched symbolically a hundred feet above the street. As the procession of Sienese begins, the marchers appear "out of a Pinturrichio fresco," waving banners suggest a Picasso design for the Russian Ballet,[31] but for the carabiniers the appropriate painter is Carle Vernet.[32]

Italy and Holland, a critic once suggested, help us to see Huxley more than he helps us to see them.[33] The point applies most clearly to one Italian painter, Piero della Francesca, whose Resurrection fresco is "The Best Picture" of them all. Besides eliciting analysis and praise, Piero forced Huxley into revelation and assessment of himself. He raised anew the question of sincerity: Piero was "genuinely noble as well as talented," sincere as well as eminently skilled.[34] Huxley wonders if he himself is one of the many shams who, taken now as "genuine," may some day prove to be false.[35] Piero's greatness, however, is due not only to his sincerity, his nobility, his praise for "whatever is splendid in humanity," but because he rejects the emotional and the dramatic and remains consistently intellectual.[36] The Christ of the Resurrection expresses "intellectual power";[37] the London paintings, on the Nativity and the Baptism, are "superb" partly because they embody no sympathetic feeling; the "turmoil" and the "emotions" of the Arezzo battle scenes "have been digested by the mind into a grave intellectual whole."[38] Huxley hopes he has Piero's sincerity; he knows he shares Piero's emotional detachment.

So superior does Huxley find cognitive to emotional reaction that he would even be willing to give up artistic talent for science. Science is "non-human," he says enviously in "A Night at Pietramala," divorced from emotion and personality; the artist is fated to live most of his life "in the emotional world of human contacts." Though *Macbeth* is widely read and electrical research is soon forgotten, Huxley would still rather be Michael Faraday than Shakespeare. Like the mathematical Guido of "Young Archimedes," men of science lead Huxley to show his own emotion behind his mask. Their "unity of purpose . . . to . . . us poor distracted mortals seems wonderfully enviable and wonderfully beautiful."[39] Denied by his eyesight the life of a scientist, Huxley could at least take solace in contemplation. High above Florence in "Montesenario," he feels that a man might learn to understand the depths of himself, the part of him he notices only in "solitude and silence."[40] As the mask is once again momentarily removed, we remember Gumbril's crystal of quiet—and sense the future mystic of *The Perennial Philosophy*.

II

IN EUROPE, as he moved through countries which had attracted him for many years, Huxley was immersed in his own cultural tradition. His first trip to the Orient, however, produced at least a mild case of cultural shock. In *Jesting Pilate* (1926), a journal rather than a series of independent essays, his cultivated, detached sensibility does not work; he cannot impose a convincing verbal form on the unfamiliar, unsympathetic Asian scene. The Hindus are merely "queer specimens of humanity," a holy man on the train to Lahore "one of the most repulsive human specimens" he has ever come across.[41] The plains, mountains, and skies of Burma are unconvincingly identified with the paintings of Claude Lorrain,[42] the social comedy at Delhi he can only see as reminiscent of Marcel Proust.[43] In one of the best passages, written about Labuan in Malaya, Huxley claims that tropical reality is too rich, too picturesque for the painter's art.[44] He does not seem to recognize the parallel involving himself—that the oddities, the inhumanities, the strange and fascinating sights are being recorded with an unfortunately shapeless effect. In the crush of devoted masses bathing at Benares, there are no eye-pleasing pure Euclidean forms.

Nevertheless, *Jesting Pilate* was an important book for Huxley, one marked at times by a deeper seriousness than the essays of *Along the Road*. Eastern religion, to become the spiritual foundation of the last decades of his life, is rejected, then tacitly at least in part accepted. Indian spirituality seems inferior to behavior at the *Point Counter Point* soirée: a little less of it, we are told, and the Indians would have more schools, "less dirt and more food," even "some kind of polite conventional social life."[45] Metaphysics and the "Other World" are a purely human invention;[46] mystics do *not* unite themselves with God.[47] Yet Huxley frankly admires the Buddha, who of all religious leaders is "the most intellectually powerful," so advanced in going beyond the concept of a personal God that it will take us hundreds of years, at least, to catch up.[48] Having observed by the end of his trip much of the world's diversity, Huxley can assert an underlying unity, with values like good-

ness, beauty and wisdom everywhere "broadly the same."[49]
He urges the traveller to seek the right proportion of values, to
"make a habit of mysticism as well as of moral virtue."[50]
Though Huxley's formula is vastly oversimplified, too abstract
to seem to touch the actual world, it shows the "perennial
philosophy" taking shape in his mind. The proper ethical
standard, he concludes, is "as timeless, as uncontingent on
circumstances, as nearly absolute" as one can make it.[51]

With its inadequacies, its inconsistencies, its illogical simplicities, *Jesting Pilate* hints at a ferment Huxley had to bring
under control. But *Proper Studies* (1927) is even more than
the effort Huxley called it to order the "confused notions"
growingly evident in his thought.[52] It is also a daring first
attempt at a comprehensive view, the first clear indication of
the astonishing range of Huxley's intellect. Only H.G. Wells
and Shaw, among Huxley's contemporaries, would have
attempted the huge demanding task he set himself—to examine
the individual, government, education, and religion and to
urge or envision a large degree of change.

Though *Proper Studies* is not Huxley's best discursive work,
it for the most part is lucid, restrained, and reasonable. Huxley
is interested in the "unmeasured characteristics" of men;[53] he
is engaged in what Vilfredo Pareto, whom he admittedly
emulates,[54] would classify as a "non-logico-experimental
science." Pareto's near invective, combining "professorial
heaviness with an almost mediaeval ferocity,"[55] doubtless
evoked and strengthened Huxley's love of irony. "We must
presume, in charity . . . that he does not mean what he says,"
is Huxley's response to Watson, the behaviorist.[56] On psychologists: "By comparison with Jung, most other psychologists
seem either uninspired, unilluminating, . . . or else, like Freud
and Adler, monomaniacal."[57] Democracy, though it "can boast
no Nero—only a Robespierre or two and some Djerzhinskys—
. . . has produced a whole Newgate Calendar of lesser ruf-

fians."[58] Huxley shares Pareto's desire to strip away facade, to get as close as possible to the actual human facts. "Human beings," one of Pareto's theorems reads, "are wont to express their instincts, sentiments, etc. in verbal form, and they are prone to embellish them with logical or pseudo-logical developments."[59] *Proper Studies,* like the more massive Pareto *Trattato,* tries to explore and expose such developments. His ironies aside, Huxley appears unprejudiced. He takes pains to analyze himself for the sake of the reader, and invites him to correct any distortion he may find.[60] The outlook, however, is primarily outward rather than inward, toward abstract systems and theories and the institutions with which they are involved. "The greater part of the world's philosophy and theology is merely an intellectual justification for the wishes and the daydreams of philosophers and theologians," Huxley claims, following Pareto in different words. "And practically all political theories are elaborated, after the fact, to justify the interests and desires of certain individuals, classes, or nations."[61] In *Antic Hay,* by projecting his inner divisions and struggles with himself, Huxley had offered imaginative comment on the meaning of his age. *Proper Studies* is his first extended and extroverted critique. Huxley needed inner unity, society wholesale reform.

Because he believes that the outer world depends upon the inner, Huxley discusses the individual and his psyche first. He traces our present "democratic social institutions" to the "fabulous," unrealistic psychology of the eighteenth-century philosophers. He agrees fully with their procedure—"given the individual," he confidently claims, "we are able to deduce the desirable institution"[62]—but not with their psychological assumptions. Their crucial mistake was in believing that men are equal in any other way except before "the infinite quantity which is God," an "irrelevant" principle in the finite world in which we live.[63] The notion of equality of reasoning ability in men, accepted or propounded by Descartes, Helvetius, and Locke, obviously cannot be made to fit the facts. One of Huxley's own crucial axioms follows: "human beings belong to a variety of psychological types separated one from another by irreducible differences."[64] This claim, to be most vigorously supported with the work of William Sheldon, is a principle of character and dialogue in *Crome Yellow,* the first novel, and the social foundation of *Island,* Huxley's last.

In an admittedly unsystematic way, Huxley explores psychological varieties. Visualizers and non-visualizers, geometers and analysts, degrees of practicality and talent are described. As we might expect, Jung's *Psychological Types* is to Huxley the single most important work, partly because Jung "is a man who does genuinely understand human beings in the profound intuitive way in which a good novelist . . . understands them."[65] For the purposes of reform to which *Proper Studies* is to lead, it is the acknowledgment of psychological variety that is important, rather than the accuracy with which it can be seen. Though Huxley claims to be "by nature uninterested in hypothetical Utopias,"[66] in his attitude toward types he virtually has one framed:

> When psychological education is less rudimentary than it is at present, people belonging to different types will recognize each other's right to exist. Every man will stick to the problems, inward and outward, with which nature has fitted him to deal; and he will be restrained, if not by tolerance, at least by the salutary fear of making a fool of himself, from trespassing on the territory of minds belonging to another type.[67]

Huxley's visions of education, government, and religion follow. Recognizing the difference between one person and another, we must in our educational endeavors "train every individual to realize all his potentialities and become completely himself."[68] We must quit sacrificing the individual to

the present system; we must recognize that the academic subjects on which modern curricula depend are simply uninterest-
ing to, and unabsorbable by many minds.[69] In the ideal system
we will "measure the capacities" of the individual and train
him "to perform those functions which he is naturally adapted
to perform."[70] Similarly, most men are not interested in government, and many who vote or rule are not really fit to do so.[71]
"That only mental grown-ups should vote, and that nobody
should be allowed to make laws who is not at least as intelligent and well informed as the men who administer them—
these are political principles which ordinary common sense
must approve."[72] By employing the appropriate "varieties of
excellence" we must establish "a ruling aristocracy of mind."[73]
In religion there are two broad categories, the "solitaries" and
the "sociables." Huxley does not know whether the objects
of "religious intuition" really exist, but assuming that they do
he will not laud one group over the other. "Both the solitary
and the social worshipper apprehend ultimate reality, each
according to his capacities and his peculiar idiosyncrasies." Just
as each man clearly knows what he finds pleasant, so each "has
a right to call his own version of reality the only one."[74]

The unrestricted liberalism of this religious view is obviously
at odds with Huxley's goals for education, which with their
suggestion of dictation from the top have a discernible coercive,
if not totalitarian air. Huxley apparently does not notice this
clash, yet he does admit that he is rationalizing his own wish.
He warns us that he cannot "transcend himself," that with his
own mind and upbringing he has distorted the facts in his
particular way.[75] Apparently he can talk about imposing training on others because he is confident congenial training would
be imposed upon himself; and since he lacks "all capacity or
ambition to govern," and finds "poetical" the "idea of being
governed well," he can promote his deliberately undemo-
cratic ideal without any sign of misgiving or personal qualm.[76]

In religion, however, he is as uncertain as before, certain only of the complexity of the truth. He will find, in fifteen years, his perennial philosophy; now, observing the variety of religious intuitions, "no conception of the nature of God is true which is not also multifarious and self-contradictory." Nothing so "beautifully rational" as Whitehead's theology is sound.[77]

Huxley's critique explores another theme conspicuous in his later work, "substitutes for religion" like politics, business, sex, and art. In ours, the "most irreligious epoch of all history," politics offers in nationalism an elaborate surrogate with ritual, music, even the real presence—of the motherland.[78] "Business in general is the supreme God," the single firm a "subsidiary deity." The orthodoxy of sex can also support the would-be ascetic. Art can supply both ritual and philosophy, and artists, along with lawyers and particularly doctors, have assumed many of the functions of the priest.[79] But the chapter linking *Proper Studies* most tenaciously to Huxley's other work is called "Personality and the Discontinuity of the Mind." Under the mask of rational, objective tone are signs of the inner discord we have so often seen before.

"Discontinuity" refers to the lack of *prevailing* identity in the mind. Huxley finds "intemittence" and inconsistency in people, and under the surface of his prose it is clear he does not like it at all. Physiology is partly the cause: hunger "breeds irritability and rancour," while a satisfied appetite may help the same person to be kind.[80] But the problem is less physical, more mental. We are brought up "to think materialistically about one set of phenomena, idealistically and even mystically about another. . . ."[81] For the "we" we cannot help substituting an "I"; it is Huxley who finds this three-part division in himself. Discontinuity does not complicate the theory of types; the emphasis instead is on the need for its correction. Huxley sees it as something the individual, hence he himself, can change. He recognizes that childhood is the "plastic" period of life, the time when the human being is "given" his distinctive "form." But he believes an adult can be a kind of artist with himself, can "feel impelled to remodel himself upon some different plan."[82] His ideal is a gloss, in highly undistinguished prose, on the author of the poetry, the fiction, and the personal essays—a personality "in which the natural discords are harmonized by some principle of unity, in which the discontinuous psychological elements are fitted into a framework of purposive ideals strong enough to bridge the gaps between them."[83] If we continue to substitute the first person for the third, the goal becomes for Huxley (his word) "indispensable." The man who wrote in so many styles of verse, whose strategy in fiction allowed the projection of various selves, must find the principle "that shall preserve him identical with himself through all the changes in the outward and inward environment of his mind."[84]

III

MOST OF THE FICTION just before and after *Proper Studies* shows unmistakably that "discontinuity" applies to Huxley himself. Not *Two or Three Graces* (London: Chatto & Windus, 1926), however, whose short stories include only fragments of worry about the problem. In "The Monocle" is another shy, divided intellectual, a less appealing, unhappier version of Denis Stone. In the title story Huxley appears as Wilkes the narrator, a music critic, a "very poor visualizer," an intellectual who remains "cool, critical, and cautious" while his friend Kingham "passionately" burns. The two bores of this nearly flawless story, Herbert Comfrey and John Peddley, provide some of Huxley's most amusing ironies. The one is "a burr-bore, vegetable and passive," the other "an indefatigable piercer, a relentless stuffer and crammer." Peddley allows Huxley to caricature his own irrelevant erudition; Wilkes lets him project himself without any personality problem, as another reasonable, fully adjusted "ideal" self. It is the two novels preceding and following *Proper Studies*—*Those Barren Leaves* (London: Chatto & Windus, 1925) and *Point Counter Point* (London: Chatto & Windus, 1928)—that graphically demonstrate the discontinuity Huxley would like to heal. Familiar fare in some respects, they represent nevertheless a new aesthetic excursion, an attempt to capture discontinuity in an original fictional form.

The new in these novels, however, is less evident at first than the familiar. Both recall the closed setting, the restricted movements of *Crome Yellow*. In much of *Those Barren Leaves*, visualized as a "gigantic Peacock in an Italian scene,"[85] the characters talk and make love while collected by Lilian Aldwinkle at her palace modeled after the Sitwells' at Montegufoni.[86] In *Point Counter Point*, pages of richly loaded, highly patterned conversation issue from Hilda Tantamount's elaborate London soirée. Both novels show the same needling and unmasking found in *Antic Hay*, achieved by combinations of Huxley's irony and wit. Amusing speech is a favorite Huxley device for poking fun. Lilian lets her predicates disintegrate in the air, Hovenden is forced to speak "th-" sounds with a "v." In *Point Counter Point* Janet Bidlake always pronounces the apostrophe in "T'ang," and Sidney Quarles, a target for Huxley's heaviest abuse, "had a way . . . of tilting his face upwards and shooting his words into the air, as though he were a howitzer," to produce "those baa-ings with which the very Oxonian are accustomed to enrich the English language."[87]

By the time Huxley was writing *Those Barren Leaves,* he found the "mere business of telling a story less and less interesting." The "only really and permanently absorbing things," he wrote in 1924, "are attitudes towards life and the relation of man to the world."[88] Hence in both novels he likes to disclose, with varying shades of irony, the basic assumptions by which his characters live. Mrs. Aldwinkle has devoted herself to what she thinks are "Art" and "Love," yet she sees a conspiracy keeping her from exciting new revelations of truth. Though Hovenden is merely a good-natured fellow lacking a mind, his mentor, Mr. Falx, is a vociferous devotee of Marx. In the more diverse, more intricate world of *Point Counter Point,* assumptions are exposed on almost every page. Mrs. Bidlake subsists on "vague, unending meditation"; Sidney Quarles on a massive sense of his own importance; his wife, as a Christian who likes "fig-leaves . . . over the mouth"; John Bidlake as a sensualist, "handsome, huge, exuberant, careless; a great laugher, a great worker, a great eater, drinker and taker of virginities." Sometimes the unmasking means a more extended irony, a more rigorous procedure. When Mary Thriplow meets Calamy on an early page of *Those Barren Leaves,* she dons jewelry to impress him with her sophistication, then has to stuff it under the cushions of the couch when she realizes she has made a crucial strategic mistake. After vigilant observance of this amusing tête-à-tête, Huxley pursues her in her moments of most private speculation, when she suffers (or stimulates) the feelings she hopes to transform into art. Similarly, in *Point Counter Point,* Sidney Quarles is followed and analyzed relentlessly, from his early promising undergraduate years to his sordid affair with his "secretary" Gladys, his cross-word puzzles and dictating equipment, and his pompous habit of writing letters to the *Times.* In Lord Edward's portrait, after noting that his ancestors had "stolen" much of their land from the Church, Huxley mentions his majority "when he was given a constituency to nurse"; recalls his brief forays in hunting, when "the massacre of birds, even in the company of the Prince of Wales," left him unmoved, "except perhaps by a faint disgust"; and cites the spiritual climax of his life, the revelation that he might have imbibed a piece of Mozart—in a schnitzel, a sausage, or even a glass of beer.[89]

When these sharply outlined figures begin to interact, they frequently weave patterns of intellectual and social satire.

[54

These are less noticeable in *Those Barren Leaves,* where Miss Aldwinkle's collection has been transferred to Italy. Here houseparty conversations sparkle in the manner of *Crome Yellow,* with Scogan replaced by the witty malice of Tom Cardan. Dealing with parasites, Cardan helps to unveil Mr. Falx; with Mrs. Aldwinkle and Mary Thriplow, he reveals conscious and unconscious attitudes toward love; and he defines himself as frankly devoted to lechery and booze. In the Tantamount soirée of *Point Counter Point,* however, ideas ring and clash with much greater wit and vigor. Mrs. Betterton, confronting John Bidlake's canvas of joyous, naked bathers, is identified as "prejudiced" toward virtue. Lord Edward blasts the fascist Everard Webley for shameful neglect, not of humanity but of—phosphorus. To Illidge the communist, Lord Edward is a rich and expendable peer who devotes his whole life to "asymmetrical tadpoles."

Point Counter Point seems to stress identity, not discontinuity, but characters in *Those Barren Leaves* have regular moments of Huxleyan conflict or unease. Mary Thriplow worries over which of her selves she should try to be; Mrs. Aldwinkle is convinced that she will never again be loved; Calamy is split between sensuality and omphaloskepsis; Irene, between painting pictures and embroidering her own brassieres. Only Falx and Francis Chelifer are sure of themselves, and Chelifer has merely reacted to the splits and struggles of his past. But most of the characters in *Point Counter Point* have sold themselves on a single, distinctive way of life. Lord Edward is the devoted physical biologist, loving his wife like a "fossil child" of the Victorian sixties. Everard Webley, the strong-willed British Freemen leader, displays his fascist assertiveness even in his pursuit of Elinor Quarles. Spandrell, more devoted even than Coleman to his satanic anti-ideal, debauches young girls, makes his mother as unhappy as he can, and in a scene out in the country even brings a blowsy prostitute to tears. Lucy Tantamount ruthlessly seeks her physical pleasure, Lord Gattenden vows to salt the absolute's tail, Carling remains a cruel and drunken Catholic, and Walter Bidlake wants even Lucy to transmute sex to his Shelleyan ideal.

Huxley liked *Those Barren Leaves* better than his earlier books,[90] and seems to have been satisfied with *Point Counter Point,* even though it became a less ambitious achievement than he had planned.[91] Some of his contemporaries were dazzled by both novels. To Leonard Woolf the earlier book was "brilliant and daring, admirably written, humorous, witty, clever, cultured."[92] Cyril Connolly found the style of the later novel "impeccable," and noted "a finer grasp of the emotional realities of ordinary people" than Huxley had before achieved with the "old cleverness" and the "old intensity" still there.[93] Joseph Wood Krutch, reviewing *Point Counter Point,* found in all Huxley's work "unflagging vivacity and . . . increasing richness of illustration."[94] But a few critics noted the disturbance underneath. To Krutch, though Huxley was the "smartest" young man of them all, actually grappling with crucial problems, he was "as lost as any of his creatures."[95] Woolf, uncertain himself, found that Huxley "does not seem to be quite certain" of what he is doing.[96] John Franklin was even more perceptive: "Mr. Huxley's real mind is and always has been moving in a direction totally inconsistent with the surface of his work."[97] Beneath the sharply etched identities at the Tantamount soirée, though superimposed concurrently upon them, is the fragmented personality of the author. A year after *Proper Studies,* where it is analyzed, discontinuity in Huxley himself shapes and colors a major novel.

Discord is most evident in Huxley's hostile tone, in a more caustic, persistent sarcasm than appeared in *Antic Hay.* When Mary Thriplow, in her first talk with Calamy, invents a Sicilian poet, carefully claps her hands, and drops the name of a well-known hostess, Huxley lets her condemn herself by merely implying her thoughts. But when she hides her jewelry to fake a less glamorous role, Huxley tries to make sure we get the point: "After all," we are told, "that was what she really was—or at least what she had determined that she ought to be." The exposure is even more ruthless later, as she prods her emotions so she can "suffer" from what she tells herself was younger love. Toward the end, having punished her enough, Huxley tempers malice with familiar comic irony. Among the images Mary exudes when she thinks she is thinking of God are three camels, a Neopolitan ice, and the grotto at Capri.

Those Barren Leaves, however, is no preparation for the merciless Huxley of parts of *Point Counter Point.* Though Sidney Quarles uses his dictaphone primarily for working crossword puzzles, he thinks of himself as the author of a most important book. A repetitive Quarles pronouncement is damningly paraphrased: ". . . as yet, he would say to anyone who asked him about the progress of the book . . . , as yet he had not even finished collecting the materials." "The largeness and the importance," Huxley adds, "justified an almost indefinite delay in its completion."[98] Quarles, doubtless, deserves such irony; Marjorie Carling surely does not. She has a nose "rather too long at the best of times"; she looks "ugly, tired and ill." John Bidlake calls her an "imbecile" with "a nose that's at least three inches too long," and Elinor Quarles remembers "those dreadful, dangling sham jade earrings," the "horribly small bites from a slice of bread" chewed "with the front teeth, like a guinea-pig." Even her voice is annoying: it is "too refined—even in misery." The poor woman, treated abominably by her self-righteous Catholic husband, has been impregnated—then almost ignored—by Walter Bidlake. Yet her anatomy rather than her pitiful plight is stressed. Even childbirth, it appears, cannot be normal for her; the doctor has discovered that "her pelvis is too narrow."

G.K. Chesterton, doubtless thinking of the treatment of

Marjorie, saw Huxley as a child whose teeth were set on edge. Dickens, he believed, "enjoyed the monstrosities" of the people he invented; but the new generation "describes normal people as they normally are; and then reacts against them with an abnormal irritation." As Puritans "got things on their conscience," Utopian idealists "got things on the brain," Huxley and his companions "get things on their nerves."[99] Marjorie's nose is much too long; Mr. Sita Ram's is cursed by a drop, which flashes and trembles under his patriotic outburst and falls with a "violent shudder" among pieces of half-consumed fish. Daulat Singh has "bright eyes" and a "noble old face" but he cannot, sad to say, refrain from chewing pan. The sick Wetherington, a memory from Walter Bidlake's childhood, inspires not pity, but "horror, fear and disgust" in a room "heavy with a horrible odour of stale sick breath."[100]

Such details may come from "nerves," as Chesterton asserts, but the sharpest satirical portrait of any Huxley novel originated from inner conflict transformed to personal hate. Middleton Murry, who ruled Huxley when he wrote for the *Athenaeum,* is reincarnated as even Murry knew in the repulsive editor Denis Burlap.[101] Burlap eases Huxley's task by condemning himself—by hypocritically impressing a rich and useful woman, by reciting Scripture to refuse Walter Bidlake an overdue raise, by blaming "Mr. Chivers" for every unpopular decision, by smiling contentedly when his rejected secretary leaves him to his mistress by committing suicide. But Burlap is handled more relentlessly than anyone else in Huxley's fiction. We are told that he is "unceasingly and exclusively self-conscious." He likes "saying mysterious things, dropping them surprisingly into the middle of the conversation." He makes his face look "arch and subtle" as if he is saying "something rather daring, witty and at the same time profound." At one point it "amused him to be baffling"; at another, he sees himself "in an apocalyptic vision as a man of sorrows." His sexual behavior is still more corrosively attacked. Burlap plays the child, we are told, in his seductions: by letting Beatrice Gilray give him hot milk and tuck him into bed, he so assuages her virginal fears that soon they copulate while splashing in the bathtub. The most biting and hyperbolic sentence in the book concerns Burlap's earlier marriage to Susan. "His ardours," we are told, "were those of a child for its mother," a child "tactfully and delicately the little Oedipus." He had a "pure, childlike and platonic way" of being unfaithful, and after returning to Susan would "roll at her feet in an ecstasy of incestuous adoration for the imaginary mother-baby of a wife" he had convinced himself she was.[102] The hostility toward Murry makes for an unforgettable portrait, but it also is evidence of unrest and obsession in Huxley.

Huxley's discontinuity erupts toward the continuous hypocrisy of a Mary or a Burlap. It also helps to account for his discontinuous narration, his deliberate strategy, in both novels, of interruption. The "Evening at Mrs. Aldwinkle's," which begins *Those Barren Leaves* with love scenes and conversation, is suddenly followed by the image of a floating human body, and the verbose autobiography of Chelifer. The transition is almost imperceptible, and artificial: the evening has ended with Mary Thriplow pondering a canoe trip with her Jim, "scratching her heart to make it bleed." In *Point Counter Point* Huxley cinematically switches from one talking group to another, exploring the themes of sex and death in an all but stylized way. Deliberately trying, as he put it, to "temper" with "counter" the "harshness of the 'points',"[103] Huxley is making some attempt at the "musicalization of fiction" outlined in the journal of Philip Quarles. But his plan supports his verbal ironies with an irony of organization. The violent clashes involving the Webleys and Illidges and Lord Edwards occur in a world which, though peopled largely by consistent individuals, is as a whole totally discontinuous and therefore ironic.

The Huxley of this period, in yet another way, is a deliberate ironist who finds discontinuity in *our* lives though it does not always appear in his fictional creations. "We live in a world of *non-sequiturs*," he says in an essay, or "we would live in such a world, if we were always conscious of all the aspects under which any event can be considered." We move between watertight compartments separated by heavy bulkheads; only the artist, by looking across them, can break them down. A single event produces discord, if it is seen through juxtaposed but contrasting kinds of accounts.[104] Huxley was unable to apply the principle as fully as he had planned, to "show a piece of life, not only from a good many individual points of view, but also . . . as scientific, emotional, economic, political, aesthetic, etc."[105] In the handling of music in *Point Counter Point,* however, his theory is evident, first at the concert at the Tantamount soirée, later when Spandrell plays a recording of Beethoven's *Heilige Dankgesang.* The harmonies of Bach which draw Lord Edward downstairs, away from his asymmetrical tadpoles and his newts, have occurred because the flautist Pongileoni "blew across the mouth hole and a cylindrical air column vibrated." When the violinists "drew their rosined horse-hair across the stretched intestines of lambs," the result was the "long Sarabande" of Bach, with its quality of "lovely and consoling certitude."[106] Similarly, Beethoven "made signs with ink on ruled paper" more than a century before; now "spiral grooves on a surface of shellac" remember the playing of four Hungarians, who have produced it from a "printed reproduction of Beethoven's scribbles."[107] Such accounts are meant to be deliberately ironical, to make reality appear "disquieting" and "exceedingly queer."[108] Discontinuity is thus also introduced into the novel, in spite of the stable identity of most of the characters' fixated lives.

Though his essay proclaims discontinuity as a condition of all of us, Huxley's fictional self-projections present *him* as an extreme and special case. In both *Those Barren Leaves* and *Point Counter Point* he appears behind an intricate pattern of fictional masks. Calamy, though the philanderer that Huxley doubtless never was, nevertheless states the ultimate question of his creator: he is the Huxley who hoped to unify himself by finding the essence, the meaning, the nature of reality. That the severe flesh-spirit split he feels is also Huxley's, is all but proved by Huxley's work from the earliest of the poems. As the houseparty develops Calamy moves, as Huxley would, toward a contemplative asceticism. Initially trapped by Mary Thriplow's deliberate sensual temptations, he later urgently wants to plumb the silences of the spirit, to understand the "mystery" he is certain floats above. He grapples with the question of ironical juxtaposition, raised by the treatment of music soon to follow in *Point Counter Point.* Calamy tries to analyze the modes of existence of his hand. In his (and ours, and Huxley's) present state of knowledge, the hand is just a shape that interrupts the light, or a myriad of electrons whirling around their nuclei, or a piece of life which itself wants to live, or an instrument of murder, of poetry, of love. Its modes of existence, that is, are many and discontinuous, and one mode cannot be explained in terms of any of the others. However— and here he hints at the last three decades of Huxley's life— with freedom, with an "open, unperturbed ... [and] quiet ... mind," he might think his way to a total explanation.[109] *Those Barren Leaves* ends with Calamy in contemplation, questioning the beautiful, terrible mystery of reality. He can at least suggest the final confidence of Huxley's *Island.* Even after his actions have been attacked by two of his friends, a mystical shining peak leaves him "somehow reassured."

Tom Cardan, one of these friends, is a much less obvious Huxley self. He is old—near death, he feels—and admits to being a parasite and a lecher who loves his booze. Yet as another compound of spirit clashing with flesh he bears a closer resemblance to Huxley than one at first suspects. His fleshliness leads him to challenge Calamy, to emphasize the physical appetites against Calamy's "protracted omphaloskepsis" which he sees denying needed "nourishment" from outside. Cardan's identity with Huxley, however, is intellectual. Gumbril the "caterpillar," exuding ideas in parts of *Antic Hay,* has here become a more amusing and effervescent authorial voice. Like the Huxley of the hastily written journalistic essays, Cardan can discourse learnedly on almost any subject—on the modern suspicion of pomp, on Etruscan phonemes, on art dealers, love and the novelist Balzac. He is Huxley the reader of the *Encyclopaedia Britannica,* fascinated by discontinuous, irrelevant multiplicity, unwilling to commit himself to any kind of search for the One.

Francis Chelifer, the third participant in the novel-ending debate, is probably Huxley's most accurate self-portrait. The image is a distorted one, of course: Huxley worked for the London *Athenaeum* and struggled with Middleton Murry; Chelifer writes for the *Rabbit Fancier's Gazette* and battles with a patronizing Mr. Bosk. But Chelifer is another romantic idealist who has turned to cynicism, like the Gumbril who rejects innocence and love in Emily, like the author of "The Defeat of Youth," like the Huxley whose voice will soon dominate *Point Counter Point.* Chelifer's cynicism has followed his experience in love: he has first idealized the bitchy siren Barbara Waters, then been worshipped by Dorothy Masson, and hence has found only unhappiness or boredom. But although he also scrambles to hide from the grasp of Mrs. Aldwinkle, after she and Cardan have rescued him from the sea, his real role is the Huxley who has been at odds with art. He writes poems which Huxley is to reprint later in *Cicadas,*[110] yet he sees all writers, including himself, as merely frauds. His long confession is full of startling comment:

[62

I write with care, earnestly, with passion even, just as if there were some point in what I were doing, just as if it were important for the world to know my thoughts, just as if I had a soul to save by giving expression to them.

I do not suppose that anything I do has the slightest importance, and if I take so much pains in imparting beauty and elegance to these autobiographical fragments, it is chiefly from force of habit.

In reality I write as I do merely to kill time and amuse a mind that is still, in spite of all my efforts, a prey to intellectual self-indulgence.

Chelifer defends the traveller's-eye view: "our habit of regarding strangers as . . . exhausted frogs," he says, "probably saves a good deal of trouble." He apologizes for letting style "pour out" of his fountain pen,[111] and sums himself up as "a competent second-class halma player."[112]

All art, not just his own, is attacked. We have already, he claims, abandoned "Religion, patriotism, the moral order, humanitarianism, social reform." Now we should "smash" art, "the last and silliest of the idols." Art is merely "the ultimate and sweetest of the inebriants"; we should sober ourselves and get rid of our "queer prejudice" in its favor.[113] His view of reality is the opposite of Calamy's; Chelifer finds no meaning in human life. Anyone who asks the fundamental questions will find himself, as Chelifer has, in "one unceasing slide through nothing." Though Chelifer does not convince Calamy in the Chelifer-Calamy-Cardan debate, and though Huxley in a letter sees the mysticism "undercutting" the sceptical view,[114] he surreptitiously supports Chelifer's argument. Calamy's confident intuition ends the last page of the novel, but Chelifer is awarded the last word in fictional time. His autobiography, though placed in the middle of the book, is composed *after* his return to "Gog's Court, the navel of reality," hence after Calamy has gazed at the mystic peak. He is allowed to patronize the metaphysic of Calamy by a notebook reference to "my poor friend." Hence Cardan is the Huxley of the easily distracted, self-indulgent mind, Calamy the man Huxley would like to be, Chelifer the uncommitted, insincere, talented Huxley that still is.

There is nothing of Huxley in Irene, Grace Elver, Chelifer, Sr., or Mr. Bosk. But the two leading females help form the configuration. Lilian Aldwinkle is (like Denis) a seeker, in her ridiculous way, for the "important, revealing, apocalyptic thing." With Mary Thriplow, even in the midst of ruthless satire Huxley exposes and scrapes one of his own most sensitive nerves. Mary Thriplow's problem is precisely Huxley's: she does not know what her real identity is. She is of course a much shallower person who could not begin to be sincere. When Cardan expands a theory of living her response has none of the Chelifer-Calamy complexity or depth. She merely plans to make a "mental note of the notions . . . [as] an idea to work up in an article."[115] Yet even here she sounds like the unguarded writer of one essay, where Huxley affixes to himself the label of "charlatan."[116] Her sentimentality as she stimulates her heart to make it bleed is a continuing quality of the poems, later projected in Denis Stone and Gumbril, and evident in the last novels of Huxley's career. Huxley reacts to it with a mixture of hatred and fear; it is a tendency he wants to castigate himself for, or purge. At one point Mary's identity with Huxley is almost exact. The public likes her books, she tells Cardan, "because they're smart and unexpected and rather paradoxical and cynical and elegantly brutal. They don't see how serious it all is."[117] Though *she* may not be "serious" underneath, Calamy, Cardan, and Chelifer prove that Huxley is.

An equally intricate pattern of Huxley selves appears in *Point Counter Point*. Here self-division is named in the novel's epigraph, and personified in the opening page by Walter Bidlake, a sketch of the Huxley who worked for Middleton Murry. Walter is torn by warring desires for ideal love and real, physical satisfaction. Deliberately modeling his feelings after *Epipsychidion,* he has convinced himself that love is "talk . . . spiritual communion and companionship," only to find that underneath he is "ardently alive." Having impregnated the idealistic but cold and homely Marjorie Carling, he burns with a "mad and shameful" passion for Lucy Tantamount. The result, of course, is a hatred of himself—for neglecting Marjorie, lusting after Lucy, and lying to Marjorie (and to himself) about both. The real-ideal motif is sounded in another key with Lucy, when Walter refuses to succumb to her carnal calculation and tries to transform their sensuality into something like a tender love. As Walter heads for the soirée he collides with a hostile lower-class pedestrian, encounters an Underground passenger who spreads a gob of spittle on the floor, and free associates to a family gardener who was once disgustingly sick—all these are not only unpleasant to experience; they are three challenges to the humanism he claims to himself to profess. Denis Stone is treated with comic tolerance, Gumbril with amusement combined with nostalgic sadness, Walter with a kind of intense compulsive passion. The stuffy "odour of humanity made him sick"; in Wetherington's sickroom he feels "an uncontrollable disgust." Mrs. Cole, Marjorie's former employer, he detests "as a bullying, slave-driving, blood-sucking embodiment of female will." He hates Marjorie "for her patient, martyred coldness," and he accuses himself of "swinish sensuality."

The split in Walter is grotesquely magnified in Spandrell, whose frustrated romanticism has produced complete decay. Although the inspiration for Spandrell is Baudelaire, not Huxley, Huxley's interest in Baudelaire arises from his interest in himself. Spandrell shares with other Huxley anti-heroes both dependence on his mother and adoration of the ideal. His mother's antiromantic second marriage has led Spandrell to practice a systematic denial of God. His suicide, the murder of Webley, the perverted seduction of Harriet are neither acts nor wishes of Huxley, but the extrapolation in extreme terms of an important Huxley self.

Philip Quarles is probably the most revealing self-portrait in all of Huxley's books. Huxley admitted to personal traits he later built into Quarles,[118] then later claimed that Philip was "in part" a portrait of himself.[119] Quarles' game leg and the resulting retreat to "private silence" closely parallel the attack and result of Huxley's *keratitis*. Like Huxley, Quarles has lost a brother; he also shares Huxley's love of irrelevant learning. Most essentially he is a man who can analyze with brilliance but rarely admit to any feelings. His failing is clearest during a scene in Italy. When their car kills a dog who has been chasing a bitch in heat, his wife shudders with sympathy and horror. Philip's response, as Huxley puts it, is "a selection from the vital statistics of Sicily, a speculation about the relativity of morals, a brilliant psychological generalization."[120] So important to self-understanding and expression was this scene that it provided the major scene and a major symbol of *Eyeless in Gaza*.[121]

Philip is not only a large part of Huxley the man; he is also Huxley the artist, at times even the Huxley who is composing *Point Counter Point*. Philip believes "it might be rather interesting to concoct a character" like himself—"a man who has always taken pains to encourage his own intellectualist tendencies at the expense of all the others."[122] Huxley, of course, is doing precisely this as he writes. Philip has some insight into his (and Huxley's) weaknesses: "Wanting to be amusing," he thinks, "that was his chief literary defect."[123] He knows that he lacks the talent for capturing the "simplicities" of life—"that talent which is of the heart, no less than of the head, of the feelings, the sympathies, the intuitions, no less than of the analytical understanding."[124] Philip's famous journal passage on "the musicalization of fiction" also applies, in part, to *Point Counter Point*. Huxley alternates and modulates upon the themes of love, sex, politics and death, even "from the aesthetic to the physico-chemical aspect of things."[125] The aesthetic parallels are never as close as between Gide and the Edouard of *Les Faux-Monnayeurs,* but the psychological identity is even closer.

Philip comes closest to Huxley when he frankly examines himself. Though he should be "himself" in his books the "question of identity" is "precisely one of . . . [his] chronic problems." Huxley analyzes Philip as a kind of psychic amoeba, absorbing first, then "oozing" on. His mind is "like a sea of spiritual protoplasm, capable of flowing in all directions . . . of filling every mould." He has "filled the most various moulds" at different times in life, and sometimes more than one at once. The choice is determined by books or by associates, from without. His cry is the question of the Huxley of *Proper Studies*: "Where was the self to which he could be loyal?" The answer is a characteristic kind of dialectic, as uncommitted as the dialectic of the poems. He has an answer to his question in "sceptical indifference," in "that mixture of pyrrhonism and stoicism which had struck him, an enquiring schoolboy among the philosophers, as the height of human wisdom." He seems to like and accept his "liberty," yet a moment later he has changed his mind again. He will visit Mark Rampion, who may be no merely temporary mould.[126]

Rampion, everyone knows, is an attempt to portray D.H. Lawrence. Just as Rampion may end the identity quest of Philip Quarles, so may Lawrence be of help to Aldous Huxley. "The sane, harmonious Greek man," Rampion says in declaring his thesis to Spandrell, is "not such a fool as to want to kill part of himself." He strikes a balance between the "conscious soul" and "the unconscious, physical instinctive part of the total being."[127] Rampion sees many of his fellow characters, along with St. Anthony, St. Francis and Jesus, as "perverts," in their various ways "trying to be non-human." They are:

> Non-humanly religious, non-humanly moral, non-humanly intellectual and scientific, non-humanly specialized and efficient, non-humanly the business man, non-humanly avaricious and property-loving, non-humanly lascivious and Don Juanesque, non-humanly the conscious individual even in love. All . . . always away from the central norm, always away from humanity.

In this "asylum" of perverts that is the world, Burlap is "a pure little Jesus pervert," Spandrell "a morality-philosophy pervert," and Philip Quarles "an intellectual-aesthetic pervert."[128] Rampion sounds like the Lawrence Huxley admired, and Lawrence's approval of the theory suggests that it may have originated with him.[129] Yet Rampion's prescription is neither the answer to Philip's dilemma nor, aesthetically, the major theme of *Point Counter Point*. By his own admission Rampion is another worrying, gibbering pervert himself. Though he is another possible end to the "Search for Truth," Philip defines the search as "just an amusement, a distraction like any other, a rather refined and elaborate substitute for genuine living."[130] Rampion's ideas are merely part of the pattern of dialectic, one part of the maze in which Huxley, even more than Philip Quarles, is trapped.

The world as well as Aldous Huxley is discontinuous and harshly ironic: "of such is the Kingdom of Heaven," says Huxley to end the novel, as Burlap, having caused the suicide of Ethel Cobbett, frolics with Beatrice Gilray in the tub. Yet even the ironies are answered in Huxley's dialectic. Their "unmitigated harshness" is opposed by the *Heilige Dankesang*, played by Spandrell from Beethoven's late A minor Quartet. During Campbell Dixon's dramatic adaptation of *Point Coun-*

ter Point, the heavenly Lydian harmonies were actually performed. To Huxley, who found Beethoven's music expressing "the most profound, . . . the most complete" philosophy,[131] "It was as though a god had really and visibly descended, awful and yet reassuring, mysteriously wrapped in the peace that passes all understanding, divinely beautiful."[132] The discontinuity of this world and the serenity of the other combine into a larger discontinuity involving both.

To the later Huxley this music would symbolize ultimate reality or essence, the Hindu Atman that is Brahman in every human being. But any such hint in *Point Counter Point* is drowned by his own discordant narrating voice—the Huxley who presents the thoughts and actions of the novel, who aims his sarcasm at poor Marjorie's lengthy nose, whose ironies comprise even the *Heilige Dankgesang.* He is least sympathetic with Burlap and Sidney Quarles, most (as we might expect) with Philip, but never fully identified with anyone. Philip, Walter, Spandrell, perhaps even the music are aspects of Aldous Huxley, but so is the composing author who tells their story.

Wylie Sypher finds Huxley using the "cubist simultaneous perspective"; he probably means the novelist's appearance within the novel and the "simultaneous" treatment of the scenes at the Tantamount soirée. Gide's *Les Faux-Monnayeurs,* however, is offered as the best example of a cubist novel. Like Picasso's *Arlésienne* it is "an inquiry . . . into the innumerable transitions between the object and the conception of the object."[133] Huxley's own personality, we might say, is the object of cubist treatment in both *Those Barren Leaves* and *Point Counter Point.* But though Huxley borrowed principles, even characters from Gide, he takes a very unGidean stance toward art and life. Gide, as Sypher puts it, "finds . . . that life is not art, that art is not life, that art cannot occur without life, but that life may be less significant than art. . . ."[134] Though Philip Quarles might subscribe to such aestheticism, Huxley himself would never have endorsed it. To him life was never less significant than art. Calamy omits the aesthetic in his catalog of modes of existence; Chelifer and later characters declare that art is not significant at all. *Point Counter Point* suggests the cubist's treatment of the object; it recalls the expressionist's distorted and highly subjective response; it foreshadows the anti-novel of a later generation in its disregard for traditional canons of form. Yet though it evokes analogies like these, in the complexity of its subjective dialectic it is a new creation, a law unto itself.

CHAPTER FOUR

LIFE-WORSHIPPER AND PYRRHONIST:

Do What You Will and *Brave New World*

Point Counter Point no longer seems a "synthesis of modern culture," a "modern *Vanity Fair*," as Robert Morss Lovett called it in 1928,[1] even though its scope was the broadest Huxley had yet achieved. Without question, however, it is Huxley's fullest statement of discontinuity, his most complex pattern of projections of the self. Yet the Huxley who had given discord unique artistic form still confronted it in the world and in himself. His friend D. H. Lawrence, on the other hand, did not seem to have the problem, before or after Huxley turned him into Rampion; and Lawrence was close enough to suggest a possible solution. As Richard Aldington puts it, Huxley and Lawrence were by 1926 "as near friends as was possible without the risk of explosions."[2] Though Huxley in one letter calls Lawrence "slightly insane,"[3] he sees him later as "the most extraordinary and impressive human being" he has ever known.[4] In his well-known introduction to the first collection of Lawrence's letters Huxley tends to emphasize the artist,[5] yet he also makes clear his attitude toward the man: "Lawrence himself" and his inner fire were what mattered.[6] Possessed by a gift, a "*daimon*" which ruled his life,[7] Lawrence to Huxley was inconsistent but not discontinuous. Rampion can almost penetrate the armor of Huxley as Philip Quarles; Lawrence becomes an invisible teacher of Huxley in *Do What You Will* (1929), the book that immediately followed *Point Counter Point*. The nature of his influence, however, we would never have foreseen.

I

In "Fashions in Love," an essay first published several years before, Huxley only hints at what would become the real emphasis of *Do What You Will*. Not surprisingly, he invokes Lawrence's aid in handling the problem of sex. The theme of post-War sexual indulgence he had treated in *Antic Hay*; now he seeks a new myth by which people can learn to exercise restraint, "without which sexual impulse cannot be transformed into love."[8] Lawrence's "new mythology of nature" attracts him because its restraints are emotional, not intellectual, more fundamental than the attitudes the nineteenth century tried to apply.[9] When Huxley reaches the problem of discontinuity, he merely turns Rampion's rhetoric into colorless prose: "The conflict is between a part of the personality and the personality as an organized whole." Only when he offers a revealing metaphor does Huxley suggest the real thesis of *Do What You Will*: a human being is "a vast colony of souls . . . souls of individual cells, of organs, of groups of organs, hunger-souls, sex-souls, power-souls, herd-souls," most of whose activities we can know but little of.[10] *Proper Studies* asserted the diversity among men; *Do What You Will* asserts the diversity within them. We are discontinuous, Huxley implies, whether we like it or not.

Huxley will not only admit discontinuity, he will virtually wallow in it. Instead of claiming any need for inner unity, he demands for "each self" "the right to exist, the right to its own values." He believes, that is, in an unrestricted vitalism, a "life-worship," as he calls it, whose God is life in *all* its vital processes, even those we think of as "repulsive" or evil. He seeks the "vital equilibrium" of "balanced excess," the fully realized life of his whole colony of souls.[11] As early as 1914 he had written amusingly of "the policy of excessivism" as "the only right one."[12] Now he seriously aims for excessive indulgence of inner discord. The life-worshipper will be "by turns excessively passionate and excessively chaste . . . at times a positivist and at times a mystic." The latest self to reach consciousness is "momentarily true."[13]

Huxley tries to justify his strange, impossible creed in the exasperating introduction entitled "One and Many." As he will later in *The Perennial Philosophy* and as he has already in *Proper Studies,* Huxley begins with human psychology—here, however, with the eyebrow-raising claim that religion is irrelevant except in psychological terms.[14]Psychologically we experience or feel both the One and the Many, hence the corollary rationalizations of monotheism and polytheism.[15] Monotheism, however, in our time leads men to worship death in the forms of automatism and mere efficiency.[16] Only polytheism can nourish the need of the spirit to worship life, to realize the true "multiplicity of the world."[17] Huxley does not deal with the ethical questions that emerge. With the help of Ernest Renan he blames monotheism (and most evil) on the Jews,[18] yet he disregards Renan's claim that the prophets first introduced ethics into religion.[19] "One and Many," though ostensibly about the needs of humanity, is a better mirror of the needs of Aldous Huxley.

Huxley spends most of his time in *Do What You Will* pointing to deficiencies in the lives of others. Instead of extolling selected life-worshipping vitalists, he prefers to expose traitors, failures, or antitheses of his creed. Wordsworth, Swift, Shelley, and Baudelaire are analyzed; Rasputin, of all people,

is juxtaposed with St. Francis of Assisi; and the book ends
with a long essay on Pascal. In examining men who allegedly
rejected instinct or passion, Huxley could again examine aspects of himself. Wordsworth, for example, is charged with
letting the "god of Anglicanism" creep "under the skin of
things";[20] had he known the jungles of Malaya or Borneo, he
might have been less "serenely certain" of the "cosy sublimities"
he found at Windermere and Rydal.[21] Eventually afraid, like
other men, of the complexity of the world, Wordsworth
founded yet another idealized, unrealistically monotheistic
and hence inadequate system.[22] Huxley's Wordsworth is
neither the youth of *The Prelude* haunted by the cataract, nor
the passionate lover of Annette Vallon. It is rather the con-
servative older man whose tendency to substitute ideas for
life allows Huxley to attack the same habit in himself. Swift's
blindness to diversity produced something else again—a "profoundly silly" misanthropy growing from an obsession with
human bowels.[23] Though Huxley had no such obsession himself, the Swift in him appears as the ascetic tendency of Calamy,
or the passionate puritanism of *After Many a Summer Dies
the Swan*. The Baudelaire of *Do What You Will* is another
life-rejecter. The model for Spandrell, the hater-of-sex in
Point Counter Point, he is treated as similarly "un-Hellenic"
in the essay, unable to understand the balanced excess, the
"radical inconsistencies of the pagan Greeks."[24] The reason
we admire this "topsy-turvy Jansenist," who found pleasure
in love only in "the consciousness of doing wrong," is that he
anticipates and epitomizes modern boredom.[25] The rationale
of Baudelaire's boredom, however, is never analyzed; the self-
consciousness of the poet is ignored. Huxley's remarks, as "sum-
mary and superficial" as he admits,[26] are again an attack on a
kind of life he is trying not to live.

In his idealism and his inner division between instinct and
intellect, Baudelaire becomes another magnified, distorted

image of Aldous Huxley. Blaise Pascal, however, is the closest, most revealing parallel of all. In the last, longest, and most important essay Huxley admits writing "sympathetically . . . in the guise of a Pascalian." He has, that is, also searched for the absolute—"in those remote strange regions beyond the borders of the quotidian consciousness." Pascal has "explored the same country"; his reports have accompanied Huxley on his "psychological travels."[27] When Huxley, in *The Perennial Philosophy,* argues the need for "dying to oneself," the Pascal in him will emerge in its most intense and consistent form. At this point, however, he insists on suppressing it. Though Pascal demolished the "vital lie" of Cartesian rationalism,[28] though he is not reproved for being racked with illness, he is blamed for trying to foist his "neuralgia metaphysic" on others,[29] for trying to convert men to the worship of Death.[30] In analyzing the *Memorial* of mystical experience which Pascal copied on parchment and wore around his neck until his death, Huxley will not accept Pascal's interpretation. He accepts the validity of Pascal's ecstasy, but not the accompanying Christian commentary. Such experiences can be explained only psychologically and tautologically; they "happen because they do happen," because that is what the human mind is like. Since they are separate events in a discontinuous pattern, any religious explanation is merely and arbitrarily superimposed.[31] Once again, though a man may want to be consistent, he is really "a colony of separate individuals" which take their turn in directing the organism.[32] Pascal did not realize this truth, the essay claims, but it and the whole collection assert that Huxley does—and that in his life he tries actively to apply it:

For me, the pleasures of living and understanding have come to outweigh the pleasures, the very real pleasures . . . of pretending to be consistent. I prefer to be dangerously free and alive to being safely mummified. Therefore I indulge my inconsistencies. I try to be sincerely myself—that is to say, I try to be sincerely all the numerous people who live inside my skin and take their turn at being the master of my fate.[33]

There is every reason to believe that life-worship could not have worked, and did not. First of all, the creed as defined is self-refuting: if Huxley is to indulge all his inconsistencies, he can be a life-worshipper only part of the time. Second, the way he develops his creed is unconvincing. Huxley first refuses to see more than a part of the truth of his subject, more than one or two aspects of Pascal or Swift or Baudelaire. His intellect then superimposes the part upon the whole. Though he refuses to see the inconsistencies and complications in others, he claims the right to be inconsistent himself. But his inconsistency is to be rational and systematic; he abstracts from *his* make-up one part again—the intellect—and then proceeds to apply it to *himself*. By reaching an irrational creed in this largely rational way, he assures not a vital response but a series of compulsions, an unbearable psychic strain. Deliberately living one's tendencies to excess would surely tear any psyche completely apart. Hence the Huxley described by Lawrence during the year of *Do What You Will* is nothing like a vital example of his creed. He is "run down and livery" in one letter,[34] "rather seedy and run down" in another.[35] His wife Maria is also looking unwell. Both, Lawrence thinks, are living "the wrong way of their nerves."[36] So salutary did Huxley find the living presence of Lawrence that he tried (but failed) to impose Lawrence's psychology on himself. Abstracting Lawrence's outward inconsistencies, he turned them into criteria for his own. To his inner fragmentation he tried to wed Lawrence's love of life, to sanction expression for all his tendencies, his selves.

Lawrence told Huxley he liked *Do What You Will*, especially the essay on Baudelaire.[37] He had felt cornered, however, by Huxley's "intellectual sympathy" in *Point Counter Point*, expressed through the "gas-bag" Rampion, "the most boring character in the book."[38] He told Ottoline Morrell that he didn't like Huxley's books, even though he admired "a sort of desperate courage of repulsion and repudiation in them." Huxley the man was for Lawrence as multiselved as we have seen him: "The Aldous that writes those novels is only one little Aldous amongst others . . . I mean it's only one of his little selves that writes the book and makes the child die, it's not *all* himself."[39] The Huxley-Lawrence friendship, an attraction of opposites, was reinforced by certain common attitudes. Both recognized the vital importance of sex and both were concerned about its tragic misuse. Both shocked the public with what they felt was the truth, and experienced the public's hostile reaction as a result. But Lawrence's letters, with all their fluctuation between depression and joy, stress the importance of centrality and wholeness, not any deliberate, conscious inconsistency.[40] Though Lawrence grew and changed as a writer, his published work has an essential unity and power that Huxley was neither equipped nor fated to match.

Huxley's allegiance to life-worship, which would have been strained under any circumstances, ended almost as soon as Lawrence died.[41] One of the stories in *Brief Candles* (London: Chatto & Windus, 1930), Huxley's last new collection,[42] supports the creed by satirizing its opposite: the intellectual, ascetic Herbert Claxton sits on a tree stump, breathes deeply through one of his nostrils, and repeats the sentence "I'm not constipated." "The Rest Cure," however, cynically echoes *Lady Chatterley's Lover* and "Chawdron" hides its heresy under an even thinner disguise. Chawdron himself, a business man with a hard head and a hog-wash heart, seems to personify the extremes of balanced excess. But Tilney, reporting on the real "truth" of Chawdron's life, claims that nothing teaches, " 'once you've gone off the normal instinctive rails.' " " 'I wonder if they really exist, those rails?' " asks the narrator. " 'So do I, sometimes'" is the answer, "'But I piously believe.'" Miles Fanning of "After the Fireworks" is more direct and more elaborate. Asked by his adoring mistress if he believes in God, he offers a properly *Do What You Will* polytheistic answer. "He said he believed in Apollo when he was working," Pamela writes, "and in Bacchus when he was drinking, and in Buddha when he felt depressed, and in Venus when he was making love, and in the Devil when he was afraid or angry, and in the Categorical Imperative when he had to do his duty." But to live as such a life-worshipper is as impossible for Miles as for Huxley. Miles would like to live by the "commandments" of the god, here Etruscan rather than Hellenic, but "'one couldn't do it even if one tried, because one's very guts and skeleton are already pledged to other Gods.'" He cannot help living and indulging in the split.

II

WHILE HUXLEY was rejecting life-worship in the stories of *Brief Candles,* he was simultaneously experimenting with the handling of point of view. He wrote another play, *The World of Light,*[43] but also demonstrated his theory, expressed a few years later in an interview, that he "must have a two-angled vision" of his characters, either showing them "as they feel themselves to be" in contrast with the way they seem to others, or presenting "two rather similar characters . . . who share the same element, but in one it is made grotesque."[44] Fanning of "After the Fireworks," for example, having wined Pamela, dined her, and lectured her on life worship and the ins and outs of art, writes a letter aimed at ending their relationship, telling her in elaborate detail how she looks to him and he seems to himself. More interesting than Huxley's exploration of his characters, however, is his sudden interest in wishing to explain himself. In one of Fanning's admissions Huxley seems to appear:[45] Fanning flees from business by letting others handle his affairs, from criticism by not reading what the critics have to say, from time "by living as far as possible only in and for the present," and from cold weather by spending the winter where it is warm. Perhaps his thinly veiled apparent frankness about such matters as these prepared Huxley for *Vulgarity in Literature* (1930), and the startling confession of a truly important, almost primal artistic sin.

Most of this long essay deals with the "lowness that proclaims itself"[46] in such writers as Poe, Dickens, and Balzac. All Poe does in "Ulalume" is "to shovel the meaning into the moving stream of the metre and allow the current to carry it along." As a result the lines "protest too much . . . and, protesting, are therefore vulgar."[47] Dickens, especially the Dickens of Little Nell, indulges in a vulgar emotional overflow. His heart, sincere though it was, "overflowed with . . . curious and even rather repellent secretions." And Balzac is vulgar in his *Séraphita* by "incessant overstatements," by "a knowingness which insists on displaying itself at all costs and on all occasions."[48] With the French tragic stage and its vulgar breaking of convention, Huxley is led to explore the classicists' "ascetic code." His remarkable confession then begins.

At a recent Parisian dinner party, Huxley says, a certain French Professor of English placed him in the "Neo-Classic school." Feeling "dismally posthumous" and depressed, he claims never to have had "the smallest ambition to be a Classic of any kind, whether Neo, Palaeo, Proto or Eo." An illuminating though casual, aesthetic statement follows: Huxley has "a taste for the lively, the mixed and the incomplete in art, preferring it to the universal and the chemically pure." He finds the discipline of classicism an escape from the task of rendering actual reality and associates it with the attitude of "mere artistic shirking." Among other things he "cannot accept the Classicists' excommunication of the body," and believes "that literature should take cognizance of physiology and should investigate the still obscure relations between the mind and its body"— although, to some, the results will be not only "vulgar" but "wicked." Huxley knows that his novels have been shocking many people, but he will not abandon the "duty" of displeasing. Following Baudelaire, Huxley finds this process an intoxicating pleasure, even though it is inseparable from bad taste. He candidly admits to being deliberately vulgar himself.[49]

In indulging himself in "the aristocratic pleasure of displeasing," Huxley allies himself with his own view of Baudelaire and virtually becomes one of the satanists of his novels. To sin against the Holy Ghost, Coleman and Spandrell became seducers; for the same exciting reason, Huxley has the desire to "overstep artistic restraints." Dickens, Poe, and Balzac are vulgar perhaps by nature and temperament; Huxley is vulgar because bad taste is "intoxicatingly delightful." Contrasting himself with Flaubert, who describes his rejection of the florid, extraneous ornament, Huxley likes to seize a phrase, an irony, a description, or a tirade and make it effective enough to be artistically irrelevant. "For a self-conscious artist," he admits in the most astonishing part of his confession, "there is a most extraordinary pleasure . . . in proceeding, deliberately and with all the skill at his command, to commit precisely those vulgarities, against which his conscience warns him and which he knows he will afterwards regret."[50]

So many "irrelevant" brilliancies appear in Huxley's novels that we cannot be certain to which "offences" he refers. The interpolated dwarf story in *Crome Yellow*, perhaps; Chelifer's poems and diary in *Those Barren Leaves;* possibly the anti-Marjorie Carling attack in *Point Counter Point*. The *Vulgarity* essay itself, with its parentheses, wise-cracks, and over-developed examples, suggests that Huxley was even displeasing himself as he wrote it. Inconsistencies in his early poems,

Chelifer's cynical comments on "the last and silliest of the idols," the undisciplined, expressionistic form of his novels, repeated statements about sincerity and talent—all proclaim Huxley's ambivalence toward the very practice of art. Yet it is startling to confront such a full and frank admission, to find a writer accustomed to masked self-revelation almost boasting of the aesthetically immoral in his work. Huxley obviously feels alienated from his public, but in a most peculiar way he is alienated from himself.

Nevertheless, this confession is more purgation than boast. Huxley may have betrayed his artistic conscience in his work, but he will not hypocritically suppress it here. Like *Brief Candles*, which preceded it, and *The World of Light*, which followed, *Vulgarity in Literature* is the product of a self-conscious mind in transition, confessing a past in order to build a wholesome future. There are hints, clearly evident at least in retrospect, of the turn Huxley's development would take. Just as provocative though less startling than his Baudelairean admission is Huxley's apparent identification with Balzac. Not with Balzac the social observer; never "a congenital novelist," as Philip Quarles' journal makes clear, Huxley would never claim to have "gigantic ... power of understanding and vividly re-creating every conceivable worldly activity."[51] The parallel involves instead the sceptical Balzac who would like to be a mystic. In syntax which allows his ideas to apply to himself, Huxley claims that "Mystical religion is the ideal religion for doubters—those ultimate schismatics who have separated themselves from all belief."[52] It is parenthetically made clear, years before *The Perennial Philosophy*, that Huxley knows the literature of mysticism well himself. But with regard to Balzac, and surely indirectly himself, he finds it "painfully easy for a sceptic, who is also an amateur, theoretical and non-practising mystic, to fall into artistic insincerity, when writing about the kind of religious experiences which interest him."[53] His target is the Balzac of *Louis Lambert* and *Séraphita,* but he may also have misgivings about the mystical ending of *Those Barren Leaves*. Balzac, it seems, was also a life-worshipper *manqué;* he wanted to "know everything and to be everyone . . . to be both mystic and mundane, idealist as well as cynic, contemplator no less than man of action." Balzac's problems are those of the contemporary novelist; his case is "instructive" and "profoundly relevant."[54]

But though Huxley was before long to become a kind of mystic, he first became an even greater sceptic—in his next collection of essays and in the best known of all of his novels. In "Beliefs and Actions" of *Music at Night* (1931) his scepticism is explicit: the rationalizations of our predecessors, he claims, presuppose "transcendental entities" about which "modern circumstances compel us to feel sceptical." His psychological bias is even more persistent than it was in *Do What You Will*. In our necessary rationalizations of feelings, desires, and moods, he continues, we employ untranscendental, psychological structures[55] and live in watertight compartments, separated by formidable bulkheads, which can be unified only by ironic juxtaposition.[56] The psychological emphasis helps to unify the collection, which ranges through tragedy, puritanism, censorship, and the beauty industry. Huxley calls himself a collector of "psychological varieties,"[57] convinced that "there is no getting behind" the "primary" nature of psychological terms.[58] His scepticism, rooted in his psychological bias, combined with decided opinions about the destiny of modern culture, became the bones and the heart of *Brave New World* (London: Chatto & Windus, 1932).

Not all of Huxley's rigid, spiritless, yet self-indulgent utopia is anticipated in the essays of *Music at Night*, but many principles are enunciated there. "If society continues to develop on its present lines," Huxley claims in one selection, "men will come to be valued more and more, not as individuals, but as personified social functions."[59] Hence the Alphas, Betas, and Epsilon-minus semi-morons, the Arch-Community Songster and the World Controllers. Another essay worries about Henry Ford's industrial religion. Anticipating the Savage in his debate with Mustapha Mond, Huxley finds no other creed demanding such cruel "mutilations of the human psyche"; it has no place "for artists, mystics, or even, finally, [for] individuals."[60] The world of the novel features the "conscription of consumption"; even the games force citizens to consume. Under the unlikely title of "Selected Snobberies" the same economics, in embryo, appear in *Music at Night*: "Organized waste among consumers" is even today "the first condition of our industrial prosperity."[61] The very spirit of Huxley's sensate, Fordian culture is suggested in the selection "Foreheads Villainous Low": "The more noise you listen to, the more people you have round you, the faster you move and the more objects you possess, the happier you will be—the happier and also the more normal and virtuous."[62] Other details and motifs are anticipated also—the feelies, the emphasis on sex, even the presence of inner conflict in the man of unusual gifts. But the scepticism of *Music at Night* is the foundation of the novel. The writer of *Brave New World*, as Huxley later put it himself, was no life-worshipper but instead a "Pyrrhonic aesthete," too "amused" and detached to care that the world was going the way he showed.[63]

Brave New World also embodies a tendency even more entrenched than Huxley's scepticism. As Huxley recognized when he called himself a Pyrrhonist, the shape of the novel is partly dialectical. It presents a successful, self-perpetuating culture in graphic, almost infinite detail, yet it also offers other choices than that culture, almost surreptitiously, and in a variety of ways.

The debate between Mustapha Mond and John the Savage is dialectic in cogent, obvious form. Disgusted by almost every-

83]

thing he has seen in Fordian culture and overwrought by his mother's death from soma, the Savage has caused a riot by heaving out the window boxes of pills. Then calmed by soma vapor and a "Synthetic Anti-Riot Speech," hustled with his compatriots into the office of Mustapha Mond, the Savage discusses with Mond the merits of civilization. Their first concern is happiness and its price. The Savage defends the beauty of *Othello*; Mustapha claims that high art must be sacrificed to maintain the stability on which happiness depends. The Savage notes the maggot-like ugliness of the Bokanovsky groups; the Controller, admitting his own dislike, sees them as "the foundation on which everything else is built, . . . the gyroscope that stabilizes the rocket plane of state on its unswerving course." Helmholtz interjects the hypnopaedic claims for science; Mustapha sees pure science as "potentially subversive."[64] The new society has made its choice: happiness depends upon stability, and stability demands the stifling of every creative act, unless it will without question reinforce the state.

As the debate continues, the enemies of happiness change from art and science to religion. Rummaging in a safe stuffed with forbidden books, the Controller hauls out the Bible, *The Imitation of Christ, The Varieties of Religious Experience,* some Newman and some Maine de Biran. In Newman, identified as an "old Arch-Community Songster," Mustapha reads that our happiness is to view ourselves as the property of God. From Biran he quotes a passage on sickness and old age, and the consequent emergence of the religious sentiment and the consciousness of God. Biran's analysis is irrelevant: the religious sentiment is supposed to "compensate for our losses," but in the brave new world the losses no longer appear. When the Savage answers feebly that it's "natural" to believe in God, Mustapha counters by making fun of F.H. Bradley, who didn't realize that "one believes things because one has been conditioned to believe them." As the Savage articulates his presuppositions and ideals, Mustapha shows that none of them applies. At the end the two men agree to disagree. Mustapha's goal remains the childlike happiness of others while the Savage insists on freedom, on the right to be unhappy, even with the ugliness, fear, and pain which that right must entail.[65]

Mustapha's side of the dialectic begins much earlier, in chapter 3, in one element of a dizzy, accelerating montage. Addressing a touring group of "Hatchery and Conditioning" students, his slant this time is psychological. His target is the now mysterious institution of the family, with all the psychological overtones that that institution implies. Claiming Freud this time as his prophet instead of Ford, he pictures the "home" in lurid, exaggerated terms, as "stiflingly over-inhabited by a man, . . . a periodically teeming woman, . . . a rabble of boys and girls of all ages." It is "as squalid psychically as physically," so "hot" is it with the frictions of life, with the "suffocating . . . insane, obscene relationships between the members of the family group." Hence the need to subdue and channel off emotion, "to make your lives," the Controller tells his hearers, "emotionally easy—to preserve you, so far as that is possible, from having any emotions at all." Desires are relieved or satisfied as soon as they arise, by entertainment, copulation, ritual and drugs. Stability is again the "primal and ultimate need." And he races through the establishment of the seventh-century A.F. world—through the death of liberalism, "Simple Life," and culture; through the development of ectogenesis, conditioning, and hypnopaedia; through the destruction of historical monuments, and the replacement of God by Community Sings and Solidarity Services; through the discovery of soma—the perfect drug—and finally the hormonal conquest of old age.[66]

Mustapha's distorted comments, of course, are dialectically countered by the words and the living example of the Savage, and not only in his idealistic statements during the novel's final debate. Brought up in his New Mexican Reservation by a "civilized" mother abandoned among primitives, the Savage represents in his grotesque suicide Huxley's "lunatic" alternative of "*Penitente* ferocity."[67] But he is a much more ingenious and effective opponent of Mustapha by virtue of his ready knowledge of Shakespeare's poems and plays. Rejected by the natives because of his mother's promiscuity, John has spent many an hour on a battered volume of Shakespeare's works. To comprehend the London he has been thrust into he must employ Shakespearean, and hence pre-Fordian, terms. Almost every cultural value represented in the plays has been discarded by the society in which he suddenly appears. Whereas frustrated love leads Helmholtz Watson to guffaw, John thinks of his beloved Lenina as the "rich jewel in an Ethiop's ear" who cannot be approached "before all sanctimonious ceremonies . . . with full and holy rite" have been performed. So imbued is he with Shakespearean morality, so ridden with guilt by any suggestion of lust, that when Lenina offers her charms he becomes the wrathful vindictive Othello, and eventually the aged Lear condemning lechery. Love, chastity, marriage and other Shakespearean socio-ethical concepts are, until John presents them, almost totally unknown. When Helmholtz hopes for creative self-fulfillment he nurtures a feeling he could not understand before his own reading of the plays. The moth-eaten volume and the priceless treasure it contains become the symbol of the values, all but forgotten, of our culture. Bernard Marx also rejects the sterile assumptions of his culture. He "doesn't like Obstacle Golf"; he even likes to be alone; and he joins in the soma battle with his anarchist friends. Obviously he too supports John's side of the dialectic.

But the most effective answer to Mustapha is another long-familiar trait—a persistent, even relentless ironic tone. The promises and values argued directly by Mustapha Mond are throughout the novel immersed in ironic dialogue. Every detail seems to embody its ironic opposite; its very appearance implies amusing and deprecating comment. When babies are manufactured on the Hatchery assembly line, we think of the mysteries of birth, now killed by the machine. "Community, Identity, Stability," the motto of the state, echoes the contrasting slogan of the eighteenth-century Jacobins. Institutional proper names immediately ridicule themselves: Human Element Manager and Assistant Fertilizer-General; the Hounslow Feely Studio, the Fordson Community Singery and the Young Women's Fordian Association; The Westminster Abbey Cabaret and Propaganda House; Electro-magnetic Golf, Centrifugal Bumble-puppy, and the Semi-Demi-Finals of the Women's Heavyweight Wrestling Championship. The characters' names are comically ironic: Benito Hoover, Polly Trotsky, Morgana Rothschild, Sarojini Engels. And so of course are the nursery rhymes: "Streptocock-G to Banbury-T/To see a fine Bathroom and W.C."

Against the mocking background of these cultural details, we watch the characters in their ironic choices and acts. No reader forgets the conditioning scene of chapter 3, where infants crawling toward flowers and books are greeted with electric shocks and clanging bells. When the men and their "pneumatic" women complete their daily routine, they play Riemann-surface tennis or indulge in unrestricted sex. Periodically pseudo-religious services are held: the communicants gather in a circle, pass around the soma-cup, sing Solidarity Hymns, listen to a piped-in, tremulous voice, and complete the ritual by copulating on the floor. The ironic knife cuts, of course, in both temporal directions. The proper names, the institutions, the cultural patterns are originally ours. During its composition, Huxley saw *Brave New World* as a "revolt" against "the horror of the Wellsian Utopia."[68] Yet he extrapolated his vision of the future from his sceptical, detached observations of the present. A projection of what our culture may become, the novel seems each day to comment more accurately on us now.

By now a classic, its title a household phrase, the novel does have significant defects. Bernard Marx is another ineffectual romantic idealist, another version of Denis, Gumbril, Chelifer and Walter Bidlake, and hence another partial projection of Aldous Huxley himself. At first he is a useful, even sympathetic figure, sensitive to the beauties of the ocean and disturbed by the treatment of Lenina as "so much meat." But Huxley cannot be serious about his alienation. Having chosen to be the amused, Pyrrhonic aesthete, Huxley cannot simultaneously—in this novel, at least—identify with the unamused, self-conscious man, Bernard. With the help of shallow psychology he is turned into an insignificant fool, and eventually shoved almost entirely out of the way. Another weakness appears in the treatment of John the Savage, whose early years constitute an overwritten, unconvincing part of the novel.

Yet on the whole the Savage is one of Huxley's best creations, effective as a Shakespearean, as a debater, as an idealistic worshipper of Lenina. At the end he helps Huxley to shatter the novel's tone, and to assert dramatically one of its most important themes. John has been cursed with an id-and-superego split, a war between ideals and the sexuality those ideals repress. Stimulated by Lenina to both romantic love and physical lust, his response is to purge his guilt in grotesquely masochistic ways, by drinking mustard-water or slashing himself with a whip. But Darwin Bonaparte's hidden cameras ruthlessly record his private life, and his activities become known throughout the Western world. When swarms of visitors, and Lenina, arrive where he has been living alone, the brave new world has trapped him once and for all. His superego collapses in an orgy, and the only thing left for him is self-destruction. Like Bernard and Helmholtz but far more helplessly, John has tried to find and live his selfhood. Selfhood, however, must be allowed and then nourished by culture. John's suicide, motivated by guilt, symbolizes the fact that in this world no true self can survive.

Hence *Brave New World* is more than another Huxley dialectic, and more than a damningly accurate vision of technological emptiness. It is an exploration in the most significant existentialist tradition of the relationship between the self and contemporary culture.[69] In *Do What You Will* Huxley had treated the self in almost total isolation and produced an oversimplified and impossible prescription. Now purged of his willed desire to "worship life," Huxley examines the problem in a fruitful though frightening way. Like Karl Jaspers' *Man in the Modern Age* published the year before, *Brave New World* asserts—though Huxley later would deny it—that the hopes of men are "no longer anchored in Transcendence."[70] Jaspers and Huxley both recognize the growing power of the state. Both are concerned about the authenticity of the self in what Jaspers calls an era of "advanced technique." Both show a kind of personal concern, Jaspers through his deeply serious, meditative tone, Huxley through Bernard, Helmholtz, the Savage, and at moments even Lenina and Mustapha Mond. But Jaspers stands beyond the incisive ironies of *Brave New World*. He believes that there "is no human existence without cleavage,"[71] yet that every man must "fight wittingly on behalf of his true essence";[72] and he is ready to comment on what mankind can become. Huxley, though he apparently still personifies the cleavage, will eventually believe that it can and must be healed. He will fight for his essence in his own unusual way, and offer his own far more elaborate views on the destiny that mankind, if it will decide to, can grasp.

CHAPTER FIVE

EXISTENCE, ESSENCE, AND PACIFISM:

Texts and Pretexts to Eyeless in Gaza

IN NOVEMBER 1936, four years after *Brave New World* was published, about seven thousand pacifists gathered at a Peace Pledge Union meeting in London's Albert Hall.[1] Writers and intellectuals, as they had the previous year, joined forces with others to arouse opposition to all war. At the first meeting Edmund Blunden and Siegfried Sassoon had spoken; this time in the unlikely company of Lord Ponsonby, the labor peer, and George Lansbury, the former labor leader, a featured speaker was the inventor of Obstacle Golf and Centrifugal Bumble-puppy.[2] Huxley's presence symbolizes a startling change in his attitude, for he never would have appeared even two or three years earlier.[3] His confession in *Vulgarity in Literature*, though it suggests a period of transition, does not hint at such newly active social and moral concern, such willingness to become existentially involved. Addressing mass meetings, however, soon became a part of the past, one phase —an important one—in Huxley's long struggle to resolve his inner conflict. Through *Brave New World* the conflict is recorded; thereafter Huxley's work shows him trying to remove it.

Huxley's search for answers, recorded in a characteristic variety of forms, took him to any number of sources, more often than not unorthodox, obscure, or even suspect. Education, science, and religion are common themes; so are little-known philosophers and artists, Oriental mystics, hallucinogens, and ESP. Never rigorous or systematic in the way he presents his quest, Huxley is frequently guilty of wishful thinking, inconsistency, logical fallacy, and fuzzy rhetoric. Yet we can always find him exploring either essence or existence, trying to capture some unblemished ultimate or urging himself (and his public) to some kind of immersion in the flux of life. Eventually Huxley envisions the understanding embracing both, in an "existential religion of mysticism,"[4] and he sees the human potential for a wholly enlightened, yet wholly practical life.

I

ONE OF HUXLEY's early steps in his search for personal answers seems to show him moving as much sideways as ahead. *Texts and Pretexts* (1932), seemingly an anthology but actually a kind of manifesto, only hints at the foundation of Huxley's final view. It is offered as a collection, largely of poetry, including major and minor English writers, some Baudelaire and Mallarmé, and prose passages of Kierkegaard, Pascal, and Maine de Biran. With the influence of religion waning, with jazz and popular songs filling the air, the need for exposure to good art, Huxley says, is particularly acute. Life still imitates art; the older poets, if they are "decoded" by comment, will be valuable to the contemporary reader.[5] Hence the passages are arranged under a score or so of different headings, with Huxley analyzing the passages he quotes. In the same year as *Texts and Pretexts* Huxley cited his need for "an acceptable philosophical system."[6] His early comments in the anthology seem to offer a metaphysic and a psychology, a rudimentary but far-reaching philosophical view. Yet Huxley at this point is unable to make his ideas cohere. Since there is, or seems to be, a "soul of the world" and since we human beings have souls, we are in "solidarity with the universe." But "psychological obstacles" prevent us, most of the time, from becoming "blissfully conscious" of this solidarity.[7] At another point the obstacles are seen as removable;[8] at still another we read that "Man and the universe are incommensurable."[9] Similarly, we can have the "*all* feeling" Melville attributed to Goethe, when "not-all feelings" are not blocking the way.[10] Yet when Huxley later rejects both instinct and intuition,[11] it is hard to see how the "all" feeling can ever appear. In urging us to form (in Keats's words) "a fellowship with essence,"[12] Huxley touches the Atman-Brahman relationship of Hinduism, the very basis of *The Perennial Philosophy* and of *Island*. He echoes the Christian existentialism of Paul Tillich, where the essence of "all" appears as "being-itself." But at this point Huxley is not yet sure of his ground. His metaphysic dissolves in inconsistency, his psychology in lack of clarity, and ethical problems are conveniently and dogmatically dodged. *Texts and Pretexts* often condemns the common habit of rationalizing, yet Huxley himself often unconsciously rationalizes.

Beyond the Mexique Bay (1934), though more valuable, is another far from convincing book. Like *Jesting Pilate* it is a journal—this time of Huxley's 1933 journey to the West Indies, Central America, and Mexico. Malcolm Cowley called the trip merely an occasion for Huxley's "noble reflections";[13] Carl Van Doren, who assessed Huxley's as "one of the most interesting minds alive," saw him as "modest," "sagacious," "consistent" and occasionally capable of turning anthropology into "pure wisdom."[14] At this distance the truth seems to lie closer to Cowley, though somewhere in between. Since Huxley was even less at home in Central America than in India or Burma, his disconcerting snobbery erupts again. He analyzes the Indian as one who saves up for "first of all, a gun, so that he can, if the need arises, murder his neighbour; second, a princely hat in which to swagger abroad and excite the general envy; and finally . . . a sewing-machine."[15] He finds in Mexico "a type of woman more horrifyingly animal, more abysmally whorish in appearance, than any [he has] seen in any other part of the world."[16] His emotional discomfort and detachment again seduce him into easy abstraction, the refuge he has warned us against in *Texts and Pretexts* and criticized Wordsworth for in "Wordsworth in the Tropics." Central America, for example, is the best place to study the European powers, since it is just a miniature Europe "with the lid off."[17] Similarly, international politics are a psychological problem; without the psychological problems, the economic ones would not exist. To this half-truth Huxley appends a disturbing, though original, solution: a "World Psychological Conference" at which experts would choose the "emotional cultures to be permitted and encouraged. . . ."[18] Occasionally Huxley is something like his earlier best in treating Mayan art,[19] or in analyzing the "rhythm of human life" as "routine punctuated by orgies . . . whether sexual, religious, sporting or political. . . ."[20] More often, however, he is too detached to be convincing. "When man became an intellectual and spiritual being," he concludes, "he paid for his new privileges with a treasure of intuitions, of emotional spontaneity, of sensuality still innocent of all self-consciousness." When Lawrence went to Mexico he failed to get his money back, says Huxley;[21] with the more self-conscious Huxley it was out of the question even to try. Instead, he visualized a life *combining* the self-conscious and the spontaneous—though not until his final novel, *Island*.

II

Though *Beyond the Mexique Bay* exposes detachment as a danger, it at least begins to hint at a corollary value. Detachment might lead to simplistic, purely theoretical solutions, but it was nevertheless an attitude helpful in analyzing cultural problems. It enabled Huxley to detect the rationalizations of others even though he might elsewhere unknowingly rationalize himself. And when he returned to Europe from his Central American journey, rationalization had assumed world-wide importance. It was supporting the spirit of nationalism, which was ominously leading the world toward a state of active war. Hence in *The Olive Tree* (1936), where he deals largely with the insidious ties of rationalization, Huxley produced a provocative, valuable book—and concurrently made his important existential choice to become involved in the pacifist attempt to prevent war.

One essay, "Justifications," displays "fantastic and far-fetched" rationalizations of sexuality,[22] like Henry Prince's claim that his public fornication was God's will. Propaganda, however, is Huxley's major target. In "Writers and Readers" he states his major point, that "social and political propaganda . . . is influential only when it is a rationalization of the desires, sentiments, prejudices or interests of those to whom it is addressed."[23] In "Words and Behaviour" the point is applied to nationalism and war. War is not only "enormously discreditable" to the leaders who begin it, but also to "those who merely tolerate its existence." Since people do not want to face either the ugly facts or their own responsibility, they find the proper words to hide the threat of the truth. "Finding the reality of war too unpleasant to contemplate, we create a verbal alternative to that reality, parallel with it, but in quality quite different from it." We then merely have to face the "fiction of war as it exists in our pleasantly falsifying verbiage." Our seemingly stupid behavior "turns out, on analysis, to be the most refined cunning."[24] This acuteness and its intensified tone are not an accident. The year of *The Olive Tree* Huxley delivered his speech in Albert Hall. By the time the book appeared he was an active pacifist.

The founder of the Peace Pledge Union, sponsor of the meetings in Albert Hall, had a personal magnetism approaching that of Lawrence, though he hardly would have subscribed to most of Lawrence's views. He was Hugh Richard Lawrie Sheppard, Canon of St. Paul's Cathedral, a man able to disturb even Max Beerbohm's isolated reserve. On October 16, 1934 Sheppard's famous letter appeared in the English press, asking for a postcard from any male willing to renounce war publicly as a crime against humanity. Within a year Sheppard had 80,000 pledges and, by early 1937, 50,000 more.[25] He was supported not only by Blunden, Sassoon and Huxley, but by A. A. Milne, Osbert Sitwell, Rose Macaulay, Laurence Housman, Murry, Cyril Joad, Bertrand Russell and many other prominent people.[26] According to Sybil Morrison, a persistent pacifist, Sheppard was a "legend while he lived . . . a man unique in his dedication to humanity, extraordinary in his reckless expenditure of himself." She describes the first mass meeting as "unforgettably inspiring, intensely exciting, and overwhelmingly successful."[27]

Huxley served the movement as both a speaker and a writer. The Albert Hall talk might have come from "Words and Behaviour," for he is reported as saying that "it was impossible to kill fellow human beings except when they are referred to in words like Fascist and Communist, which deny their humanity and specify only their principles."[28] In *What Are You Going to Do About It?* (London: Chatto & Windus, 1936), the movement's first official pamphlet, he borrows from biology, history and the Bible to refute potential objections to the cause. As "editor" and probably major writer of *An Encyclopaedia of Pacifism,* Huxley offers the social psychology of *Beyond the Mexique Bay:* "Nationalism is the most powerful of contemporary religions, and in all countries children are systematically instructed in the tenets of the local nationalist creed."[29] Psychology is sometimes subordinated to economics: under "Causes of War," "pursuit of wealth" is listed first, followed in turn by "glory" and "creed." The idea of a "Class War" is accepted, though "without necessarily accepting the Marxian analysis of our social order."[30] Prophetically, the *Encyclopaedia* would establish a kind of Peace Corps, a "system of peace-time national service," consisting of "tough jobs and civilian risks," to supply a sufficiently exciting equivalent for war.[31] The weakness of the pamphlet is the weakness of pacifism—its refusal to establish any meaningful moral scale. We hear no echo of Huxley's attacks on Naziism and Hitler; England, not Germany, seems to come off the worst. The ethic of the *Encyclopaedia* is the most pointed we have seen, a resolute, uncompromising insistence on nonviolence. It would operate in pacifist cells, "pledged to put pacifist principles into action in all circumstances of life. . . ."[32] The *Encyclopaedia* analyzes its own central concept:

> Non-violence does not mean doing nothing. It means making the enormous effort required to overcome evil with good. Non-violence does not rely on strong muscles and devilish armaments; it relies on moral courage, self-control and the knowledge, unswervingly acted upon, that there is in every human being, however brutal, however personally hostile, a fund of kindness, a love of justice, a respect for goodness and truth which can be reached by anyone who uses the right means. To use these means is often extraordinarily hard, but history shows that it can be done—and done not only by exceptional individuals, but by large groups of ordinary men and women and even by governments.[33]

Even though the pacifist movement had many intellectual supporters, its demise was hastened by intellectual opponents. Huxley's *What Are You Going to Do About It?* was attacked by C. Day-Lewis, in *We're Not Going to Do Nothing.*[34] George Orwell made biting references to the "Fascifist gang."[35] As the opposition increased the Church took an increasingly active part, with the Bishop of London calling the pacifists the real dangers to peace and the Archbishop of York referring to the "Christian duty" to kill.[36] Sheppard came to America to preach sermons and raise money,[37] but after he died in October, 1937, disputes within the movement helped to weaken it. By 1939 pacifist leaders allegedly were in touch with a German propaganda organization.[38] When war broke out more than 50 percent of the Union's membership resigned, as Sheppard himself had predicted before he died.[39] But Huxley turned his pacifist experience (and much more) into *Eyeless in Gaza* (London: Chatto & Windus, 1936), the most vivid of recent unread British novels and one of the most important statements of his life.

Huxley's letters show clearly that *Eyeless in Gaza* was the most trying of his novels to write. Huxley began "meditating" it as early as 1932[40] and was "working feverishly" on it in 1933.[41] But the following year he was "stickily entangled";[42] in 1935 he reported "chronic trouble," and Maria referred to a six-month period of "insomnia . . . , gloom, irritation [and] lack of work."[43] Supposedly, Aldous' difficulties were behind him when (in May) she wrote this, yet in November the book still would not "get finished."[44] When Huxley first began to think of writing *Eyeless in Gaza,* before he became involved in pacifist work, he retained his *Point Counter Point* theory of various "universes of discourse," discontinuous with each other so far as men could know. No cosmology was more than imaginative exercise.[45] During his pacifist involvement, in the midst of composition, Huxley saw no "remedy for the horrors of human beings except religion or . . . any religion that we could all believe in."[46] *Eyeless in Gaza,* discounting the abortive *Texts and Pretexts,* records the true beginning of Huxley's quest to find one. The difficulties of composition surely reflect the strain involved. Huxley not only looked squarely at himself; he tried to see how he (and the rest of humanity) should answer the basic questions of essence and existence, how he and they should really try to live. Though Huxley never actually tells us so himself, *Eyeless in Gaza* is the frankest, fullest confessional he ever wrote.

The friends and relatives of Anthony Beavis, Huxley's protagonist, were so clearly drawn from life[47] that Huxley had to write his stepmother in self-defense.[48] In many other ways Anthony's life runs parallel to Huxley's, yet the crucial resemblance is a matter of change in attitude: Anthony, like Huxley, wants to become a better man. In the midst of his struggle Huxley wrote of the "horror" he felt "at any kind of personal contact with people, other than those in the immediate neighborhood—and even with those!"[49] To another correspondent he confessed to "my besetting sin, the dread and avoidance of emotion, the escape from personal responsibility. . . ."[50] Hence *Eyeless in Gaza* follows Anthony's attempts to purge his indifference, his traveller's-eye view refusal to "be bothered about people." Like Huxley, Anthony writes *about* the problem of personality, with the help of recent psychology, of McTaggart, Bradley, and Hume. Yet such intellectual excursions are precisely Anthony's (and Huxley's) most dangerous moral temptations—rationalizations and withdrawals, self-justifications of the lack of inner unity. With Anthony, as with Huxley, the problem at this point is not a matter of theory; it is one that has to be existentially solved. As *Eyeless in Gaza* opens (*in medias res*) Anthony is jolted out of detachment by the force of life in the raw. An airplane dumps a yelping dog right next to him and his mistress, and in a moment both of them are splattered with its blood. Though Anthony's first reaction is a shocking jocularity, he soon revolts against his insensitive detachment and succeeds in fully immersing himself in life. A trip to Mexico, instead of *Beyond the Mexique Bay* detachment, includes a night of bedbugs, an attack of dysentery, a dangerous jungle trip, and a barroom threat to his life. Only then can Anthony learn from James Miller, a kind of anthropologist-doctor, that pacifism with the love and nonviolence it is based on can modify his character and prove that change has taken place. After the existential challenge (well before "existential" became a common word), Anthony gains much more—a tenable ethic and politics, a "fellowship with essence," an understanding (presumably shared by Huxley) of good, evil, and ultimate truth.

A weakness of Huxley's scheme for Anthony's regeneration is its obviously heavy dependence upon Miller. Like Rampion before him and Propter and Bruno still to come, Miller is one of those prophetic, morally flawless Huxley spokesmen whom critics find extremely hard to take. Once identified as Dick Sheppard combined with Gerald Heard,[51] Miller is more likely Huxley's image of Dr. Theodore Pennell, the man who subdued hostile Indian tribes with nonviolent psychology in 1892.[52] But he is also a spokesman for F. Matthias Alexander, author of (among other books) *The Use of the Self.* Though Miller immediately spots Anthony's negative scepticism, he is more interested in Anthony's appearance and physique, which sound like the seedy Huxley that Lawrence's letters describe. He finds a significance in the forehead and lips, doesn't like the sallow skin, guesses correctly about scurfy hair, headaches, stiff necks and lumbago, and blames Anthony's attitude on intestinal trouble and the condition of his spine. He concludes that Anthony has divided his natural unity in three—"An admirable manipulator of ideas, linked with a person who, so far as self-knowledge and feeling are concerned is just a moron; and the pair of you associated with a half-witted body." He later gives Anthony a lesson in the proper use of the self, an exercise in getting properly in and out of a chair. The diagnosis and the exercise are Alexanderism, "a technique for translating good intentions into acts."[53] Huxley was an Alexander pupil, and one of his most loyal and outspoken supporters. Alexander cured the insomnia the novel had helped to cause in Huxley—so at least Maria Huxley claimed. But he also "made a new and unrecognizable person of Aldous"; he "brought out, actively, all we . . . know never came out either in the novels or with strangers."[54]

Alexander, a friend and instructor of John Dewey as well as Huxley, has himself described the genesis of Miller's method. Once a successful amateur reciter of Shakespeare, he tells us, he decided to take up reciting as a profession but ran into serious trouble with his throat and vocal chords. When his physician could not tell him what it was that caused the trouble, he started to use a mirror to find out for himself. A habit of putting his head back, he learned, was associated with the problem, yet correcting it was by no means a matter of either "feel" or will. "When a wrong habitual use has been cultivated in a person for whatever purpose," he writes, "its influence . . . is practically irresistible." Only continued, rigorous training in a new bodily procedure allowed him to destroy the old objectionable habits, and to develop, as he put it, "constructive conscious control" of the self.[55]

Although Alexander seems to have been a fad—his books are now all out of print[56]—Huxley seems to have had full confidence in his techniques, greater even than Anthony displays in *Eyeless in Gaza*. In a book review five years later Huxley finds them one of the two solutions (the other is the mystic's) for "the problem of bridging the gap between idealistic theory and actual practice." Alexander makes possible "creative conscious control" of what to Huxley is still a "psycho-physical organism."[57] Hence Alexanderism, like the "balanced excess" of Huxley's earlier life-worship phase, has a deliberate, self-conscious *mental* element. Habituated for years to the free ranging of his mind, with sceptical negativism as a corollary or result, Huxley apparently found congenial answers to his needs in the control and the consciousness stressed by Alexander, the discipline rationally understood.

The confident tone of the review, however, belies the difficulty *Eyeless in Gaza* and the letters suggest that Huxley faced. Anthony's journal records his inner struggle even after the meeting with Miller, now to check "all improper uses of the self." He notes one significant advance after one of Miller's lessons; he is learning to "refuse to be hurried into gaining ends by the equivalent (in personal, psycho-physiological terms) of violent revolution," to concentrate, before he acts, "on the means whereby the end is to be achieved. . . ."[58] Still tempted, as Philip Quarles was, by the Higher Life, Anthony devotes a whole journal-essay to the problem. It is, among other things, "A more complete escape from the responsibilities of living than alcohol or morphia or addiction to sex or property."[59] Even by attacking the Higher Life Anthony can live it once again.

Eyeless in Gaza is more than autobiography and self-analysis, however. It is a moral vision as well as a series of self-directed moral lessons, a vision of evil combined with an answering vision of good. The lessons are largely packed into Anthony's journal; the vision emerges from the most vivid scenes in Huxley's fiction. At Bulstrode school one morning, for example, Anthony is summoned to another cubicle, where a silent but seething crowd of boys peers unseen at a schoolmate, Goggler Ledwidge. With thick glasses, a rupture appliance and a woolen undervest he has long ago outgrown, Goggler has just been caught in the act of masturbation. Anthony's moral cowardice is then shown, not merely told. Though his friend Brian urges pity rather than scorn, Anthony laughs, shouts insults, and hurls his slipper like the others. Anthony's moral condition later is much worse. He breaks a promise to Brian so as to have dinner with Gerry Watchett, about to become the most repulsive of all of Huxley's villains. Gerry's circle means a chance for observing with detachment. Anthony can feel "amused astonishment," like the Huxley who, in *Beyond the Mexique Bay,* saw himself as a kind of explorer among the "blackamoors."[60] In the same scene detachment is shown through imagery. As a younger boy Anthony saw the world as a "vast and intricate jewel," but after ten years the single jewel has split into fragments. Each glass of wine on Gerry's table is a "great yellow beryl, solid and translucent." Apples and oranges are transformed to "enormous gems." Even sound is "frozen and crystalline"; a bawdy limerick is "sculptured jade." Although Anthony is drunk when he sees this dazzling array, the images help to communicate the usual state of his mind. Their supernatural brilliance is somehow "remote" and "strangely irrelevant." The objects he sees all reside in an aquarium, where he himself is a god-like fish, separate in spirit from his own physical being.[61]

Anthony's moral irresponsibility develops partly through a quadrangle involving Mary, his mistress; his friend Brian; and Brian's fiancée, Joan. Brian, victim of a compulsion to check with shocking suddenness his ardent advances to Joan, asks Anthony to mediate with her about this psychological distress. Instead, Anthony turns it into an amusing tale for Mary, then takes Mary's dare to seduce Joan for himself. An *Othello* performance, a powerfully ironic background for the seduction, produces in Joan a state of intense "movedness," with her emotions harmonized into a "precarious miracle" before Anthony takes advantage of her state. Joan's innocent intensity and Anthony's cool, sophisticated detachment are handled by Huxley with imaginative sureness and unusual depth of understanding.

The recognition scene, however, the moment of existential shock, is the most memorable incident in all of Huxley's work. This symbolic event, with copulation interrupted by the cries and blood of the dog, alone suggests much of what Huxley is trying to say. A man-made object moves in the material realm above the lovers; it gives "birth," in an act also suggesting defecation, to animality, to violent death, to all the precariousness and ugliness evident so often elsewhere in the novel. That night Anthony is awakened by a long-familiar but haunting symbolic dream. As he eats some food in the "obscure but embarrassing presence of strangers," it expands, grows rubbery, sticks to his mouth and almost asphyxiates him. The nightmare, we are told, has "some kind of vague but horrible connection with the dog." Anthony's selfish detachment, the dream suggests, is caused by his inability or unwillingness to cope with actual experience, and is allied with the fear of hostile judgment by people unknown. The dream leads to an important free association: he thinks of his mother, of his first mistress, of the "sun-warmed flesh" of the Helen who has left him, the fly-infested corpse of Brian, and of the carcass of the dog. These images, symbolic of the main elements of his life, return to remind him of his selfish, harmful past.[62] A few days later he begins to understand, to embark on the road to involvement and self-change, to universal compassion, nonviolence, and love.

The vision of evil and ugliness encompasses more than Anthony's life, for a main theme is the distortion of love, its degradation into objectionable or repulsive forms. Helen, for example, has known only a gross, largely physical attachment. Before her affair with Anthony she has succumbed to Gerry Watchett, with a sick kitten involved this time, instead of a dead dog. Although the animal is "heavenly" when it is healthy, its sudden illness disgusts her, like the kidneys she stole years before on her shopping tour with her sister Joyce. Gerry, after curing the kitten, takes advantage of Helen's distress to seduce her. As she lies awake later in a sordid room in Paris, shortly after the fright of her abortion, the hallucinations which plague her are just as terrifying as her actual plight. In a suggestive dream analogous to Anthony's, she watches, near a huge statue of Voltaire, a play of intrigue about violence and love. After "revoltingly delicious" public love-making with Gerry, she starts to kiss her nephew's fingers. The child is transformed into the dying kitten, the kidneys she once stole, and the horrible remains of her own operation. The falling dog means to her all these things she fears and abhors and alerts her to her substitution of the flesh for love. Yet she never understands the irony of her attachment, never is able to feel love's liberating power. Her physical being appeals to her husband—Goggler Ledwidge, of all people—no more than the disgusting kidneys did to her, yet she treats him with cruelty when he transforms their marriage into a beautiful, lyrical novel. Her affair with Anthony leads to a fuller love for Ekki Giesebrecht, the Communist, but with the suddenness of the falling dog, he is abducted by the Nazis for certain torture and death. While she waits for him by the symbolic river Rhine she sees it as "swift and purposive," rushing by "like life itself, like the power behind the world, eternally, irresistibly flowing." Seeing herself as "a partaker of its power," she misinterprets its meaning. In her full acceptance of Ekki's anti-Nazi passion, she does not see that all physical existence is transitory, and that human love is worthless if it is allied with political, militaristic hate. She knows only that at any time another dog may fall.

The curse of the absence or of the distortion of love also strikes the older generation, and Anthony's unrepressed, anti-Victorian London friends. Mrs. Foxe, the real cause of Brian's Oedipal distress, is as possessive as the mothers in *Those Barren Leaves* and *Antic Hay,* but more dangerous, with her glittering unselfishness as a disguise. Anthony's father, convinced he is showing true love for his dead wife, really participates in self-congratulating rituals, for he suddenly forgets his loss and abruptly marries again. James Beavis, Anthony's uncle, has no use for women at all, but rather a strong though unexpressed attachment to younger men. Beppo Bowles fizzles and giggles over the deviants of Berlin cafes, argues with a blackmailer and is forced to pay him off, and propositions the attendant at a public convenience in Hyde Park. Mary seduces Anthony, gives herself (and her money), before Helen does, to Gerry, and ends up a morphia addict with delusions that she can still appeal to men. Her life is symbolized, appropriately, by a needle; Beppo's, by a row of urinals lined with boys. Mary's daughter Joyce and her husband Colin are merely respectable, and so devoid of conjugal feeling that they are as miserable as the rest. The spontaneous, romantic, naive Joan Thursley has little chance to survive in such a world. Victimized by the tortured, inherently selfish scruples of Brian, her innocent warmth drags her, too, under the tide.

Unhappiness and degradation, unnatural restraint and mis-directed desire, selfish, possessive egocentric love, permeate the imagined world of *Eyeless in Gaza*. A few scenes, like Helen's parlor game with her kitten, display Huxley's annoy-ing tendency to overexplain what hardly needs to be explained at all. And near the end the horrifying vision becomes almost unbearably intense, with the scream of a dope-fiend, a night-marish abortion, and unsparing description of Mark Staithes' gangrenous leg. Yet Huxley's vividness and directness are al-most always under complete control. Though the world he creates is not one we could take for very long, it is one we can be-lieve in, however frequently we are disgusted or appalled. Hux-ley selects or exaggerates the sordid in reality—as do Faulkner, Dostoyevsky, Swift, and the author of the Book of Job—so that both Anthony and the reader will be immersed in the evil he envisions. Commitment to people means commitment to people at their worst. If we ignore the unpleasant, then we cannot find the truth.

Huxley's vision, which appears at first to be disordered, is cast into deliberately anti-traditional form. The opening love-scene, itself one of the last episodes recounted of Anthony's life, is interrupted by several leaps backward and forward in time, before (in chapter 12) the yelping dog actually plunges to the roof. Five separate partial narratives are intertwined, each tracing less than two years, each interrupted by Anthony's journal discussions of pacifism, love and many other themes.[63] One result is the rejection of naturalistic form: like a George Moore or Zola heroine, Mary Amberley declines from happy motherhood to dope addiction, yet no environmental causal forces are ever detailed. Another is Huxley's rejection of tragedy: Brian Foxe, a talented, eager youth ready to sacrifice himself, is destroyed by circumstances combined with a single flaw; yet Huxley makes the dramatic least of these elements by "recalling" Brian's suicide before it is described. Similarly, social criticism, psychological analysis, and melodrama appear, yet none is allowed to shape the novel's form. Instead Huxley sets personality against time, and asks whether old patterns and habits can be changed. For three romantic idealists they apparently cannot. Brian, "extraordinarily decent" from his days in Bulstrode school, anxious to devote his life to helping mankind, comes to love his ideals more than other people. Since his spirit has power to urge rejection of the flesh, he is crushed like John the Savage between superego and id. To Hugh "Goggler" Ledwidge his wife is only an internalized beautiful image. Working in a museum, away from the realities of life, he contemplates her spirit in the presence of primitive spears before idealizing her in the pages of his novel. Mark Staithes is a Chelifer-like idealist become a cynic, who sees human beings as "like dogs on an acropolis . . . only too anxious to lift a leg against every statue." His contempt springs from his total, idealizing love of himself.

Anthony Beavis would like to believe that he can ignore his past but *Eyeless in Gaza* shows that he cannot. He hates the thought of his "personal enemy" Marcel Proust, "squatting, horribly white and flabby, with breasts almost female but fledged with long black hairs, for ever squatting in the tepid bath of his remembered past."[64] He learns, however, that personality *is* continuous, that people are (as Hopkins puts it) "their sweating selves, but worse"—unless they follow the way of nonviolence and love. Idealists, cynics, nymphomaniacs, communists, all imprison themselves in the burrows of their egos. The burrow may be deeply sensual, or it may be an "intellectual other-world" of the kind inhabited by Anthony's philologist father. The meaning and the result are essentially the same. But even before the dog descends, Anthony begins to feel that the truth resides on another, deeper level. The smell of Helen, as he bends to kiss her shoulder, reminds him of a voluptuously happy childhood game with Brian. He wonders if the original experience may have had "a point, a profound purpose . . . to be recollected here . . . as his lips made contact with Helen's sun-warmed flesh." In the midst of his "detached and irresponsible" act he is reminded "of the things that Brian had lived for." Even Brian's suicide, he concludes, "was mysteriously implicit" in Helen's hot skin.[65]

From these thoughts emerge an ethic, an aesthetic, and a supporting metaphysic, fathered more by physical science than by any theology. In the hostile Mexican's pistol, in the blood from Brian's body, the "same constellations" of energy-units appear, the same in the sun as in the "living flesh" it warms. Every organism is unique, yet united with every other; a secretion from one species can save another's life. Minds are identical also, because the "mental pattern of love can be transferred from one mind to another and still retain its virtue, just as the physical pattern of a hormone can be transferred." United and separate concurrently, people are brought together by good and divided by evil. Hence separation and diversity, as the Buddhist element in Huxley's final view will have it, are the very condition of life, without which the good and the beautiful cannot be known. Vigilant love and compassion will expand the area of good and perhaps even unify existence with the intellect—intuitively, with completeness of understanding.

"No more discourse" is Anthony's goal, "only experience, only unmediated knowledge, as of a colour, a perfume, a musical sound." His aesthetic is a brief phase of Huxley's life-long battle with art—literature as a "complete expression . . . leading to complete knowledge . . . of the complete truth." The final symbolic vision is Huxley's rudimentary metaphysic: two cones meet at their tips, the upper with its base in the heaving surface of life, contracting to a calm in the darkness lying below; the lower expanding into the infinitude of light, the ultimate source of everything that exists.[66]

In a period when didacticism is authorial sin, it is no wonder that *Eyeless in Gaza* has been thoroughly ignored. There are additional reasons for sniping at it, of course—the occasional woodenness of Anthony, the emphasis upon the Alexanderist fad, the appearance yet again of established Huxley types. Joseph Conrad, a novelist now admired more than Huxley, suggests an instructive parallel and contrast. Trying to uncover "the truth, manifold and one, underlying . . . every aspect" of the "visible universe," Conrad hoped to "render" it by his impressionist art in what he called a "single-minded" fashion.[67] For Huxley the truth was far more complex, far less accessible, and hardly to be captured by any recognized mode or genre or style. Like Joan Thursley at *Othello,* Huxley knew the power of tightly disciplined art; he had even shown that he could, at times, produce it. In *Eyeless in Gaza* he realized he had to exceed artistic limits, to present (if necessary in a somewhat cumbersome way) his own pursuit of a tenable total view. A comprehensive theory of essence and existence was now almost an obsessive goal. It might be nourished by the art of others, but it would be served by and expressed in the fiction Huxley wrote himself.

CHAPTER SIX

REFORM AND SAINTHOOD:

From *Ends and Means* to *Time Must Have a Stop*

A<small>T THE END OF</small> *Eyeless in Gaza,* Anthony Beavis is ready to give a public lecture on pacifism, even to a hostile audience. Whatever the hecklers may do he feels he is mentally ready, armed with his vision of both immediate and ultimate reality. Aldous Huxley, however, only five months after *his* speech in Albert Hall, left the pacifist movement and even England itself, accompanied by the jeers of his opponents of the Left.[1] He had originally planned a visit to America of no more than a year,[2] but partly because he was able to write scripts in Hollywood, the visit became a permanent move to the area in and around Los Angeles.[3] Though at one point Huxley at least considered a return,[4] he doubtless could see the pacifist movement losing ground as the tensions bound to lead to war increased. *Eyeless in Gaza* ends before Anthony is actually tested in his lecture; the life of Aldous Huxley, however, had to continue. Not long after his apparently successful speech, Huxley decided he was "completely unsuited to political life."[5] He would have to find other ways to change the world, and himself. Anthony merely *plans* to search for " 'complete knowledge ... of the complete truth' "; Huxley had already, and with great intensity, begun.

I

By the time he and Maria arrived in New York in April, 1937, headed for Colorado and then Frieda Lawrence's ranch in the mountains of New Mexico,[6] Huxley had journeyed a remarkable distance in his quest. He had written much of *Ends and Means* (1937), one of the most ambitious of all his many books. As his portentous subtitle puts it, he is inquiring "into the Nature of Ideals and into the Methods employed for their Realization." His goal includes his own reform and understanding, but even more obviously Huxley hopes to reform the world. Ideals or ends involved in reform, James Miller claims in *Eyeless in Gaza,* are determined by the methods or the means. In *Ends and Means* Huxley's strategy is both to present his ideal goal and to use it to test the available means. As in the novel but even more emphatically, the means are still nonviolent groups like Sheppard's small cells of pacifists. The members must "accept the same philosophy of life;" they must hold property and income in common, and assume unlimited liability for each other; they must be governed, preferably on democratic lines; they must engage in study, and discipline the spirit; and they must do practical work "which other social agencies, public or private, are either unable or unwilling to perform."[7] They must also be able to "go out into the world"[8]—even into business, and in the "most scientific, the most unprimitive way."[9] Since Huxley deals with politics, economics, education, and religion, his aim, though it is not stated so baldly, is to dissolve the entire power structure of the world.

The most obvious quality of *Ends and Means,* its casual, confident naiveté, is suggested by the epithet of "cookery book." Huxley offers "recipes" for almost every kind of ill—"political recipes, economic recipes, educational recipes, recipes for the organization of industry, of local communities, of groups of devoted individuals."[10] He can claim, without qualification or embarrassment, that "to create the proper contexts for economic reform" all we have to do is to "change our machinery of government, our methods of public administration and industrial organization, our system of education and our metaphysical and ethical beliefs."[11] Small wonder that Alfred Kazin scorned the work. "It is strange to find Aldous Huxley a perfectionist," he said in his review. "It is stranger still to find him demanding an inclusive perfection of all men. . . ."[12]

The weaknesses of *Ends and Means* are easy to spot or mock. On record as aware of the dangers of abstract language, Huxley employs a vocabulary rarely informed by the real and concrete. He can speak of the "attachment" of "rulers" to "pride,"[13] of undesirable "contexts of reform,"[14] or of people suffering from "defects in the economic machine."[15] He is embarrassingly ignorant of the world of affairs: he thinks an examination system will "rid our business and our politics of imbeciles and the more simple-minded types of crook."[16] Instead of exploring a problem he has identified, Huxley tries to solve it with someone else's recipe. Anxious to decentralize modern industry, for example, but knowing nothing first-hand about it himself, Huxley finds his answer in *A Chacun sa Chance* by the die-maker and reformer, Hyacinthe Dubreuil.[17] If Dubreuil's plan were adopted and even the largest industries were reorganized into small self-governing groups, Huxley believes that "genuine democracy" would arrive at the factory.[18] So (by definition) it would, but nobody would ever let it happen: only two years had passed since American labor had finally won the collective bargaining battle. Though *Ends and Means* itself warns against the love of simplification,[19] Huxley finds a single work by a single man sufficient guidance in an area of immense complexity.

Given the massive gaps in Huxley's argument, how do we

account for the appeal of *Ends and Means*? Malcolm Cowley found Huxley "sometimes magnificently right";[20] less surprisingly, Julian Huxley's tribute refers to that "great book";[21] Harrison Brown speaks of its "particular influence" on him when he read it as a graduate student years ago.[22] Most unexpected are the comments of professional sociologists, the group one would expect to show least sympathy. Otto Kraushaar knew that the book would not "appeal to professional intellectuals, to the academically minded, or to scholars who insist above all on a technical and rigorous logic," and described Huxley as "shallow, journalistic, unlearned, raw, impractical, and utopian." Yet he found the "general direction" "refreshing indeed."[23] And Talcott Parsons, on the verge of publishing his own most influential work, found, in spite of many misgivings, *Ends and Means* to be "full of shrewd and interesting observations on particular points."[24] These men apparently recognized the perceptiveness of Huxley's comments on the weaknesses of both academic and technical education; or his wise suspicion of the purely intellectual; or his advanced view of the drama as a kind of therapy; or his awareness, ahead of George Orwell (Huxley's political opponent), of the great need for early training in analyzing propaganda. But they were doubtless also attracted by Huxley's tone and attitude, whereby at a time of increasing darkness the spirit of the Enlightenment could glow. The Italians had invaded Ethiopia, Spain was immersed in Civil War, Hitler had reoccupied the Rhineland. Yet Huxley, by analysis and with emotional restraint, could plan for a better future, tender the hope for nonviolence and peace. He had the courage to offer a comprehensive vision.

Behind the weaknesses and the insights of Huxley's handbook for reform is the heart of a dramatically appealing, apparently new religion. It is not the religion of any sect or creed, but rather a kind of universal essence. Miller's wish in *Eyeless in Gaza* has in a sense come true: the meditative practice not tied to any theology, which he would prefer to the Christian prayer of Purchas's groups, is wholly consistent with the postulate of *Ends and Means*. Though Huxley had not yet begun to use the actual name, he was introducing the "perennial philosophy," the most exciting idea of his career.

The core of this idea, stated negatively but forcefully in the seventh paragraph of *Ends and Means*, is that the ideal human being is "non-attached." Non-attachment means not only the rejection of strong sensations or emotions and the refusal to seek power, material gain, or social status. It applies to any kind of tempting "exclusive love," even philanthropy, science, speculation, and art. Yet it is negative only nominally, as Huxley understands it, for it "entails the practice of all the virtues," specifically of charity, courage, intelligence and generosity. It is crucial, Huxley claims, to both Eastern and Western tradition. It "has been formulated and systematically preached again and again in the course of the last three thousand years."[25]

Huxley's ideal, embodied in James Miller and several spokesmen to come, probably reflects some influence of Gerald Heard, who had made the trip from England with the Huxleys. The two men had met in 1929, when Heard was an editor of *The Realist*. In their pacifist work they became the closest of friends,[26] later even a combined target for attack,[27] and Huxley for a while thought of his book as a collaboration.[28] In Heard's voluminous, opaque, sometimes unreadable work—even Huxley once called Heard's writing "frightful"[29]—Heard speaks of non-attached leaders whom he labels "Neo-Brahmins"—men completely free from themselves, free from possessiveness and the fear of pain, damage, or death, with integrity, understanding, and a power of personal appeal.[30] But Huxley had the idea in embryo before Heard had written and before the two had met: with non-attachment clearly his goal, Calamy is a potential Neo-Brahmin at the end of *Those Barren Leaves*. The nature of life assumed by non-attachment is implicit in the early poem, "The Burning Wheel." Even Gumbril talks about becoming a saint, albeit "an unsuccessful flickering sort of saint," and in *Point Counter Point* the mystical source of non-attachment lives, through Beethoven, in the *Heilige Dankgesang*. Heard supported what Huxley already knew. His pacifist work had meant abandoning *de*tachment, but his psyche, his temperament, apparently demanded a related substitute. *De*tachment was transformed into the morally justifiable *non*-attachment.

Huxley's attempted justification appears at the beginning and the end, briefly in the opening chapter and more extensively *after* the recipes for reform. Without yet attempting to prove it, Huxley first asserts that individuals, not organizations, are the proper means for reform. The individual has to be an ideal type, essentially *un*involved—universal rather than "the fruit of particular social circumstances." Is there such a type, freed from the "prejudices" of time and place? Yes—those who have been liberated from circumstances by the "practice of *disinterested* virtues [italics added]," and "through direct insight into the real nature of ultimate [not everyday] reality." This insight is an inherent gift (not yet inducible by drugs) which cannot be completely manifested without the proper virtues. The ideal type is now identified: it is the "mystics and the founders of religion." They combine virtue with metaphysical insight; they are "the most nearly free men"; and "at all times and in all places" they "have spoken with only one voice." The best single term to describe them is "non-attached."[31]

Huxley's words are a forceful, unconscious revelation of the nature and the assumptions of his quest. The highest value is neither existential nor essential; it is not even phrased in philosophical terms. It is instead psychologically conceived, as "freedom" or "liberation" of the mind. The will is not to be directed toward any particular goal but rather freed from its prejudices and passions, rendered "disinterested," emotionally cleansed. Though the critical intellect may help, it is subservient to the will, subject to the rationalizations Huxley has already shown.[32] Ironically, this process is happening as Huxley writes: Huxley argues for total freedom because of a need to free himself. He cannot permit a specific or positive doctrine with the personal restrictions logically entailed. His critical intellect has shown him, in *Point Counter Point* and *Eyeless in Gaza*, that such doctrines are burrows, rationalizations of selfishness. Yet sceptical detachment cannot nourish Huxley's idealistic spirit; it leads to the dialectic, the Pyrrhonism of *Brave New World*. The answer to Huxley's problem is simply liberation from it, into a state of mind with no compromising attachments at all.

Though *Ends and Means* reveals the need and the direction of Huxley's mind, it attempts to explain to others the nature and the needs of the whole world. When Huxley returns to his argument at the end, after two hundred pages of plans for reform, he argues his ideas about the mystics and non-attachment in a less subjective, much more convincing way. He assumes, without trying to prove, that the world has meaning and value, a premise supported by our "intuitions of value and significance."[33] He dismisses the philosophy of meaninglessness of *Antic Hay* as wrongly identifying the scientist's world with the ultimate.[34] Apparently following Emile Meyerson and Whitehead, he sees a man defined by his relationship with the universe. But though he has to hollow out his home,[35] a man does not have to live in an *Eyeless in Gaza* burrow, to mistake his small confinement for the whole. Again echoing Jaspers and other existentialists, Huxley accuses science of leaving the world as a whole devoid of meaning and indirectly driving men to put meaning into parts—specifically and particularly into nationalism. The philosophy of meaninglessness is now rejected because it leads to the repulsive activity of war. For further information about what its acceptance can produce, we are directed to its logical conclusion—the Marquis de Sade.[36] Huxley finds support in the theory of evolution. Man has developed a habit of "gratuitous and voluntary" intra-specific competition, a tendency to specialize in the killing of his fellow men.[37] Evolutionary progress, however, depends upon intra-specific cooperation; cooperation demands, among other things, intelligence; but intelligence will not work "where it is too often or too violently interfered with by the emotions, impulses and emotionally charged sensations."[38] The path of future progress is therefore that of non-attachment.

Like others Huxley wants to find the true to be identical to the good.[39] He admits to wishful thinking but adds that "wishes are a reliable source of information." Even if the existence of righteousness cannot be proved, the fact that people crave it is important. And even if "good" and "virtue" depend on location or on the color of the skin, two significant principles emerge. The first is obviously important—that "the category of value is universally employed." The second is neatly circular: "as knowledge, sensibility and non-attachment increase, the contents of the judgments of value passed even by men belonging to dissimilar cultures tend to approximate."[40] But the truly important empirical evidence is offered by the mystics. (Objections by sceptical nonmystics are not allowed; only the trained person has the right to judge, and anyone who wishes can undertake the training.) The mystic, by his meditative practices, is united with "an ultimate spiritual reality that is perceived as simultaneously beyond the self and in some way within it." Furthermore, while the mystics prove that the ultimate exists, the "best" mystics show that it is not personal.[41] Just as Huxley's ideal human being is non-attached, so is Huxley's God impersonal. Together they form the basis of Huxley's final view of life, of its essence and of its proper aim.

When Huxley returns to the nature of God in his study of "Religious Practices," he anticipates by almost thirty years recent Christian discussions of the problem. Precisely like Bishop Robinson, who recently reached a comparable public with his *Honest to God*,[42] Huxley dislikes the idea, as he had twenty years before,[43] of "somebody *out there,* apart from the percipient and different from him."[44] Robinson depends largely on Bultmann, Bonhoeffer and Tillich; Huxley, though familiar with the neo-orthodoxy of Barth, mentions Augustine, Calvin, and particularly Kierkegaard. As Kierkegaard's phrase puts it, a God apart from men is capable of "the most monstrous 'teleological suspensions of morality.' " Again he is interested in the fruits of such a doctrine: belief in "the complete transcendence and otherness of God" is not only "probably untrue" but has always produced "extremely undesirable" results.[45] Huxley does not explore the provocative paradox, that a transcendent, personal God has worse effects than an impersonal, "immanent-and-also-transcendent principle."[46] He bridges the apparent gap, however, between impersonal ultimate reality and human goodness. To know God one must be good; for the fullest possible knowledge, one must be "as good as it is possible for human beings to be." To reduce my separation from God, I must not separate myself from other human beings. The end of *Eyeless in Gaza* is re-echoed: "Evil is that which makes for separateness; and that which makes for separateness is self-destructive." Goodness, supplemented by recollection and mediation, is a *method* for reducing our attachments, for diverting attention from "our animality and our individual separateness."[47] For all shades of belief and unbelief, these should be challenging if not unanswerable claims.

During his surprisingly elaborate argument Huxley introduces two unorthodox scientists, each of whom remained an influence and a friend. One is the parapsychologist J. B. Rhine, whom Huxley visited at Duke after his first arrival in America and regularly thereafter for many years. Asserting his faith in Rhine and his work for the first of many times, Huxley claims the presence of "a 'psychic factor' within a psychic medium," which "exists independently of the spatial and temporal conditions of bodily life." He is convinced that telepathy and clairvoyance exist, and is virtually certain of the existence of prevision.[48] His interest in psychic phenomena here and later, however, is wary. He does not identify the whole world beyond the senses with the ultimate reality reached by religious mystics, and later warns of the dangers of confusing ESP with mystic vision. Far more closely connected than Rhine with the argument of *Ends and Means* is another investigator, William Sheldon, who impressed Huxley immediately when they met in 1937.[49] Each human type, the work of Sheldon indicates, can practice religion in its own congenial way. To Sheldon the three basic kinds of physique—or components, since they represent the extremes—are identified by terms now rather generally known. They are the "endomorphic," in which the digestive viscera are highly developed and the subject is usually fat; the "mesomorphic," when bone, muscle and connective tissue dominate; and the "ectomorphic," characterized by long and poorly muscled extremities, great exposure of the sensory system, and stooping posture. The portly endomorph is supposedly "viscerotonic"—fond of eating and public ceremony, tolerant and complacent. The mesomorph is "somatotonic"— aggressive and competitive, liking adventure and risk, tending to be noisy and callous. The "cerebrotonic" ectomorph prefers his privacy, is emotionally restrained, and tends to be apprehensive and hypersensitive to pain. Sheldon, who compiled his data by taking frontal, lateral and dorsal photographs of naked males, claims about eighty per cent correlation between physical type and predicted temperament.[50] Other psychologists, in America at least, have questioned his conclusions and have not been able to reproduce his results.[51] For Huxley, however, Sheldon's claims were always valid, and in *Ends and Means* a necessary link in the argument about the practice of religion.

[118

Sheldon's assertive, physical somatotonics, Huxley claims, will find ritual dances appropriate.[52] Meditation, he implies, will work best for the introspective cerebrotonics. Of most consequence, however, is the method of the social viscerotonics, "an intimate emotional relationship between the worshipper and a personal God." This *bhakti-marga,* as he calls it, is preferred by the majority of Christians (presumably, whatever their physique) and has more power for change than any other religious activity. But it raises the dangerous spectre of attachment; it leads worshippers to rationalize their desires "in terms of a personalistic theology," and it produces the typically Western "enormous over-valuation of the individual ego."[53]

Such separateness is examined again in the concluding chapter on "Ethics." Sex, though by no means evil in itself, is evil as individual vanity or lust.[54] The emotional "sins" of anger, envy and fear are based on our "animal separateness from one another." We should deny that individual ambition is a virtue and identify the "power-seeker" as disgusting.[55] To behave ethically ourselves we need intelligence; to transcend personality we must become persons first, as thoroughly aware of ourselves as possible. Though Alexanderism will help, the non-mystical doctrines of Christianity will not. Preoccupation with sins, because it leads to preoccupation with the self, is another example of improper means.[56]

II

Ends and Means, with all its faults, exemplifies the magnificent range of Huxley's mind—his drive toward a theory of *all* of reality, his interest in the practice his theory implies, his willingness to make use of almost any possible aid for more accurate description of human beings and their world. But as a specific cure for specific ills *Ends and Means* could never work. It depends upon non-attached yet extremely active groups, yet how these could avoid attaching themselves is not made clear and cannot be visualized. Huxley must have seen that his recipes were inadequate in a world where violence was more and more becoming the rule. He was sure of the absolute, the ultimate reality, and of the original, essential relationship between it and every man. But men in the world had allowed themselves to be conditioned; they had become attached to the very patterns and attitudes *Ends and Means* rejected and abhorred. Quietism was no solution. Ultimate reality, in Huxley's view, demanded the practice of charity and compassion; without these virtues it could not even be found. But how they could be practiced in the careening world of the thirties was a problem the Huxley of *Ends and Means* was unable to solve. In the ultimate reality of the mystics Huxley had found his essence. But he had no settled view of the way we should try to manage our existence.

Hence *After Many a Summer* (London: Chatto & Windus, 1939), Huxley's next book, is a loud cry of ethical frustration. In this bizarre combination of mysticism and sex Huxley tries to dogmatize ethical problems away. Ostensibly wishing to solve the problems of attachment, he instead offers the most extravagant restatement. He himself once called the book "a wild extravaganza, but with the quality of a most serious parable";[57] later he saw it as "a kind of fantasy, at once comic and cautionary, farcical, blood-curdling and reflective."[58] It is set largely in California, in that state's most exaggerated mode. In October, 1937, after his summer in Colorado and New Mexico, Huxley visited Hollywood, and the following spring the Huxleys and Heard settled in Los Angeles.[59] But the site of the novel is William Randolph Hearst's San Simeon, the fabulous castle some miles up the Pacific coast. As rendered here, the castle dining room combines a Fra Angelico with furniture from the Brighton Pavilion; the elevator is adorned with a Vermeer; waiters and butlers roller-skate on a private tennis court; baboons munch bananas not too far from a Christian Science Reading Room; and the leading lady makes her own chocolate sodas a few feet from her private replica of the grotto of Lourdes. "Greece, Mexico, backsides, crucifixions, machinery, George IV, Amida Buddha, science, Christian Science, Turkish baths . . . every item is perfectly irrelevant to every other item."[60] The evil of attachment is combined with the evil of separateness.

An important change, however, has taken place in Huxley's thought. In *Ends and Means,* to transcend personality we had to develop into persons first. In *After Many a Summer,* personality is categorically rejected. Given the characters in the novel, such rejection is no wonder. Jo Stoyte, the American businessman owner of the place, is attached with all the intensity of his hair-trigger emotions to sex, to the fear of death, to money and possessions. Virginia Maunciple, the stupid, naive, daughter-figure is his mistress. Besides her sodas and Our Lady, she is attached to "yum-yum" (sex), mink coats, and Schiaparelli. She cheats on Stoyte by sleeping with Dr. Sigmund Obispo, whom Stoyte has hired to care for his heart trouble and to keep recharging his declining virility. Obispo's attachment is to the scientific view, already shown to be limited by *Ends and Means.* "Facts are facts; accept them as such" is his motto. Hence his rigidly unromantic seduction of Virginia, on the principle of "sensuality for its own sake. The real, essential, concrete thing. . . ."[61] His assistant, Peter Boone, is precisely his opposite. He idealizes not only Virginia but politics; his main attachment is the Loyalist cause in the Spanish Civil War. Jeremy Pordage, a fourth principal, is attached to the Higher Life. Jeremy not only knows of the mystics, he has even read them, but almost as pointedly as Obispo he ignores them. He has no pretensions about the value of his scholarly work; he just likes "scrabbling about in the dust-heaps" of the English Romantic period. Raised by a dominant mother, another of his attachments, he is accustomed to bi-weekly visits to two sordid prostitutes. Virginia, however, does not tempt him for a minute; he sees himself instead as Bluebeard to his scholarly work. The Hauberk papers he has been hired to edit are "unravished brides of quietness" from the past.

If the evils of personality are not evident in the characters, they should be in the plot, the briefest but most ingenious one in Huxley's work. While Obispo and Boone search for ways to prolong life, Jeremy discovers that the Earl who wrote or owned the Hauberk papers has made similar attempts himself and, now 203, is still alive. At the same time Stoyte, discovering Virginia and Obispo in dishabille by the pool, mistakenly shoots not her seducer but Peter Boone. After camouflaging the homicide, Obispo, Stoyte, and Virginia escape to England, where in a stinking subterranean dungeon they find the aged, concupiscent Earl. He and his house-keeper mistress, who have survived by eating the entrails of carp,[62] spend their time either shouting or copulating in the dark. Jo Stoyte is so obsessed with the fear of death that he sees their ape-like existence as a rather attractive fate.

Lest we still fail to grasp the total worthlessness of their lives, Huxley makes it explicit. No good exists on "the plane of the emotions" as it did in *Ends and Means*. Nor has Huxley maintained his reasonable, essentially optimistic tone. With conspicuously weary and bitter disillusionment, he finds that:

> Men and women are continually trying to lose their lives, the stale, unprofitable, senseless lives of their ordinary personalities. For ever trying to get rid of them, and in a thousand different ways. In the frenzies of gambling and revivalism; in the mono-manias of avarice and perversion, of research and sectarianism and ambition; in the compensatory lunacies of alcohol, of read-

ing, of day-dreaming, of morphia; in the hallucinations of opium and the cinema and ritual; in the wild epilepsies of political enthusiasm and erotic pleasure; in the stupors of veronal and exhaustion.

The human being, as Huxley sees him, wants to "escape"; to forget his "own, old wearisome identity; to become someone else or, better, some other *thing*—a mere body, strangely numbed or more than ordinarily sentient; or else just a state of impersonal mind, a mode of unindividualized consciousness." The human state is one of "fundamental wretchedness"; the human being lives in "the hideous world of human persons."[63] Such phrases never appear in *Ends and Means*.

Huxley uses Propter as a partner in the attack. In one of the metaphysical lessons he gives to Peter Boone, Propter grants that personality ought to be respected. But one does this in order to make possible liberation, the realization that "all personality is a prison." Personalities are "illusory figments of a self-will disastrously blind to the reality of a more-than-personal consciousness, of which it is the limitation and denial." Propter and Huxley see personality as one kind or another of craving, for sex or longer life or an ideal or even for time to read. But they take a long step beyond the Huxley of *Ends and Means* by claiming that evil is also associated with time, to Propter "the medium in which evil propagates itself, the element in which evil lives and outside of which it dies," in the last analysis even evil itself. Time and craving are "two aspects of the same thing; and that thing is the raw material of evil." Good can exist only on the animal level and on the level of the spirit—as the "proper functioning of the organism" or as "the experience of eternity." But it cannot exist on the human level.[64] Morality, in the ordinary sense, becomes impossible. The recipes of *Ends and Means* are thrown away.

Nevertheless, along with this vision and explanation of evil,

After Many a Summer does at least explain a view of the good. Propter as well as Obispo is a cynic. He admonishes Pete to be "specially cynical about all the actions and feelings you've been taught to suppose were good," which are really "merely evils which happen to be regarded as creditable."[65] But he does have a way of establishing a better world. Only the "wildly pessimistic" believe that human beings are "condemned by their nature to pass their whole lives on the strictly human level." Human nature can be transcended and transformed, not by evolutionary growth as Gerald Heard would have it but "here and now . . . by the use of properly directed intelligence and good-will"—at least in a simple environment with decentralized government.[66] Propter lives near Stoyte but in a smallish bungalow, grinds his own flour, does his own carpentry. He tries to liberate the transient workers Stoyte's men are exploiting. A Kansan arrives from the dust bowl with his family, full of hostility and the lust to indulge himself. Propter tries to teach him, little by little, to think of his ego as "a kind of nightmare, a frantically agitated nothingness" but capable of knowing God.

According to Propter, there is only one right track, "only one God and one beatific vision." But to make this vision clear he (and Huxley) find a near impossible task. Commenting on the Spanish mystic Miguel de Molinos, whose letters appear among Jeremy's Hauberk Papers with pornography by the Marquis de Sade, Propter finds the only available vocabulary is "intended for thinking strictly human thoughts about strictly human concerns." Metaphysical terms are not much of an addition, and the professional psychologists who interest themselves in the problem really know nothing about the mystical experience.[67] Propter's solution is the one later developed at length in *The Perennial Philosophy:* he quotes the words of the true mystics as his own description of the nature of man and God. Man, according to the seventeenth century Cardinal Berulle, is " 'A nothingness surrounded by God, indigent and capable of God, filled with God, if he so desires' "; and God, according to Propter and the German mystic John Tauler, is " 'a being withdrawn from creatures, a free power, a pure working.' "[68] These propositions, which Propter meditates, are in an important sense the main thesis of the novel.

The abstract metaphors which Berulle and Tauler employ do not fully clarify what Huxley and Propter mean. They do reinforce Huxley's belief, however, in the worthlessness of the ego and his continuing rejection of a personal conception of God. During Propter's meditation, an unlikely time for critical exposure, they are used to show that even Propter can make mistakes because he is a human being. His speculations on the nature of God and man, and their application to the problem of the hostile man from Kansas, are acceptable as metaphysical propositions. But he has made the mistake of letting them express his *own* personality. Aiming initially "to realize for a moment the existence of that other consciousness behind his private thoughts and feelings, that free pure power greater than his own," he has let himself be distracted from this spiritual goal. He is not attached to sex, to money, even to the scholarship in his excellent *Short Studies in the Counter Reformation*. He has let his mind wander, however, in memory and random speculation. So complete is Huxley's rejection of personality that even these apparently harmless modes of thought are condemned. Shutting his eyes again, Propter then begins a purgative atonement, a real spiritual exercise. His vigilance starts as willful "thrusting back" of irrelevant thoughts; it transforms itself gradually into "a kind of effortless unattached awareness"; the awareness is realized as a "partial expression" of the "impersonal and untroubled consciousness into which the words [of Berulle and Tauler] . . . were slowly sinking." The words lose their intellectual character, become "intuitive and direct," and Propter discovers "the felt capacity for peace and purity, for the withdrawal from revulsion and desires, for the blissful freedom from personality. . . ."—until he is interrupted by Jeremy Pordage and Peter Boone.[69] Gerald Heard's goals and exercises are almost clear.

Propter, of course, has taken a beating from the critics; even Thomas Merton found him the "dullest character in the whole history of the English novel."[70] And according to contemporary critical principles he has little business in any novel at all. The novelist is supposed to embody his ideas, to show rather than tell, to produce not lessons but illustrations and images of the truth. Huxley was always more or less at odds with these standards; in *After Many a Summer* he tosses them away. "Art can be a lot of things," Propter tells Jeremy and Pete; "but in actual practice most of it is merely the mental equivalent of alcohol and cantharides."[71] Eventually, he states more elaborately Huxley's latest position, at least on literary art. Building on *Ends and Means,* where literature was seen as idealizing the average sensual man, Propter claims that it has "enormous defects"—because it accepts "the conventional scale of values"; because it treats "as though they were reasonable the mainly lunatic preoccupations of statesmen, lovers, business men, social climbers, parents"; and particularly because, using "the most magnificent and persuasive language," it helps "to perpetuate misery by explicitly or implicity approving the thoughts and feelings and practices which could not fail to result in misery." Propter praises satire as "more deeply truthful . . . and . . . much more profitable than . . . tragedy,"[72] and thereby explains a basic strategy of Huxley's extravagant fable. As a satire *After Many a Summer* is often accorded praise, while Propter and the didactic sections are treated with contempt. The book is also, however, a satirical allegory needing Propter's ideas for the fable to be fully understood.

After Many a Summer tells a story about a philosophical triangle, in which potential good is separated from true, timeless good by various kinds of time-obsessed, hence evil craving.[73] Propter, of course, is timeless good, and as such an attraction to several of the others. Jeremy likes to talk with him; Pete listens and actually tries to learn; even Jo has built his castle near Propter's plot of land. But Jeremy prefers his self-centered isolation, Pete confuses timeless good with false ideals, and Jo is cursed with a whole collection of attachments—not only sex, youth, possessions, power, and money but the Sandemanian Calvinism burned into his soul by his father and the Christian Science ceaselessly shouted by his wife. All but Propter need what the Buddhists call "right knowledge." Jeremy has read but ignores the mystics, and devotes his intelligence to scholarship in romantic dustheaps; Pete is only beginning to lose his naiveté; Jo is sworn to the two false theologies he has absorbed; Obispo has sold his intelligence to science; and Virginia Maunciple seems to have no mind at all. She can only think of Propter as "Old Proppy," whereas Obispo, sure that religion is less than "a good belch," never talks to Propter or even mentions him. He and Stoyte are both attached to the prolongation of life, and their evil destroys potential good when Peter is shot.

Almost everything in the novel supports the allegory. Obispo's well-known baboons, corralled for experiments in longevity, are human beings in their jealousy and passion. Giambologna's nymph symbolizes obsession with the flesh; with the other nubile statues in Beverly Pantheon, the Personality Cemetery, it is Huxley's comment on Forest Lawn, the object in *The Loved One* of Evelyn Waugh's satiric attack. Virginia's shrine points to the dangers of personal (and Christian) religion, as well as to the childish attachments of Catholicism. Jeremy in the swimming pool parodies a meditating Buddha; Dr. Mulge, President of Tarzana College, "torch-bearer" of culture to the Pacific, is Huxley's idea of melioristic humanism. At dinner, Mulge spouts bilge about "Creative Self-Expression" and "Enjoyment of the Best in Drama and Music." The only human-level thinker who makes sense is represented but masked: labeled "The Book of Common Prayer" is a Hauberk pornographic journal, of that best philosopher of meaninglessness, the Marquis de Sade.

Huxley's allegory helps to justify Propter's didacticism. It does nothing to minimize another aesthetic problem, however, born of the temptations of the omniscient point of view. Instead of matching Propter's understanding and compassion, Huxley seems to crave and indulge in authorial power, to overwhelm his characters with his sophistication. The monstrous ego of Obispo may deserve his urbane comment: shooting testosterone into his employer, Obispo appears to Huxley as "simultaneously his own ballet and his own audience . . . Nijinsky, Karsavina, Pavlova, Massine—all on a single stage."[74] Peter Boone and Jo Stoyte, however, are pitiful creations in their different ways, yet are dissected with such complex and formidable techniques as understatment, word play, and intricate ironic prose. Assailing personality in the abstract is one thing, attacking individual creatures is another. By glorying in the weaknesses of personalities he has created, Huxley exposes a lack of charity in his own. Though the novel reaffirms Huxley's essentialist metaphysic, it is a backward step in the quest for a workable ethic.

Grey Eminence (1941), however, shows a startling change: ethical inconsistency has suddenly been transformed into ethical dogma. In this study of Father Joseph, Richelieu's secretary of state for foreign affairs, Huxley writes as though even the world of politics need not involve a trace of ethical ambiguity. Huxley follows Joseph, born François Leclerc du Tremblay, from his childhood sobbing at the story of the Crucifixion, through his year at court as Baron de Maffliers and his acceptance into the Capuchin order of Franciscan friars. He is particularly interested in Joseph's life during the Thirty Years War, when his influence was allegedly at its greatest and most pernicious. He shows how Joseph operated as a politician—in his machinations, for example, at the Diet of Ratisbon, where he handled the Emperor Ferdinand, Wallenstein, and Maximilian of Bavaria in "a miracle of diplomatic virtuosity."[75] But the political narrative of *Grey Eminence,* admittedly incomplete, is immersed in a study of religion—religious forces, religious tradition, and the techniques of religious meditation. During his pacifist activities Huxley had concluded that the abolition of war was less a political than a religious problem; thereafter he decided that the religious answer must itself be purified of political elements. By 1940 he was "profoundly pessimistic about great masses of human beings,"[76] including presumably those represented in the semi-political Peace Pledge Union. Huxley's aim in *Grey Eminence* is to demonstrate that religion cannot be reconciled with politics—that an ethical act must be religiously inspired, and remain wholly unpolitical, religiously wholly pure.

Hence *Grey Eminence,* though a biography, is another manifesto as well. It offers the most rigid ideal we have yet seen— more rigid than the disciplined but occasionally negligent Propter, stricter than the non-attached man of *Ends and Means.* Huxley calls his ideal the "theocentric saint"; he has in mind certain mystics like Meister Eckhart, St. Teresa, and the anonymous author of *The Cloud of Unknowing.* He visualizes not occasional or even frequent ethical acts, but rather the full rigor of a truly saintly life. Until most people actually live as saints, says Huxley, society will never be significantly improved. Meanwhile the few theocentric saints alive at any time "are able in some slight measure to qualify and mitigate the poisons which society generates within itself by its political and economic activities." They prevent the social world "from breaking down into irremediable decay."[77] Not all mystics meet Huxley's criteria and have thereby such a salutary effect. *Grey Eminence* presents Father Joseph as a true contemplative, with all the spiritual discipline he needed. But because he did not accurately understand the ideal, he became a powerful enemy of the truth and of mankind.

Father Joseph interests Huxley, surely, because of his "dialectical" life, because Huxley could recognize in him another divided man. Joseph tried to unite service to God with service to France, founding and nourishing the order of Calvarian Nuns, yet helping Richelieu with a war so devastating that its miseries would linger for literally hundreds of years. In several ways he resembled certain Huxley characters. Like Calamy he combined a hostility toward women with the contemplative zeal and ability of the mystic. Like Mark Staithes he was a kind of ascetic masochist. Like Maurice Spandrell, Lord Edward and Mr. Falx, he was dominated by his passion. But because Father Joseph was actually immersed in history, because he shaped and was himself shaped by real events, he offers Huxley the opportunity to do something really new—to examine in a person rather than in the abstract, the search for ultimate truth, the destructive split within the self, and their relationship to the actual, living, material political world.

Using what he claims to be the available primary sources, Huxley examines as well as he can the texture of Joseph's inner life, the spiritual state and content of his tough and vigorous mind. Though he tries to imagine, to reconstruct on his own from time to time, he quotes occasionally from the letters and journals of Joseph himself. Most emphatically, however, he stresses Joseph's spiritual training, in particular the influence of the English-born mystic, Father Benet of Canfield. In the longest chapter of the book, to define and explain the later impact on Father Joseph, Huxley explores the mystical tradition before Benet appears, particularly the anonymous *The Cloud of the Unknowing*.[78] He describes Benet's own analysis of the "Exterior, Interior, and Essential" will of God in Benet's own book, *The Rule of Perfection*.

Huxley's analysis, longer even than any speech by Propter, is aimed largely at showing Benet's primary mistake.[79] While most of *The Rule of Perfection* is well within the "pure, undogmatic" tradition of mysticism, Benet departs in one important way. He insists "that even the most advanced contemplatives should persist in 'the practice of the passion'," that they should "meditate upon the sufferings of Christ" even when they can unite their souls with the Godhead beyond.[80] Huxley has charged worship of a personal God, in *Ends and Means*, with a pernicious influence. In *Grey Eminence* his suspicions have become an extended wail warning of danger.

There is no doubt, Huxley's study suggests, that Father Joseph, the lovable Benet, and Joseph's friend (and Propter's authority) Cardinal Berulle, were advanced contemplatives capable of annihilating themselves and becoming absorbed in the essential will of God. But those who meditate on Christ, as Benet and others insisted we should do, are subject to "a kind of illegitimate corollary, the thesis that suffering is good in itself and that, because voluntary self-sacrifice is meritorious and ennobling, there must be something splendid even about involuntary self-sacrifice imposed from without."[81] Joseph as a child was moved by the sorrow and horror of the Crucifixion. Huxley claims that after "half a lifetime brooding upon the torture and death of a man-god," his "zeal for a crusade was too burningly hot to be extinguished by anything short of a sea of other people's blood."[82] Using Benet's techniques of meditation, he was able to develop the "peculiar strength which belongs to the self-abnegated man," the ability to wield "the authority of a power infinitely greater than himself."[83] But although he harnessed the power of goodness, he used it for a cause imbued with evil. When Joseph died, he was in popular eyes "L'éminence Grise," the hated lieutenant who had helped the hated Richelieu prolong the war and with it their personal misery. Even the "beautifully saintly" Charles de Condren refused on grounds of conscience to preach the funeral sermon.[84]

Historians are not agreed about Father Joseph's real importance. He may have been, one suggests, less an influence on than a tool of Richelieu.[85] But to Huxley he was even worse than a mere Machiavelli who helped prolong the Thirty Years War. His spiritual errors and consequent degeneration were, we are told, "among the significantly determining conditions of the world in which we live today."[86] And since they helped Joseph along his unfortunate way, both the lovable Benet and "the brilliant and saintly" Cardinal Berulle, no longer the spiritual hero he was in *After Many a Summer*, "take their place among the men who have contributed to the darkening of the human spirit."[87] Put simply, the policies which Joseph's misuse of the spirit promoted "created the social and economic and political conditions which led to the downfall of . . . [the Bourbon] dynasty, the rise of Prussia and the catastrophes of the nineteenth and twentieth centuries."[88]

Out of these conclusions grows Huxley's new dogmatic ethic. Except for those who are proficient in the "art of mental prayer," action simply is not safe. Ordinary people, "sunk in their selfhood and without spiritual insight, seldom do much good."[89] Benet of Canfield's *Rule*, though it dealt with personal intention, ignored "those acts which the individual performs, not for his own sake, but on behalf and for the advantage of some social organization, such as a nation, a church, a political party, a religious order, a business concern, a family."[90] Political solutions are of no use whatsoever; good cannot be "mass-produced," it is strictly "a product of the ethical and spiritual artistry of individuals."[91] The theocentrics who can help must remain in units sufficiently small, like those of the Benedictines and the Society of Friends. And like these groups they must operate only on the *margin* of the state.[92]

No one could accept Huxley's fantastic oversimplification of history, where so many people and so many kinds of causes are confidently and blandly ignored. It is no easier to swallow total rejection of the political and social, the suggestion that no government has ever done any lasting good at all. Eventually Huxley would modernize his view of the saint and demand, besides compassion and love, a degree in science and acquaintance with many different fields.[93] *Grey Eminence* is nevertheless one of the most interesting, best written books Huxley ever produced.[94] The opening image of Joseph, barefoot, plodding the scores of miles to Rome is as effective a beginning as that of any of the essays. Some of the best passages appear in digressions or asides, like the description of the "Rubens" painting of Richelieu being treated for piles,[95] or the vision of horror and evil in the etchings of Jacques Callot.[96] Yet the book as a whole is effectively organized, even though dramatic narrative alternates with the theory that forms the purpose of the book. Perhaps it is one of its author's most successful books because Huxley, though not yet inwardly unified, had continued to develop a "fellowship with essence" by living with a pure and powerful idea of God.

III

A FEW YEARS LATER Huxley published *Time Must Have a Stop* (New York: Harper & Brothers, 1944), the book he called his "most successful" novel. He liked it, he told his interviewers, because he had "integrated what may be called the essay element with the fictional element better there than in other novels."[97] Perhaps he had in mind the effective pattern of symbols, where an ever-present Romeo and Juliet cigar suggests indulgence as a way of life—its teat-like quality, its owner's childishness; two Degas nudes, art and the ephemeral quality of human beauty; and a treatise of François de Sales, the ultimate essential truth. Perhaps he also felt that Sebastian Barnack and his years-long inner struggle were an accurate masked projection of what he had gone through himself. Sebastian has turned "sensuality, abhorrence and self-hatred" into an "all too fascinating" volume of poems. In a Quarles-like journal he has also traced the difficulty of trying to love God, if necessary "without any *feelings*—by the will alone."[98] But he surely must have been thinking also of Sebastian's Uncle Eustace Barnack, who dramatizes almost all the important Huxley themes.

A descendant of Tom Cardan of *Those Barren Leaves,* Eustace has succeeded, where Cardan failed, in marrying into wealth; hence he can satisfy his desires almost at will. He smokes the cigars, dines on exotic food, lives amidst Venetian furniture and yellow Chinese carpets, and ends a phone call from his arthritic former mistress to attend to a coy and voluptuous local prostitute. Though Eustace is clearly as attached as all the others, he knows it and even defends his way in argument. He can thus act as critic and exposer, the role that Huxley, even at great aesthetic cost, could not hitherto resist taking for himself. It is Eustace who indicts the disguised selfishness of his political brother John, the morbid imaginings of self-pitying Fred Poulshot, the soft-headedness of Paul De Vries—at one point by means of his "New World Suite" of dirty limericks. Eustace also voices Huxley's preference of Chaucer to Dante, who would be ignored if he weren't "the second greatest virtuoso of language that ever lived"; he sees Christianity producing "violence and rapine, practised by proselytizing bullies and justified in terms of a theology devised by introverts"; he speaks sarcastically of "war and massacre in the name of Humanity," with "its price . . . a state of things that absolutely guarantees you against achieving the good which the massacre was intended to achieve." Those who, like Eustace, practice "life as a fine art," are never taken seriously but "demonstrably do much less mischief than the other fellows."[99] His views, of course, are by no means always Huxley's. Moreover, he acts in the objectionable way of the attached, not only by indulging his sensual desires but by urging Sebastian to devote his life to art and deliberately undercutting the saintly influence of Bruno.

Yet Eustace also lets Huxley express the crucial part of his growing vision. More directly than even the inhabitants of *Island,* Eustace encounters ultimate reality. During his life he is able to sense it once or twice, in a passage he reads in the *Treatise* on the availability of grace, in a sudden view of "enormous and blissful brightness" induced by Bruno Rontini. But the crucial, revealing moments are those that follow his death, as he lies collapsed in the bathroom with a fatal heart attack. In a half-dozen chapters alternating with the plot, Huxley dramatizes the ultimate as a dazzling light. The dead Eustace is seen as an "absence" becoming aware of the light and simultaneously becoming known by it. At first this awareness is subsumed with hunger and joy; when it realizes that greater knowing will mean annihilation, it changes under the light to anguish and hideousness, repulsively opposite to the beautiful and the real. A kind of dialectic ensues: the clot of partial awareness realizes it can escape annihilation, simply by refusing to participate. As it does so, the brightness begins to lessen, an image intervenes between the light and the "suffering awareness of the light."[100] The image, of course, is Eustace, who is joined by another image of his expensive cigar.

Then his memories, his experiences—his personality—are seen as part of an immense cosmic pattern, "A vast ubiquitous web of beknottednesses and divergences, of parallels and spirals, of intricate figures and their curiously distorted projections— all shining and active and alive." A more personal battle ensues this time, more obviously parallel to Eustace's living struggle with Bruno. Through the interstices of the lattice he is aware of the light. It is an austere beauty, a "vast undifferentiated silence" that is "fascinating, desirable, irresistibly attractive." But realizing that it will mean the annihilation of his shameful self, Eustace averts his attention to a memory of Mimi the prostitute, then to one of a sensual joke on Mozart's *Ave Verum Corpus*. Another memory appears at another intersection of the lattice—a near-mystical moment when he was a boy at school. Just as he now is turning away from the light, so did he then reject a similar, living experience, of something totally new from a "more real order of existence" breaking through the "blue nostalgic canopy" of the sky.[101] Other meaningful fragments are scoffed at and treated with hate, until a more blissful experience suddenly arrives. His mother-in-law has arranged a seance for several of the living, and the medium is trying to get in touch with him. She does, for Huxley shares the Hindu belief in the possibility of such psychic power, but she misinterprets all of Eustace's remarks. So, we learn elsewhere, are all such activities mistaken, often serving as barriers to the true metaphysical quest.[102]

Eustace is finally identified with universal laughter, the attitude of the cosmos toward the self-willed, unenlightened efforts of men. Various absurdities pass in an array: frightened Negroes after the Gettysburg Address, advertisements for whiskey after the "Triumph of Education," lies and imbecility after Maxwell and Faraday made it possible to use the ether. With the light, and the tender, silent blue completely denied, the grotesquely comic vision of evil painfully expands. It is an "age-old slapstick of disaster following on the heels of good intention":

A counterpoint of innumerable hilarities—Voltairean voices, yelping in sharp shrill triumph over the bewildered agonies of stupidity and silliness; vast Rabelaisian voices, like bassoons and double basses, rejoicing in guts and excrement and copulation, rumbling delightedly at the spectacle of grossness, of inescapable animality.

But the laughter, persisting even against Eustace's will, suddenly leads him to "remember" part of the future. Jim Poulshot, his nephew, has been wounded years later in the Pacific war, and three yellow men drive bayonets into his screaming face. In France, Weyl and his wife are now frightened refugees. As the planes strike at a convoy they are trudging behind, Mme. Weyl is run over by a speeding truck. Though Eustace finds himself identified with their trembling, sobbing son, he prefers even this state to the annihilating light.[103]
Eustace has faced and rejected the Clear Light of Reality, the Clear Light of the Void, to use the language of the *Bardo Thödol*. In this treatise on how to die, commonly called *The Tibetan Book of the Dead,* the subject, while dying, can be liberated by recognizing and accepting Reality, realizing that the "voidness" of his own intellect is Buddhahood. If he cannot do so he will (like Eustace) have another chance, for the Clear Light appears in both Primary and Secondary Forms. Failing here also, he will be given additional opportunities. He can obtain refuge in the dazzling light of wisdom, instead of fearing it, and avoid fondness for the series of duller lights which represent anger, jealousy, and other aspects of the human world. His final opportunity is to close the door of the womb into which he may be tempted for rebirth. Should he also falter here, he is still instructed as to the best kind of womb to seek.[104] Huxley has obviously selected wisely from the *Book,* a sacred text to him for many years. He has ignored the instructions involving rebirth and the womb, avoided any references to the various gods, omitted the guru and his role of adjusting the subject's body and of applying certain pressures at the appropriate time. More important, he has remained true to the spirit

of his text in treating Eustace's death as a lesson for those alive.

As one Lama puts it the *Bardo* "reveals the secret of life" though it appears to be a study of the "science of death";[105] its value is "only for those who practise and realize its teaching" while they live.[106] Similarly, Huxley offers the *living* person two choices. He can decide to live, as all but Bruno have, on what *After Many a Summer* calls the purely "human" level. At best, he will then be like Sebastian's aunt and cousin Susan, who are not lustful, self-indulgent Eustaces and Veronicas, but personifications of "sound, honest, better-than-average goodness." Without such people society would collapse; with them, it was "perpetually attempting suicide."[107] Hence in ultimate terms they, and even the pain of their loved ones, are hilarious, absurd because their best actions are done in ignorance. This is the way of "apotheosis," of the exaltation of personality. But the individual can also follow the way of "deification," where personality is annihilated in charity and union with God.[108] Awaiting him if he will but realize it is "some new unprecedented kind of beauty." The clash between the beauty and the ugliness Huxley sees is nowhere made so clear and powerful as in these pages of *Time Must Have a Stop.* The novel may not be what Huxley thought it, a "piece of the *Comédie Humaine* that modulates into a version of the *Divina Commedia.*"[109] But it has a lyrical and dramatic originality and daring nowhere visible in Huxley's other work, and it makes clear that Huxley's odyssey will eventually and happily end.

CHAPTER SEVEN

THE PERENNIAL PHILOSOPHY

For at least a few years during the early 1940's, Huxley tried to live the life of spiritual discipline envisioned in *Ends and Means,* illustrated in *After Many a Summer,* and at least implied in *Time Must Have a Stop.* With Gerald Heard and others he founded the monastic haven called Trabuco College, in Trabuco Canyon southeast of Los Angeles. The 1942 prospectus of the College begins in humility, then emphasizes human failure, shame and spiritual starvation. The "way out," as Huxley's works were all maintaining, is not "social reconstruction," a new political creed, or even an international organization. Instead it is "a slow hard lifetime of study, prayer and disciplined, ascetic living" aimed at learning "that God is the only Reality, and that the whole visible world is real only in so far as He constantly sustains it." Trabuco was planned as a community devoted to sponsoring such a life. The residents were to do manual or household work, perhaps help to cultivate the land, subsist on a rigidly simple diet, and engage themselves spiritually in research, experiment, and properly disciplined living. For Huxley's public, research was the important activity, research in the "enormous mass of existing literature, from many countries and ages, on techniques of prayer, ways of self-integration and methods of psycho-physical development."[1]

Trabuco College was sponsored by an older institution still flourishing today, The Vedanta Society of Southern California. The Society, which occupies an attractive temple in Hollywood and publishes a periodical, *Vedanta and the West,* has claimed Huxley, Heard, Isherwood and the late John Van Druten as members. Its founder, Swami Prabhavananda, has had a strong personal influence on a variety of people.[2] Like other Centers, however, the Society is under the spiritual authority of the Ramakrishna Order of India.[3] Sri Ramakrishna was a saintly nineteenth-century Indian spiritual leader; the movement began at the turn of the century when one of his pupils, Swami Vivekenanda, showed up at the World's Parliament of Religions in Chicago. He quickly became the most popular speaker there, remained in America for a highly successful speaking tour, gave classes in New York, and thereby founded the first American Vedanta Society.[4]

"Vedanta" means literally the "end of the Veda," the Vedas being the four collections of primary, canonical Indian scriptures. More loosely the term refers to Hindu wisdom, or the religious wisdom centering in the Upanishads, which are themselves certain philosophical parts of the Vedas. But Vedanta societies take the Vedanta to include the whole body of explanatory comment, including the *Gita,* the ninth century works of Shankara, even such Occidental efforts as articles in *Vedanta and the West* and most of the later works of Aldous Huxley.[5] For some Vedanta is doubtless merely a source of exotic appeal embodied in such strange works as *The Tibetan Book of the Dead.* Yet Vedanta also makes undeniably impressive claims. For many who have explained the reasons for their commitment, its appeal lies in the very lack of exclusiveness, the claim that in essence all religions are one.[6] Secluded in the contemplative atmosphere at Trabuco, Aldous Huxley pursued research aimed in part at proving that claim. He there[7] wrote one of the major books of his career with the Vedantist title, *The Perennial Philosophy* (1945).

I

The Perennial Philosophy is a sequel to *Ends and Means,* based on the mystics who had inspired that earlier work. It is not visionary or imaginative, but again derivative and discursive— not a text for Eustace Barnack, who sees the light of ultimate reality at death; but one for Sebastian, who needs a set of principles to live. In his journal, a vehicle for many of Huxley's ideas, Sebastian is led from Hotspur's phrase that "time must have a stop" to produce what he calls a "minimum working hypothesis." Its Vedantist propositions, echoing Hinduism, Buddhism, Taoism, and Christianity, admirably summarize what Huxley now develops:

> That there is a Godhead or Ground, which is the unmanifested principle of all manifestation.
> That the Ground is transcendent and immanent.
> That it is possible for human beings to love, know and, from virtually, to become actually identified with the Ground.
> That to achieve this unitive knowledge, to realize this supreme identity, is the final end and purpose of human existence.
> That there is a Law or Dharma, which must be obeyed, a Tao or Way, which must be followed, if men are to achieve their final end.
> That the more there is of I, me, mine, the less there is of the Ground; and that consequently the Tao is a Way of humility and compassion, the Dharma a Law of mortification and self-transcending awareness.[8]

The basic ideal of *Ends and Means* was non-attachment; the mystic's basic claim in *The Perennial Philosophy* indicates why that ideal can be achieved. His claim is the Sanskrit saying of the Upanishads, to be repeated again and again in Huxley: *"tat tvam asi,"* "That art thou."⁹ As the Zen Buddhist Yung-chia Tashih puts it, "One Nature, perfect and pervading, circulates in all natures"; in Shankara's words, "Though One, Brahman is the cause of many"; in the Christian William Law's, God "is everywhere present, yet He is only present to thee in the deepest and most central part of thy soul."¹⁰ "That" is the divine principle or essence, Sebastian's Godhead or Ground, and "thou" an aspect, an element of every human being which can be in Sebastian's words "actually identified" with the Ground. Though to achieve this identification is "the final end and purpose of human existence," to do so one must live in a humble and self-denying way. *The Perennial Philosophy* develops all these claims, and in keeping with the Trabuco aim "to meet contemporary needs"¹¹ shows how they apply to a whole range of modern life. Like *Texts and Pretexts*, it is an anthology of hundreds of quotations supplemented by analysis and comment. In spite of many weaknesses, substantive and stylistic, *The Perennial Philosophy* is a bold and challenging book, full of acute insights into the major problems of our world.

Huxley's theology and ontology, now more fully developed than in *Ends and Means,* are dramatically phrased by Meister Eckhart, the heretical mystic Huxley perhaps admired most. The difficult passage has almost overwhelming implications:

> When I came out of the Godhead into multiplicity, then all things proclaimed, "There is a God." . . . But in the breaking through I am . . . neither God nor creature; I am that which I was and shall remain, now and for ever more. . . . By this thrust I become so rich that God is not sufficient for me. . . . For in thus breaking through, I perceive what God and I are in com-

mon. . . . For there I am the immovable which moves all things. . . .[12]

An impersonal Godhead precedes and stands above the personal God. In relationship to this Godhead beyond them both, Eckhart finds himself *equivalent* to the personal God. The human being is not a mere creature, subject only to the will of a wholly other personal deity; he is in some sense the divine spirit, the Godhead itself. He and God appear at the same time. The Church, not surprisingly, has often viewed the mystic with suspicion when faced with assertions such as these.

Since Huxley's audience is Western and probably largely Christian, unaccustomed to the concept of the Divine Ground, it must be warned again, from the new point of departure, of its proneness to worship an exclusively personal God. Huxley grants that the Godhead, the "Absolute Ground," has a personal aspect even in Eastern religions. The Hindu pantheon, for example, includes Isvara the Lord and its own trinity of Brahman the creator, Vishnu the preserver and Shiva the destroyer. The human incarnation of God is also often seen, in the Krishna of Hinduism, the "Three Bodies" of Mahayana Buddhism, and the Allah of the mystic Sufis of Islam.[13] But the Christian's belief in but one incarnation, one avatar, has saturated history with "more and bloodier crusades, interdenominational wars, persecutions and proselytizing imperialism" than any religion of the Orient.[14] And the worship of a wholly other, transcendent God or Father is a greater danger than quietism or antinomianism stemming from the worship of a God who is exclusively immanent.[15] Huxley reveres certain Christians like Eckhart and William Law, but like other Vedantists is less Christian than Hindu and Buddhist.

The huge barrier separating the human being from the Ground is the separate self, Sebastian's "I, me, mine." Personality is the "final and most formidable obstacle." The Savonarola of *After Many a Summer* reappears, seeing us captivated by, identified with

> ... the pleasures of gluttony, for example, or intemperance, or sensuality; with money, power or fame; with our family, regarded as a possession or actually an extension and projection of our own selfness; with our goods and chattels, our hobbies, our collections; with our artistic or scientific talents; with some favourite branch of knowledge, some fascinating "special subject"; with our professions, our political parties, our churches; with our pains and illnesses; with our memories of success or misfortune, our hopes, fears and schemes for the future. . . .

The " 'stinking lump' of selfness" has to be mortified;[16] mortification, "deliberate dying to self" is demanded by every theocentric saint from just about every religion of the world.[17] This principle, though like others expressed in *Ends and Means,* is broached here with more evidence, and in an uncompromising tone. "Total selflessness" is the goal. Mortification is necessary in willing, desiring, acting, knowing, thinking, feeling, and fancying[18]—all of which, in *Do What You Will,* would have been wholly encouraged and indulged.

Predictably, *The Perennial Philosophy* evoked vigorous rebuttal. Winfred Garrison of the liberal *Christian Century* found no virtue in Huxley's syncretism; in Huxley's predilection for Buddhism, he had even raised the spectre of Nirvana. The good Christian phrase "dying to self" had been besmirched; the "annihilation of personality" was really Huxley's goal.[19] Huxley's answer would doubtless be that this was precisely his goal; the reviewer's obvious attachment would clearly show the goal to be sound. Since the time of Calvin and Luther, Huxley claims, Protestants have tried to avoid "that distasteful process of self-naughting, which is the necessary pre-condition of deliverance into the knowledge of eternal Reality." "Waiting on God is a bore," he might repeat, "but what fun to argue, to score off opponents, to lose one's temper and call it 'righteous indignation' . . . ."[20] Had Protestants followed Hans Denk instead of Martin Luther and the tolerant Sebastian Castellio instead of the intolerant Calvin,[21] disputes on dying to self would probably not even arise.

Unfortunately, the most doubtful of Huxley's claims is that there *is* a "perennial philosophy," a "highest factor" common to *all* the great religions. The religions themselves do not confirm the claim unless one selects only what one wishes to see. Confucianism is barely mentioned in *The Perennial Philosophy*;[22] except for some atypical elements, Judaism also is all but ignored. Yet Confucianism has had the allegiance of literally billions of Chinese. The significance of Judaism is even more apparent, but Huxley nowhere shows that he cares what Judaism is. Confucianism, we remember, has no mystical tradition; its emphasis is heavily personal and moral. Judaism has its mystics from the early Hasidim to Martin Buber, but it demands allegiance to a highly personal God, inseparable from the ethical concepts of justice and mercy, actually and deliberately moving in history. Both religions are ejected before the discussion begins.

Another claim is also clearly false—that the mystics agree on the nature of their experience. To most Christian mystics, "That" is *not* "thou" and never can be. In the words of St. John of the Cross, the mystical union with God is a "union of love and of likeness, not division of substance." The soul "will indeed be God by participation," but "the soul's natural being—notwithstanding the soul's supernatural transformation—remains as distinct from the Being of God as it was before. . . ."[23] Even within Hinduism there is a basic disagreement. Huxley merely follows the main line of Hindu thought emanating from the ninth century sage, Shankara. It is Shankara, founder of the "non-dualist" school of Vedanta, who emphasizes that Atman is Brahman, that "That art thou."[24] God is inferior to

Brahman and finally not even real. He is instead in Heinrich Zimmer's words merely "phenomenal—a majestic, lordly face painted on the sublime blank of Brahman, true being, which is devoid of physiognomy as well as of all other attributes and definitions." The love of God, though "priceless," is a means toward a higher form of personal liberation.[25] Yet the opposite conclusion is reached by Ramanuja, a major figure two centuries after Shankara. To Ramanuja God is both real and *higher* than Brahman. The mystic may realize his identity with Brahman, but this is not the highest state he can achieve. Brahman, merely "that which is unconditioned by space and time," was originated by God, the mystic's "proper goal."[26] Like other opponents of the traditions Huxley has chosen, Ramanuja is never mentioned at all. Huxley admitted some years later that he was "not a scholar" and could "lay no claim to exhaustiveness or accuracy."[27]

Though as theology and religious history *The Perennial Philosophy* has many defects, it is again and again a trenchant critique of modern man. Huxley knows "man's deep-seated will to ignorance and spiritual darkness,"[28] and he knows the many outlets and forms the darkness can take and assume. He cites the "organized lovelessness" of racial contempt, of the exploitation of Nature, of the violence inflicted by one sovereign state upon another.[29] He knows that the most urgent and difficult problem is the human craving for some kind of power. He recognizes in the belief in progress our characteristic "overvaluation of the things of time."[30] He finds us accepting as "axiomatic" the separateness of our egos, our treating them as above the moral law, as even above the laws of causality.[31] Perhaps as clearly as anything else, Huxley knows the dangers of our emotions and of the way they are used to justify the separate self. Finally, he realizes how our institutions—churches, press, and governments—can reinforce the pressures which make us behave as we do.

Huxley's analysis of our problems is often totally convincing, but the degree of his insistence on mortification is a mistake. Richard Chase once cogently noted the hazards of worshipping pure spirit, the possible outcome of "narcissism, . . . cosmic sleight of hand and . . . practical cruelty."[32] Huxley ostensibly recognizes these dangers: he favors the Mahayana over the Hinayana Buddhists for rejecting "spiritual knowledge exclusively in the heights of the soul,"[33] and he applauds the Christian rejection of quietism.[34] Yet he would still apparently *isolate* being as an essence. The standard Vedantist view sees Brahman, spirit, as the being of *everything*.[35] Within the human person, but beyond his thoughts and feelings and desires, is "that greater reality that he really is. . . ."[36] Huxley's emphasis on mortification seems far more negative. Instead of accepting personality as *maya,* or "illusion," he wants to reject it and let only the spirit survive. *The Perennial Philosophy,* though still a powerful social critique, is another elaborate response to Huxley's sense of inner division. The strongest drive in Huxley is still toward liberation; after mortification *he* hopes to feel psychically free.

The drive toward the ascetic shows that like other men Huxley is led or driven by his own psychology. In a sense he admits this in his opening chapter, where he sees human psychology as "the focal point where mind and matter, action and thought have their meeting place."[37] But his awareness does not comprehend his own psychology, at least in the theory he offers in his books. It is significant that throughout his life Huxley rejected Freud, though the tone and intensity of his rejection varied.[38] Given Freud's emphasis on sex and Huxley's near-obsession with it, the rejection implies unconscious resistance incompletely understood. Here perhaps is a source of Huxley's compulsiveness, of his exclusion of the arguments against total mortification and his emphasis on undiluted spirit.[39] Reinhold Niebuhr, who had just published *The Nature and Destiny of Man,* like Huxley identifies an ego-centered self and the destructiveness resulting from its belief in progress. But Niebuhr accepts its presence and finds in it some good, some *"justitia originalis."* He will not have it dissolved in mysticism.[40] Another kindred spirit Huxley might have learned from was Paul Tillich. Though no Vedantist, Tillich speaks of the "all-pervasive power of the Brahman," with which the mystic as Tillich sees him strives to identify. But since "everything that is participates in the power of being," Tillich believes in the *acceptance* rather than the mortification of self.[41] Some years later Huxley would fully agree. His characters would accept themselves while believing *tat tvam asi*; they would exemplify both "Good Knowing" and "Good Being."

There are signs Huxley realized that total mortification could not work. With a metaphor to be more fully developed later, he sees the human psyche at one point as "amphibious," unable always to be identified with the spirit and "to some extent" necessarily associated with the body.[42] Unaware of inconsistency or contradiction, he sees *human* grace emerging in many ways, from the "mother, father, nurse, ... beloved teacher" or friends; from "men and women morally better and wiser than ourselves"; even from our ideals and our *attachments*—"to country, party, church or other social organization."[43] Huxley actually denies his essentialism in the process of writing his book. *The Perennial Philosophy,* though it argues for mortification, is itself a dynamic, unmortified assertion. As a young man Huxley found writing a "wholly moral action";[44] in his middle age, it might be said, the act is existential. The intellect articulates the psyche's longing for liberation; the self will have its attached and contradictory way, arguing the psyche's ideal within a book. Yet such inconsistencies must be set against real values—a new comprehensive vision, a sense of urgency, and faith in an available, permanent source of the good.

II

WHEN HUXLEY was interviewed in New York in the fall of 1947, he noted "a sense of general precariousness" and saw "the whole social order running down in the most hopeless way." The Germans were living a "troglodyte existence," the news from India was "horrible." Even America was in a "fantastic" state, with "a widespread sense of insecurity."[45] On Huxley's mind was not only the condition of the world but also the dreadfully significant fact of Hiroshima. As soon as *The Perennial Philosophy* was finished there were increasingly urgent reasons to apply it. It became immediately the shaping force in Huxley's work.

Two of his earlier and most successful ironic works, Huxley now saw through new perennial-philosophical eyes. He turned "The Gioconda Smile," his brilliant story of 1921, into a didactic play illustrating his cluster of beliefs. Dr. Libbard, formerly a cynical, tight-lipped, tired figure, has become the loquacious teacher of Mr. Hutton, who learns about progress and man's attitude toward Nature, about the danger of living "discontinuously by virtue of being rich," about "one's own insufferable self." Still innocent of the murder, Hutton insists he belongs in jail for the crime of "resisting the spirit of God within."[46] Though the play ran for many months in London, Broadway did not want to hear what Libbard and Hutton had to say: Brooks Atkinson deplored Huxley's "mixed styles" and "banal writing"[47] and *The Gioconda Smile* was an immediate flop. *Brave New World* Huxley did not actually revise—the true revision would be the valedictory *Island*—but he used a 1946 foreword to the novel to make clear how the perennial philosophy should work. Much of it is an exercise in sarcastic attack, deliberately written "with a certain brio."[48] Criticized as "a sad symptom of the failure of an intellectual class in time of crisis," Huxley suggests an ossuary "Sacred to the Memory of the World's Educators" to be placed "among the ruins of one of the gutted cities of Europe or Japan."[49] Yet he does also briefly outline his social ideal. In the right state, he tells us, politics would be "co-operative," derived from the anarchist theory of Peter Kropotkin. Economics would be decentralist, in line with Henry George. Religion of course would be "the conscious and intelligent pursuit of man's Final End, the unitive knowledge of the immanent Tao or Logos, the transcendent Godhead or Brahman."[50]

Another requirement he cites, the need for decentralization, he had argued ten years before in *Ends and Means*. Now nuclear fission made the claim even more urgent: the nuclear scientist he sees as "Procrustes in modern dress," preparing for us our new totalitarian bed.[51] His fears are expanded in *Science, Liberty and Peace* (1946), an essay unhappily full of unanalyzed abstractions and metaphors,[52] yet alert to the danger, before the phrase was even coined, of the military-industrial complex. Huxley's concern for the individual, for independence and self-government, his continuing interest in our "Final End"—all are clearly evident, even though the connection between symptom and cure is not really shown. The more complete, more graphic statement is *Ape and Essence* (New York: Harper & Brothers, 1948), Huxley's first novel of the atomic age.

This most appalling of all of Huxley's books depicts the future that follows (and some of the history) when the perennial philosophy is ignored. The "Arch-Vicar of Belial" and "Bishop of Hollywood," a new but sloppy Mustapha Mond, enunciates with vigor Huxley's basic social ideas. Our Nationalism is merely "the theory that the state you happen to be subject to is the only true god." What we call Progress is "an orgy of criminal imbecility." We think we are "conquerors of Nature"; we really are "slaves of wheels and ledgers," about to suffer from upsetting Nature's equilibrium.[53] He adds paren-

thetically a hint of human potential: if we had combined Eastern mysticism with Western science, refined "Western energy"
with "the Eastern art of living," and tempered Eastern totalitarianism with Western individualism, we would have been
able to find "the kingdom of heaven."[54] The perennial philosophy is implied as early as Huxley's title. Isabella of *Measure
for Measure* finds man "an angry ape," ignorant of "his glassy
essence," playing "such fantastic tricks before high heaven/As
make the angels weep."[55] In *Ape and Essence* the "glassy es-
ence" of the spirit has been denied; angry apeness and simian
cleverness remain, to play the "fantastic tricks" made possible
by nuclear science.

The Arch-Vicar's surroundings bear no resemblance to *Brave
New World*. Instead of the gleaming efficiency of the hatcheries
and crematoria, the setting offers only large piles of rubbish—
Los Angeles a few generations after World War III. Human
skeletons are piled in doorways and ruined filling stations; dust,
tattered clothing, cheap jewelry and brassieres cover what was
once an undergraduate science laboratory; dunes of sand drift
through the street; trains and automobiles, rusty and unused,
clutter the landscape. Women draw water from a well into a
goatskin; food is so scarce that books are pulverized for bread.
The graves of prebomb movie moguls are robbed for jewels and
clothes. Many inhabitants are deformed; the gamma rays have
produced babies with four rows of nipples, or without any legs
or arms, or with eight or more fingers on a hand. The adults
live a life of outlandish beliefs and shocking rituals. World
War III to these people is "The Thing"; the Devil whom they
call Belial, was the cause—but he used human beings and
science "as His instruments."[56] In the "Shorter Catechism"
which all young people learn, "The Chief end of Man is to
propitiate Belial, deprecate His enmity and avoid destruction
for as long as possible."[57]

The first social leader we meet is a secular official, the whip-wielding "Chief" who robs a grave for a suit of clothes. But religious officials really are in charge. The Arch-Vicar, (also Lord of the Earth, Primate of California, and Servant of the Proletariat) leads a hierarchy—Archimandrites, Patriarchs, Presbyters, Postulants, and Satanic Science Practitioners. More significant than their titles is the fact that they are gelded, for the efficient cause of evil to this society is sex. The Shorter Catechism declares Woman to be "the vessel of the Unholy Spirit, the source of all deformity," and "the enemy of the race, punished by Belial and calling down punishment on all those who succumb to Belial in her."[58] These are no *Brave New World* pneumatic, willing females, at least for the largest proportion of the year. Here women wear "NO" to cover the strategic places on their bodies. To fill his ranks the Arch-Vicar spots the idealistic males and convinces them to submit, as he did, to castration.

The focus of this culture is two appalling annual rituals, one following quite naturally after the other. In the genetic "Purification Ceremony," deformed babies are put to the knife, if they have more than three pairs of nipples or more than seven fingers or toes. Familiars and Postulants survey the population, shave the heads of the offending mothers, administer a preliminary whipping, then ship them to one of the Purification Centres where the ceremony is held. In the torchlit Los Angeles Coliseum against the music of xylophones and bone recorders, an antiphonal chant to Belial proceeds. It is a parody of orthodox Christian ritual, organized to echo the odes of Attic tragedy. A harelipped Mongolian idiot, the "characteristic product of progressive technology," is taken from the mother's arms, and the chant concentrates on her "filth unutterable." To the hungry shouts of "Blood, blood, blood," the Patriarch butchers the infant and spills some of its blood on the altar, then throws it away as two Postulants whip the mother with bulls' pizzles.

But one visceral emotion leads to another, and the race must reproduce as well as purify itself. The gamma rays have made sex seasonal. "Romance has been swallowed up by the oestrus, and the female's chemical compulsion to mate has abolished courtship, chivalry, tenderness, love itself."[59] As the spectators begin leaping down from the Coliseum seats, the annual orgy of copulation begins. The Arch-Vicar genuflects, lights a phallic-symbol candle, and a briefer chant about lust and craving follows: "This is the time,/For Belial is merciless,/Time for Time's ending./In the chaos of lust."[60] The "NO" brassieres and pants are ripped off and the two weeks of mating begin. Between the butchery and the orgy the Arch-Vicar squeaks his message explaining the power of Belial while munching on pigs feet and swilling them down with wine.

The man who listens to him is Dr. Alfred Poole, a protagonist out of the same mold as Bernard Marx with a mother fixation much worse than Jeremy Pordage's or Gumbril's. A botanist arriving on an expedition from New Zealand, an area un-affected by The Thing, Poole has been captured but given special treatment because he has useful scientific skills. While the Arch-Vicar, finished picking his teeth, goes off to light the candle, Poole succumbs to the orgy and the heroine Loola, a *Brave New World* Lenina with an extra pair of nipples. Their story, with the background of primitive goings-on, is cast in the form of a movie scenario replete with directions like "Dissolve to the interior of the Unholy of Unholies," or "Vaseline-like, the strains of the Good Friday music from Parsifal make themselves heard on the sound track."[61] The most obvious quality of the script is grotesque exaggeration, particularly in its emphasis on sex. We are nationalistic, bumptious wor-shippers of science; yet sex, it is suggested, is behind it all, and sex will get worse after the world we know is destroyed.

What seemed mere tasteless vulgarity when *Ape and Essence* was published now appears at least aesthetically prophetic. Huxley's book anticipates the theater of the absurd, for Ionesco's rhinoceri postdate more Huxley baboons. Before the Poole-Loola-Arch-Vicar story begins, human beings of *our* America actually appear as angry apes. A mauve-muzzled female baboon intones provocative love songs. A baboon housewife listens avidly at the radio. The "Right Reverend the Baboon-Bishop of the Bronx," holding a crozier and chanting "in nomine Babuine . . . ," pronounces a benediction upon the Field Marshallissimos of the baboon army. Michael Faraday, though in the human form of an old man, walks on all fours with a dog collar on his neck; when he tries to stretch, the baboon singer strikes him with a switch. A few shots later, two Albert Einsteins appear tied to leashes held by baboons. When they are finally forced to release the nuclear bomb, the "Thing" and the consequent "Judgment" are on their way. Though these baboon images look like creatures of Ionesco, *Ape and Essence* is too didactic to be an absurdist work. It is also too bewildering to be a good one, for no other Huxley tale has so many narrating selves.

Number One is William Tallis, the author of the script, who has lived in a desert house suspiciously like the Huxleys'.[62] Though Tallis is referred to he never actually appears; his script is discovered by Number Two, the narrator of an introductory chapter, a man even more suggestive of Aldous Huxley than Tallis. This narrator treats Mahatma Gandhi as Huxley has treated Father Joseph: Gandhi made the mistake the theocentric saint must always avoid of getting himself involved in nationalism. He also exposes in Huxley style the weakness of one Bob Briggs, a "bovarist" who is "bound and committed to adultery." After he and Briggs have visited Tallis' house, the script of "Ape and Essence" begins, and two more Huxley personae soon appear. Number Three, though he sometimes gives camera men the directives, particularly likes to make fun of Dr. Poole. Number Four is a one-man chorus, a Narrator proper in the script. He also badgers Poole about his mother fixation; he sometimes comments patronizingly to the audience; his alliterative verses on "Cruelty and compassion" replace Huxley's favorite lines from Fulke-Greville; he repeats familiar ideas on Pascal, on Progress, and on tragedy; he recites the passage from *Measure for Measure* and his own verses on the ape and essence theme; and he introduces the baboons before Poole's expedition begins. He is clearly Huxley the philosopher, religious thinker, and social critic, equipped with more sarcasm and greater range in tone.

Yet in spite of the various derogatory comments on Poole, there is a final important connection between Poole himself and Aldous Huxley. Poole, of course, is initially the shy, inhibited, Huxley type of hero, a type Huxley originally based upon himself. But after the orgy, finding his lust metamorphosed into love, he decides that he and Loola are meant for each other alone. In this culture's argot their monogamy classifies them as "Hots" and makes them liable to burial alive if they are caught. Undaunted, Poole leads Loola toward Fresno and the colony of Hots. Inspired like Walter Bidlake by *Epipsychidion,* which he has rescued from the oven, Poole first applies Shelley's metaphors to Loola, then attacks the Arch-Vicar's satanology. Belial, says Poole, can "never resist the temptation of carrying evil to the limit. And whenever evil is carried to the limit, it always destroys itself." The "Order of Things" is certain to reappear. At this point even Number Four's condescending tone has gone. He evokes the "wholeness of art which is analogous to holiness," and suggests that "beyond *Epipsychidion* there is *Adonais,* and beyond *Adonais* the wordless doctrine of the Pure in Heart."[63] And so it is as script and novel conclude: when the lovers reach the desert, they stumble on William Tallis' grave on which appropriate words from *Adonais* are inscribed. In their love, their unselfish consideration for each other, they qualify as obviously Pure in Heart.

One wonders how much of this ending Huxley understood,

or how much, at least, was consciously calculated. A decent but inhibited young academic, "surreptitiously burning" with sexual fantasies, finds himself in an orgy where any woman is fair game. His inhibitions gone with a yank or two of the panties, and the fantasies are now wholeheartedly indulged. But his sensuality reveals no egoistic attachment; it releases first the power of idealistic love, then the transcendent power of the spirit. There is no suggestion in *The Perennial Philosophy* that man can discover his "glassy essence" like this. Shelleyan idealism and uninhibited lust, romantic love and the transcendent mystical spirit—in the strands of fantasy and the bewildering group of Huxley projections, we are back among the confusions and contradictions of the poems. Had Huxley restricted himself to his baboons, or kept the theme of apeness versus essence really clear, we might have had the first classic of the atomic age. Instead, we face another masked revelation of Huxley's mind, with the contemplative stability he had established now upset. The instinct of sex could not be excluded or ignored, nor could romantic intuitions of the ideal. The rigidities of *The Perennial Philosophy* were going to have to give.

III

THE PROCESS OF SOFTENING in Huxley's creed was gradual, sometimes almost imperceptible. "Variations on a Philosopher," for example, the first essay of *Themes and Variations* (1950), seems like a return to Trabuco orthodoxy. Huxley's subject is Maine de Biran, the French epistemologist of Napoleon's time, who like other empiricists saw the source of knowledge in sensations produced by the external world. Unlike Condillac and others, however, who had no use for (though they assumed) the concept of a perceiving self,[64] Biran claimed that while sensations come and go, our active willing to move or not move still remains. He believed that the force "of a willed effort against a felt resistance, is the ultimate source of our knowledge of ourselves and the world."[65] Though Huxley explores Biran's epistemology, he is far more interested in Biran's inner life. If Huxley's creed is really perennial, it should apply to a Frenchman of an earlier century.

With the help primarily of the *Journal Intime,* Huxley explores the recesses of Biran's mind. We learn, of course, what Biran was most concerned with, but—equally important—the crucial things he did *not* think. In this "imaginative account," as it has accurately been called,[66] Huxley assumes the omniscience of the novelist. We are told what Biran felt at six o'clock in the morning, what he said as he was putting on his clothes, and what he thought when he left the house and headed for the baths—all inferences rather than explicit *Journal* statements.[67] Though Huxley's comment on the philosophy is generally accurate so far as it goes, Biran is barely distinguishable from a Huxley protagonist, and in important respects almost a double for Huxley himself. Like Denis Stone he wonders "over and over again" why he had to be "born with a different face."[68] He has the shyness of Denis, Gumbril, and the rest of the Huxley line and at one point at least the shyness of Aldous Huxley. Biran almost vomited in front of Louis XVIII; so did Huxley, Huxley tells us, in view of the Prince of Wales.[69] Like Walter Bidlake and Anthony Beavis, Biran refused to "insist on his rights," hated conflict, and did not collect his debts.[70] Biran had the "consciousness that he was not a born writer";[71] Huxley knew he was not a "congenital novelist." And Biran is seen as an "empiricist of the spirit,"[72] a phrase Huxley would happily have accepted for himself.

The *Journal* confirms the qualities Huxley attributes to Biran, if not all the thoughts Huxley pushes through his mind. Yet Biran becomes finally not a version of Aldous Huxley but an opportunity for Huxley to feel superior. By analyzing Biran

and the way in which he failed, as Huxley had in his life-worship phase with other figures in *Do What You Will,* Huxley
implies that he himself would not have made the same mistakes,
or at least that he is not going to make them now. As Biran's
qualities are extracted and dramatized, Biran is checked against
Huxley's set of beliefs. He is seen as one of Sheldon's "extreme
cerebrotonics," "one of those slender, small-boned, thin-muscled
persons, in whom the nerves and vital organs are uncomfortably
close to the surface . . . [who tend] to turn inwards, away from
their surroundings. . . ." He is one of Jung's introverts—too
much so "to be concerned with other people's unconscious behavior." He is one of those self-conscious people preoccupied
with moral problems, but not, it is strongly implied, a "twice-
born Christian, a twice-born Buddhist or Vedantist."[73] He is
not, that is a perennial philosopher.

Huxley once wrote Hermann Broch that Virgil had "wanted
to see God," but not quite strongly enough—or "he would have
subjected himself to the purificatory discipline of one of the mystery religions."[74] Biran is also deficient; he does not know the
proper Huxley answers. Toward music he was a "voluptuary"
who failed to devalue "delicious" sound. Art was "merely a stim-
ulant"; it had nothing to do with "the divine not-I, which tran-
scends the ego and is its ground." There follows a disquisition
on what art really means. Biran tended to abstract from reality
instead of grasping "life as it is." Had he read Meister Eckhart
(or, we might add, seen the weakness in Aldous Huxley) this
tendency might not have long persisted. He was a good judge
of the "facts and fictions" of animal magnetism and wise
enough to accept the reality of ESP. But he never got his
magnetist friends to cure his illness, which prevented him from
seeing an important part of the truth. If his "I" was to surrender, it would be to Plato rather than Mesmer, and the surrender would "be purely voluntary and self-suggested, not
imposed from without by a study of other 'I's.' "[75] How he

could have studied involuntarily is a question Huxley does not ask. The Biran essay, one of Huxley's favorites, is less the "historical and biographical" effort of his label[76] than a recapitulation, with some changes, of his own ideas. He reasserts what his intellect has accepted with an attitude of lofty confidence. Biran, almost always "our philosopher," seems to shrink in importance as Huxley's digressions appear ever more frequently. Since Biran cannot respond, Huxley is an easy victor— but a writer who plays this kind of psychological game has abandoned mortification, no matter what he says. The intellect may believe and the will continue to assert, but the self shows the actuality of change.

As Huxley softens the demand for mortification and gradually loosens the framework of his ideas, he shifts his emphasis from essence to existence. The saints of *The Perennial Philosophy* are almost essences, ripped or abstracted from the context of their culture. Biran, however, is treated as an actual person, born with actual attributes in a specific place and age. A Trabuco contemplative, living a life of "unwavering rectitude,"[77] Huxley had affirmed himself existentially in the process of writing *The Perennial Philosophy*. Now he has advanced much farther down the existentialist path.

In his many comments on art in *Themes and Variations* Huxley displays again and again this interest in experience. Though art brings insight and rapture analogous to the mystic's, it does so by looking around and not above, by "redeeming the squalid chaos of human life."[78] We must not equate images with the reality whence they proceed: "we must never expect to find in art a reflection of contemporary reality as it is actually experienced. . . ."[79] Looking at the baroque art of seventeenth-century Rome, one can only speculate about the actual life from which it grew,[80] but the implication is that the effort is worth the time. In "Variations on a Baroque Tomb," in his most effectively personal style, Huxley asks why, at a particular moment, the death's head should appear on royal tombs. After answering he relates the abstract to the lived. His essay is "on the level of intellectual abstraction." As a member of a particular generation, he is "on the level of history." But when he actually comes to die, he will be on "the level of exclusively individual experience." And he praises some of the most clearly existentialist works of art—"The Death of Ivan Ilyitch," Goya's *Disasters,* and *The Naked and the Dead.*[81] The emphasis of his essay on Piranesi's prison etchings is experience at its existential worst. Piranesi is delineating "metaphysical prisons, whose seat is within the mind, whose walls are made of nightmare and incomprehension, whose chains are anxiety and their racks a sense of personal and even generic guilt."[82] Though the theocentric Saint Catherine is mentioned, the perennial philosophy as a system of abstractions does not appear. The final words of the essay refer instead to "the inhabitants of a hell which . . . bears the stamp of self-evident authenticity."[83]

There is no such de-emphasis in *The Devils of Loudun* (1952), Huxley's grotesque, often painful tale of demoniac possession, one of the most vivid and carefully written of his books. Here the perennial-philosophy cluster of ideas reappears in frequent miniature essays. Yet as Huxley traces the lives of Grandier, Soeur Jeanne, and Surin he shows none of the aloof superiority directed toward Maine de Biran. There is little of the "they might have known better"; instead we have a rigorous attempt to recreate the existential context of the subjects' lives. Much detail is imagined, perhaps once again projected, for Huxley again assumes the omniscience of the novelist. Yet no other Huxley book is so thoroughly researched. He had begun his work by 1941, more than ten years before the final result appeared.[84] He obviously became deeply absorbed in what he found—"the entire gamut of the religious life from the bestial to the sublime."[85]

What attracted Huxley to the grotesquerie of seventeenth-century France when *The Perennial Philosophy* was reaching publishable form? Richelieu and his totalitarianism, superstition and torture feature the part of the age Huxley decided to explore. And at Loudun the horrors were as shocking as they could become. Huxley's interest is partly historical; the period, as seen in *Grey Eminence,* planted the seeds of European nationalism, which in turn bore fruit in the wars of our own time. But far more important is a psychological tie to the meaning of the alleged possessions themselves. They represent for Huxley a plunge into the abyss, a Dante-like excursion into hell.

For most people the abyss was identified by Pascal as the awesome marvels of infinity and nothingness. When this early existentialist faced the implications of man's state, he decided to wager on the existence of God. Perhaps Huxley had confronted a kind of nothingness when, as the "amused Pyrrhonic aesthete," he responded with *Brave New World.* He would soon face human helplessness as it is even more commonly known, in what *Island* refers to as the "Essential Horror." But until he had finished *The Devils of Loudun* (1952), the abyss was located in the extremes of personality. His own extremes are projected in his work, particularly in the period ending with *Point Counter Point.* In *The Perennial Philosophy* they are explained and in theory relieved by Vedantist dicta about what people really are. To test these principles and thereby, vicariously, himself, Huxley had studied the problems and responses of Maine de Biran. But human personality in its most appalling form was the sensuality, the hypocrisy, and the sadism of Loudun.

Huxley tells us how Princess Soeur Jeanne and the other Ursuline sisters became obsessed with strange visions, shameful thoughts and inclinations, including the belief that they had been deflowered by demons. The gruesome process of exorcism then commenced, with spells chanted and enemas administered before a public who would travel many miles to observe. Father Urbain Grandier, a lascivious priest who had seduced almost every woman in the area except Soeur Jeanne and her nuns, was named as the villain and convicted, tortured, and burned for being a witch. A third principal, Jean-Joseph Surin, entered the scene to rid Soeur Jeanne of her devils; in the process he became virtually possessed himself. Such extremes as these are developed fully though sometimes fictionally. Experiments with the alleged "strange and alarming properties of menstrual blood,"[86] Grandier's speculation about "apple-round breasts" and youthful coquetry,[87] Soeur Jeanne's thoughts of Grandier as an "obscenely fascinating image,"[88] her "horrible" but "wonderful" sensations as she undergoes "the outrage of a forcible colonic irrigation . . . the equivalent, more or less, of a rape in a public lavatory"[89]—such details as these help to build the world of Huxley's study, a world which makes *Eyeless in Gaza* seem almost a pastoral idyll.

When Huxley has plunged himself (and us) into these details, reporting where he has some evidence, imagining where he does not, he finds a significant form in the horrors of Loudun. The principles of comedy and tragedy again apply. "Jeanne des Anges," he claims, "was one of those unfortunate human beings who consistently invite the outward approach, the purely comic treatment." The fact that the evidence shows her possession was a fraud demands for her histrionics a comic emphasis. Had she admitted in her journals that she had lied in accusing Grandier she would not have been the comic actress we now know. Surin, in spite of his excesses, Huxley sees as "essentially tragic," one whom we know "as he knew himself—from inside and without disguise."[90] This literary analysis, however, is an afterthought rather than a shaping principle. The narrative we read is a drama of the personality and the spirit, two principles which clash and become perverted before a final resolution. In Grandier personality denies the spirit to allow indulgence of the senses. In Soeur Jeanne personality descends to lower depths: her imaginary excesses, as abysmal as those actually practiced by Grandier, are compounded by a greater hypocrisy, for her lies send another person to an unbelievably painful death. In that death, however, personality is first expressed and then brought to a symbolic end. Even while Grandier's body is being crushed—the body to which he has let himself become so attached—he is saved by his confession and spiritual grace. His spirit wins a victory over his personality, and over the sadistic men who insist, quite falsely, that he is guilty as charged. Grandier's astounding courage at his death, a frightening but dramatic victory, provides the emotional climax of the book.[91] It ends with the end of the story of Surin, to Huxley "a very remarkable man" and an important reason for his interest in Loudun.[92] Surin recovers from psychosomatic illness, from the obsessions his role as exorciser has produced. Though he is another personality who has been in the abyss, he nevertheless is able to emerge. Yet Surin's enlightenment might have come more readily had he not made spiritual mistakes. Like too many other Christians desiring unity with the Son, he has been led to reject the divinity of nature,[93] and to see it instead as totally depraved—a temptation Huxley sometimes faced himself. To be invaded, as he puts it, by the peace of God, Surin had to stand naked "before the given facts," both of his life and of the created world.[94] Hence in drawing conclusions from Surin's experience, Huxley abandons the claim that nature should be mortified. We should mortify instead our tendency to replace it. We should discard "the verbal patterns to which we expect reality to conform,"[95] the essentialist purity, for example, of *The Perennial Philosophy*. As Huxley's final work will try to demonstrate more fully, our fundamental problem is ecological.[96] Hence *The Devils of Loudun* is yet another Huxley dialectic: even as Huxley leads us through his seventeenth-century hell, he tells us how we can escape today's.

CHAPTER EIGHT

THE PRIVILEGE OF BEING:

Island

THE WORLD OF *The Devils of Loudun* is a hell of evil, grotesque behavior, and pain. Women are impregnated by a lustful priest, devils make it possible for a Sister to do the splits, a man's legs are completely crushed as wedge after wedge is ruthlessly malleted home. Yet embedded in Huxley's story of demoniac possession, hidden by the weird narrative and the controlled urgency of tone, is a newly flexible and comprehensive view. We are born with Original Sin, Huxley interpolates, but we should remember also our "Original Virtue."[1] We should still seek to live the "primordial fact that That art thou," but not try to find the Ground only in its eternal essence.[2] We must, hence by implication we can, "live with the cosmos on all its levels, from the material to the spiritual."[3] The people of *Island,* Huxley's last major book, have learned to do so. A happy childhood begins a life of acceptance and understanding, sexual harmony, congenial absorbing work, and communion with the divine. From being an analyst of repulsive excesses of the past, Huxley becomes at the end of his life a prophet of possible fulfillment in the future.

I

In *The Genius and the Goddess* (New York: Harper & Brothers, 1955), a weak novel which flopped as a play, Huxley is masked as an older man, John Rivers, an omnivorous reader who seems at times to be omniscient. While sipping his highball and telling the story of his youth, he casually refers to Michelangelo and Thomas à Kempis; to "First Corinthians, thirteen" and the Amalekites; to Hera, Demeter, and Aphrodite; to Goethe, Poincaré, Hilbert, and Late Victorian Rebellion; to psychologists, composers, pornographers, and prophets. He has opinions on any number of topics. "Fiction has unity, fiction has style. Facts possess neither." "Goethe was absolutely wrong." "Most people inhabit a universe that is like French *café au lait.*" He knows that children have an appetite for thrills, that the third-act prelude to *La Traviata* is irresistible, that a tragedy described from the outside is a farce. But he does not really know which thinkers are nearest the truth; he isn't sure whether to give thanks or to despair that a World War I love song is "still warbled" during Korea; and at the end of the novel he remarks that everyone will be drunk, since he is in a Christian country and it's Christmas day. He is most uncertain about the nature of reality. It may be "too undignified to be recorded, too senseless or too horrible to be left unfictionalized."[4] His statement as the novel opens is a startling one from Huxley: "Reality never makes sense," except "maybe" from God's point of view.[5]

Rivers has been made learned, opinionated, often wise, yet in crucial matters essentially uncertain. As a youth he was priggish and inhibited, a pharisee, "an athlete who couldn't say 'Bo' to a girl."[6] Mother domination kept him an innocent virgin who thought that decent couples coupled only once per child. During the part of his life which is the gist of the novel, however, Katy the goddess, worn out and desperately needing animal grace, crept cold and shuddering into his bed. The seduction allowed her to establish contact with "life at its simplest . . . as physical companionship, as the experience of animal warmth. . . ."[7] But as Rivers fell totally in love with the reborn goddess, animal grace was replaced with human attachment, and Katy's daughter Ruth, in the throes of puberty, fell in love with him and became intensely jealous. On the way to a picnic before Rivers was to leave, Katy and Ruth argued until their car was smashed by a truck. A *machina ex deo,* it has been said,[8] ended this tragedy of Rivers' youth.

As Rivers, older, tells this story to a narrator (and so to us), he makes clear the extent and the limits of his wisdom. He draws a kind of ethical graph of the seduction, with a line for himself, a second line for Katy and a third line for the man he is now. He uses metaphor which neither he nor we can understand. Katy should have "come down" to his level and "gone further," while he should have "climbed to her level," then "pressed forward to join her at the place where one is genuinely beyond good and evil in the sense of being, not a superhuman animal, but a transfigured man or woman."[9] Rivers cannot tell us what "pressing forward" really means, or show us, himself, what it is like to be transfigured. He does recognize sainthood when he sees it, for Beulah the maid is "well along" that road. He knows from the accident which left the goddess completely disfigured that there is a "Predestination of events," and he is also aware of the "Predestination of two temperaments." Animal, spiritual, and human grace, "aspects of the same underlying mystery," combine with Predestination to determine the course of our lives.[10] But Rivers is a Huxley wary of mere verbal understanding. Speculations about "being in love with God," suddenly interrupted by the crying of Rivers' grandson, yield to comments on the power of sex and the inevitability of aging and death. Rivers believes in the Clear Light of the Void, yet he and Huxley know that mere *belief* is not an active lived awareness. Only his late wife Helen really knew how to die and to live—"to live now and here for the greater glory of God."[11] And Helen is only briefly mentioned in his tale.

Rivers only briefly was able to live as well as Helen did. He knows that experience is "intrinsically golden," "poetical by its essential nature," but he can feel the poetry only from time to time. Before the seduction, however, his life was completely transformed, when he first joined the goddess' genius husband as his assistant. In spite of Henry's remote self-centeredness, Rivers felt happy, good, and religious, aware for the first time of what the Epistles really meant. He actually lived the newness of the spirit, grace, faith, hope and charity. As an "honorary Maartens," friend of the children as well as of Henry and his wife, he realized that he had never loved or felt really unselfish before. His awareness did not survive the existential test of immersion in sensuality, love, and destructive jealousy. Yet for a while his world was "totally transfigured," though he cannot show us the transfiguration of adult experience. "People, houses, trees, T-model Fords, dogs at lampposts—everything was more significant." They were both their own being and "Being with the biggest possible B."[12] When Joseph Anthony, directing the dramatic version of *The Genius and the Goddess,* wanted to change Rivers into a "sloppy neurotic," Huxley reacted with an intensity very rare in his published correspondence. "The life of my Rivers," he insisted, has "rich significance."[13] Perhaps he was recalling the source of his hero's ontological raptures in one of the most important single days in his own life.

II

ONE "BRIGHT MAY MORNING" in early 1953, under the supervision of Humphry Osmond, a psychiatrist friend, Huxley swallowed four-tenths of a gram of mescaline, closely related chemically to LSD. It allowed him, he tells us in *The Doors of Perception* (1954), to feel as gloriously close to pure Being as Rivers had, without mortification or any other preparatory exercise. He had expected to see visions like those of AE and William Blake; instead, while looking at three flowers in a vase, he claims to have discovered what Eckhart meant by *Istigkeit* or Is-ness. The medium of language, under suspicion since *Eyeless in Gaza,* was no longer a barrier. Huxley "understood, not on the verbal level, not by inchoate hints or at a distance, but precisely and completely" what The Beatific Vision and *Sat Chit Ananda* (Being-Awareness-Bliss) referred to. The clash between time and eternity was resolved: *in* the flowers, in their "minute, unique particulars," "by some unspeakable and yet self-evident paradox" was the Dharma-Body of the Buddha, the "divine source of all existence."[14]

Language no longer bars Huxley from *Istigkeit,* yet the language of his interpretation is revealing. It is still in part Vedantist and religious: he has not actually had the Beatific Vision himself; he is "not so foolish as to equate" *any* drug experience with the "realization of the end and ultimate purpose of human life." He sees the experience as a gratuitous grace[15] allowing what he now calls the "Not-self" to be released from the possessive grip of the self. The psychological emphasis becomes physiological. Huxley accepts C. D. Broad's suggestion that our brain, nervous system, and sensory apparatus are largely "*eliminative* and not productive." They protect us from being swamped by all that is happening around us, and allow us to perceive only what is likely to be useful. At this point "Mind at Large," another new term, is suddenly born. "To make biological survival possible, Mind at Large has to be funnelled through the reducing valve of the brain and nervous system."[16] Mescaline allowed Huxley, for "a few timeless hours," to see "the outer and inner world . . . as they are apprehended, directly and unconditionally, by Mind at Large. . . ."[17] Physiology takes us back to Vedantist metaphysics, for "Mind at Large" is indistinguishable from the Buddhist "Universal Mind." Now as never before Huxley is an "empiricist of the spirit," and supports the mystics by the visions he has himself.

Physiology, psychology, metaphysics—ethics also are involved. To the Not-Self Huxley had become under the influence of the drug, there was nothing less appealing and relevant than human self-assertiveness, even that of his observing wife and friend.[18] He asks himself how "cleansed perception" can be reconciled "with human relations, with the necessary chores and duties, to say nothing of charity and practical compassion." He concludes that he knew contemplation at its "height," but not its "fullness." Mescaline produces a state analogous to quietism; and superior to the quietist, as he has maintained in *The Perennial Philosophy* and *The Devils of Loudun,* is the "active-contemplative," the Eckhart or Bodhisattva, who will even abandon his heavenly vision to bring compassion to a human brother. Yet the passive contemplator not only does no damage; he can also bring back reports of his self-transcendence, and have "some beneficent influence" in "a world of darkened selves."[19] Here in abstract and sophisticated form is the drug-trip rationale of the contemporary hippy.

Though Huxley will not—yet—equate his experience with the Beatific Vision, his remark that he knew contemplation "at its height" is a large and provocative claim. Annoyed by the various confident assertions, R. C. Zaehner, Spalding Professor of Eastern Religions and Ethics at Oxford, decided to try taking mescaline himself. In a BBC interview later published in *The Listener,* Zaehner describes his experience as a total contrast. Everything became to him "inexpressibly funny"; it was "the very antithesis of a religious experience."[20] So significant and dangerous did Huxley's challenge seem that a few months later Zaehner published a full-length book—*Mysticism: Sacred and Profane—An Inquiry into some Varieties of Praeternatural Experience.*[21]

Here Zaehner's own experience is detailed in an appendix, where his laughter is documented and his testy reactions are reported verbatim.[22] Zaehner's real interest, however, is "not so much in the drug itself," but "rather in what Mr. Huxley experienced himself and in his assumption that his experience had religious significance."[23] He does not see why we should "be asked to believe that a vision of nature transfigured in any way corresponds to the vision of God Himself." On the contrary, in both Huxley's case and that of the psychotic manic, "the personality seems to be dissipated into the objective world, while in the case of Suso [a Christian mystic whom Huxley quotes in *The Perennial Philosophy*], as of other theistic mystics, the human personality is wholly absorbed into the Deity Who is felt and experienced as being something totally distinct and other than the objective world."[24] And later, how can one say that experiencing identity with "a minute proportion of the phenomenal world" is equivalent to experiencing oneself as "the Absolute for which the phenomenal world is simply not-being?" Mescaline, Zaehner concludes, allowed Huxley to feel what a "nature-mystic" feels. It is not to be confused with religious mysticism[25] like that of Suso or St. John of the Cross; instead it is similar to other recorded ecstasies of writers like Wordsworth, Arthur Rimbaud, and Marcel Proust.

The contrasting responses grow from and may be caused by contrasting preconceptions. As a Roman Catholic Zaehner believes in a wholly other God, precisely the concept that

Huxley had already rejected for himself and, by implication, also for Heinrich Suso. Zaehner was admittedly not predisposed toward mescaline;[26] Huxley was confident of learning something significant. Yet Zaehner is properly sceptical about Huxley's interpretation. Huxley is not wholeheartedly the scientific analyst, is not so objective as his authority, C. D. Broad. He admits to taking a "trip" through a *chemical* "Door in the Wall," yet he also felt he had reached the "world of transcendental experience."[27] We cannot help feeling that he found what he wanted to find, that he saw or "understood" what he had convinced himself was there. But though Huxley's interpretation raises as many questions as it answers, mescaline was obviously of the greatest importance to *him*. At last the doors of his own perception were cleansed, with less interference, as Humphry Osmond put it, "from his enormous rationalizing brain."[28]

When Zaehner's friend Stuart Hampshire reviewed *The Doors of Perception* he suggested the parody of "a Drugstore for the Soul, built in Indian or Aztec style, supplying the wisdoms of the East in the new synthetic forms. . . ."[29] Huxley's book already takes Hampshire at his word: "If the psychologists and sociologists will define the ideal, the neurologists and pharmacologists can be relied upon to discover the means whereby that ideal can be realized or at least . . . more nearly approached. . . ."[30] Though Huxley will continue to find the saint the highest type, from now on he seeks new horizons for non-saints, including the non-saint who is himself. The rigid demands of *The Perennial Philosophy* are rejected, contradicted, or ignored. Religion and its vocabulary have given ground to science.

In *Heaven and Hell* (1956), two years of reflection and new trials later, the process is decidedly advanced. Here "visionary experience" and mysticism are first philosophically distinguished: "Mystical experience is beyond the realm of opposites.

Visionary experience is still within that realm."[31] But in an Appendix the two are juxtaposed so frequently that this abstract, undeveloped distinction is thoroughly blurred: "visionaries and mystics are a good deal less common. . . . to be a mystic or a visionary is no longer creditable"; the "mental climate . . . is unfavourable to the visionary and the mystic." More surprisingly, both groups are seen in psycho-physical terms. Huxley will not say their experiences are "nothing but" chemically induced, but he frankly and fully admits that they are chemically conditioned. Nothing any longer is "purely 'spiritual' "; most contemplatives, the historical record shows, "worked systematically to modify their body chemistry."[32] In *The Perennial Philosophy* the "stinking lump" of selfness had to be "passionately repented of and . . . completely died to," before God could be known in "purity of spirit." Now "the aspiring mystic should turn for technical help" to—pharmacologists, biochemists, and experts in ESP![33]

Yet Huxley's picture of the mind employs first neither philosophy nor science, but rather a lyrically geographical metaphor:

> A man consists of what I may call an Old World of personal consciousness and, beyond a dividing sea, a series of New Worlds—the not too distant Virginias and Carolinas of the personal subconscious and the vegetative soul; the Far West of the collective unconscious, with its flora of symbols, its tribes of aboriginal archetypes; and, across another, vaster ocean, at the antipodes of everyday consciousness, the world of Visionary Experience.[34]

If the Atman that is Brahman is to find a place at all, it will have to be at the antipodes, along with various visions. The new category, visionary experience, now claims Huxley's interest, far more than the experience of the mystics, no longer the only ones who have true visions. Huxley did not live to see the burgeoning cult of LSD, a drug much easier to prepare than mescaline, or confront the growing evidence of its frequent unhappy results. Though he admitted that some drug-takers travel to "hell" instead of "heaven," he seems clearly to have underestimated the potential terror of the journey. For him the experience apparently remained a glorious one. We have it on the authority of Gerald Heard that Huxley felt LSD was "a sacrament, a perfect psycho-physical aid to sustain the mind at its utmost reach."[35]

Much of *Heaven and Hell* is devoted to visionary art—of many modes and of many lands and many eras. Huxley notes the resemblance between visionary experience and the "heavens and fairylands of folklore and religion," for the typical vision includes "vast and complicated buildings" which pass "from richness to more intensely coloured richness, from grandeur to deepening grandeur"—a "new creation," like a paradise of ancient times.[36] Precious stones, Huxley feels, are "precious because they bear a faint resemblance to the glowing marvels seen with the inner eye of the visionary." More conscious sophisticated religious art, best illustrated by Paolo Uccello's "extraordinary" Resurrection window, has always used vision-inducing materials.[37] They have been devalued, however, by modern technology. The evening lighting of a city, Huxley notes in the manner of his early personal essays, once "reserved for victories and national holidays, for the canonization of saints and the crowning of kings," now "occurs nightly and celebrates the virtues of gin, cigarettes and toothpaste."[38]

Visionary experience is still not mystical, but it brings the Divine Ground surprisingly near. Get to heaven by taking the drug, and you reach a "vantage point" from which you can see it "more clearly . . . than on the level of ordinary individualized existence."[39] Later in 1956 Huxley moved to the farthest end of the limb. Addressing a professional conference of the New York Academy of Sciences, he asserted categorically that

by taking drugs "Human beings will be able to achieve effort-
lessly . . . the ['loving kindness, peace, and joy' that] could be
achieved only with difficulty, by means of self-control and
spiritual exercises."[40] His books do not explore or develop this
astounding declaration, yet his letters suggest that he fully
believed it. One "extraordinary experience with mescaline," he
wrote to Humphry Osmond, gave him a "direct, total awareness . . . of Love as the primary and fundamental cosmic fact."
He felt "intensely aware" of the human world "from the stand-
point of the living primordial cosmic fact of Love."[41] He took
a vision-inducing drug perhaps once or twice a year, yet the
total amount he ingested in ten years was less than some people
now take in a single dose.[42] Huxley was far more cautious than
Timothy Leary and well aware of the need for controlled research. He assured Thomas Merton that the psychedelic experience was "in no circumstances a thing to be entered upon
light-heartedly or for enjoyment." Its importance, however,
is indicated by his comment on the result—"An unspeakable
sense of gratitude for the privilege of being born into this
universe."[43]

III

HUXLEY HAD CLEARLY FOUND personal salvation. He had tried
to resolve his conflicts by searching for a mystical essence, by
the process of mortifying personality. Yet simultaneously he
had groped along an existentialist path, even while maintaining his rigorous essentialist view. Alfie Poole's intensely physical love for Loola was a step toward becoming one of the Pure
in Heart; Maine de Biran should have and could have grasped
life as it is; even *The Perennial Philosophy* gestured toward
human grace. Helen Rivers dies to "there and then and tomorrow" to give herself completely to the present. The self has

to be used up but no longer rejected or "naughted" away. Huxley's personal battle with life, inward and in the world, was transformed into a vigorous and forward looking acceptance and the feeling that there was immense potential for mankind.

Huxley's drug experience codified his view of the role of the artist. A painter like the van Gogh of *The Chair* is not really able to recreate the Nature of a Thing, though his work will be "incomparably more real" than the results of ordinary perception. Instead he produces "emblems" which in turn will help "to prepare the mind . . . for immediate insights on its own account." Like the mescaline-taker, the artist has "a knowledge of the intrinsic significance of every existent."[44] To recapture the early raptures of John Rivers, to live with something like the immediacy of Helen, we will have to learn from all the "non-verbal" humanities.[45] In *Adonis and the Alphabet* (1956), largely collected from essays in *Encounter, Esquire,* and *Vedanta and the West,* this and other possibilities are vigorously explored.

In Huxley's rapidly changing terminology, the way of Helen Rivers is the way of "understanding," the liberated state in which we can make "direct, unmediated contact with the new, the mystery, moment by moment, of our existence."[46] But understanding is inhibited by "knowledge," our system of concepts in the form of words or other symbols. We need knowledge to "become human," to "turn into persons," inhabitants of a world no longer "hideous" but nevertheless of diminished understanding. For the knowledge we accumulate, though possibly *based* on understanding, can be no substitute for it; it cannot replace experience itself. "Existence is prior to essence," Huxley says, now openly agreeing with the familiar proposition. But to live, to establish contact with existence, we must—once again the term appears—*liberate* ourselves "from the tyranny of words, conditioned reflexes and social conventions. . . ."[47] We cannot consciously try to understand; the more we try, the less we succeed. It is not the insistent, infatuated, word-valuing "I" which understands, but a "not-I"; a beneficent worker "which looks after my body and gives me my best ideas."[48]

Huxley has referred to the "not-self" from time to time before,[49] but now it becomes part of a theory of personality more elaborate than any he has previously developed. Casually yet almost dramatically his mind continues to reach out and grasp, from any field of inquiry which will help. Every human being is both ego or conscious self and "five or six merging but clearly distinguishable not-selves." The first is the one psychiatry deals with, the not-self of habits, reflexes, and repressed impulses; the second the not-self of our physiology, in charge of the lungs, the heart, and the glands. The remaining not-selves bring us closer to ultimate truth. One, the not-I which leads to understanding, is also defined as the not-self "responsible . . . for every enhancement of wisdom, every sudden accession of vital or intellectual power." Another not-self is the Jungian, inhabiting the world of "great shared symbols." The last two bring us farthest into the realm of "understanding." One is the not-self of visionary experience; the other, the "universal Not-Self," "immanent in every mental or material event"—Suchness, the Atman-Brahman, or the Clear Light of the Void.[50]

Huxley has a final metaphor: we human creatures must live *amphibiously* in the two worlds of understanding and knowledge, of experience and abstraction—each, of course, a complex place in itself. Yet though proper living will never be easy, the amphibian can be improved by education. Instead of the highly verbalized education rooted in our culture since the Middle Ages, we need training in the non-verbal humanities, illumination by our not-selves that will let us get out of their light. Much of the training involves proper use of the body, by Alexanderism, the Bates method for vision, and "systematic relaxation." The most important kind of training is in spiritual insight, aimed not at mortification but at rediscovering "a virgin not-mind capable of non-verbally not-thinking in response to immediate experience."[51] Huxley is not only reacting against his own tendency to abstract and verbalize, but revolting against the history of Western man. Since Descartes, at least, men have more and more divorced their thinking minds from the world. As J. Hillis Miller says, "the ego . . . has defined all outside itself as the object of its thinking power."[52] Like Yeats, Eliot, Wallace Stevens and many others, but far more deliberately and consciously, Huxley wants to heal the split, to reunite the thinking subject with the rest of the world. His method involves "constant and intense self-awareness free from preconceptions, comparisons, condemnations."[53] With proper training John Rivers may be able to live as well as Helen does.

Several of the essays in *Adonis and the Alphabet* remind us of the less didactic early Huxley. In "The Desert," there are as many jet planes as Joshua trees, and new Reservations with technicians instead of Indians, "surrounded by barbed wire and the FBI." Huxley's conclusion: "The wilderness has entered the armament race, and will be in it to the end."[54] Yet even in the more personal essays the new didactic emphases emerge. "Hyperion to a Satyr" describes Huxley's discovery, on his walk with Thomas Mann, of thousands of discarded condoms on a beach. Continuous as the stars that shine, they stretched in never ending line—until the Hyperion Activated Sludge Plant got to work. The clever animadversions on sludge and contraceptives lead to another attack on the dangers of words and symbols. A more tantalizing passage appears in an essay entitled "Mother," in which F. W. H. Myers, Zen and Tantrik Buddhism appear with the notions of "working hypothesis" and "operational procedures."[55] A foreword to a psychiatrist's book about Zen makes somewhat clearer where Huxley is really headed. The author's theory of personality and of knowl-

177]

edge and understanding must, says Huxley, be tested, and if
it can be verified should then be put into use. Oriental philosophy provides the proper model because it is "transcendental
pragmatism" rather than pure speculation. When transcendental pragmatists test their metaphysics, "the mode of their existence changes, and they know everything, including the
proposition 'thou art That,' in an entirely new and illuminating
way." We can, if we wish, "become adjusted to the Nature of
Things," both in the universe and in our own mind-bodies.[56]
Huxley's final books attempt to show us why our society pre-
vents us and how an ideal society might proceed.

IV

THE HOPE FOR HUMANITY is mental liberation; the danger lies
largely in a complex pattern of mental restriction. Hence Huxley was intrigued by the suggestion of *Newsday* in late 1957
that he write a series of essays on new methods of persuasion.[57]
A few months later a long supplement to the paper, "Tyranny
over the Mind," appeared. Since the point of departure was the
prophetic *Brave New World,* the book in which the *Newsday*
essays were reprinted was called *Brave New World Revisited*
(1958). Huxley felt that the prophecies of 1932 were being
realized much sooner than he had predicted. The nightmare
he had envisioned happening seven centuries after Ford "is
now awaiting us, just around the next corner."[58] Borrowing
a theme from *Adonis and the Alphabet,* he stresses over-popu-
lation as the quickest route to the Brave New World, since it
"leads to economic insecurity and social unrest," which then
produce "more control by central governments and an increase
of their power." Advances in technology compound the problem, by lowering the death rate and increasing centralization.[59]
America, though not yet over-populated, is cursed by a power

elite, and our lives are becoming so standardized as to impair our mental health. A new "Social Ethic" assumes that the social whole is more important than the individuals which compose it—to Huxley "merely a justification after the fact of the less desirable consequences of over-organization," bound to produce "a kind of servitude."[60] Most of these ideas are admittedly borrowed ones, available in William Whyte, C. Wright Mills, and Erich Fromm.

Huxley's greatest concern is again for the pitfalls of language, for the new sources and dangers of propaganda. Motivation analysts of the advertising agencies, mastering and exploiting human hopes and fears; Communist brainwashing techniques developed from Pavlov's work with strain in dogs; tranquilizers, subliminal persuaders, and LSD; recent successes with hypnopaedia—all may serve the would-be tyrant in controlling his subjects' minds, as often as not with at least their unconscious assent. Huxley still feels such psychological techniques are the real danger, as he had in his 1946 Foreword to *Brave New World,* rather than the Stalinist methods of Orwell's *1984.* His solution repeats what has been said in earlier work: education both "in facts and in values," and in the abuses as well as the uses of language; and development of smaller, more autonomous units of government, "self-governing voluntarily co-operating groups."[61]

Brave New World Revisited, already almost a forgotten work, lacks the imaginative power of the original novel, now a classic, a modern myth. It is concentrated and unified but as a consequence shorn of Huxley's usual liveliness of style. However, at about the time his essays were produced, and perhaps for a period of almost thirty years,[62] Huxley was gestating a more important sequel to *Brave New World.* In the original novel Helmholtz Watson, punished by exile for being too creative, happily left for a distant island of free men. In the 1946 Foreword Huxley had outlined that island's life. In an essay on "Human Potentialities" for Sir Julian's *The Humanist Frame,* he indicated some of its primary ends and means.[63] Now, hardly more than a year before he died, he published a Utopian novel to make all his beliefs and values clear. Appropriately titled simply *Island* (New York: Harper & Brothers, 1962) it is Huxley's final major statement, the culminating effort of his life.

Read as a novel, as a product of the artistic imagination, *Island* is a failure, as most early reviewers hastened to point out. The characters seem flat, stereotyped, oversimplified, given less to feeling and acting than to explanatory talk. But as a frankly didactic statement about cosmic truth and the nature of man, *Island* is a challenging and courageous vision. A dialectic of opposing forces characterizes much of Huxley's earlier work; in *Island,* the dialectic involves the primordial forces that move in the world. Evil appears in grotesque forms as the "Essential Horror"; so does good, as the islanders' ideal of "Good Being." Two ways of living parallel these principles, one horrified, hence cynical and uncommitted, but attached; the other capable of accepting all of life, liberated by a comprehensive understanding. This understanding, a product of transcendental pragmatism, orders the society in which Huxley's islanders live. Their upbringing and education maintain and promote it, their religion confirms it, their way of life expresses and uses it. They embody or represent all that Huxley himself had come to accept. *Island* as a whole is far more important than the sum of its separate parts, some of which involve questionable, untested claims. It is valuable for what it tries to do—to present a reasoned, undogmatic view of human life, where potentialities and aspirations are actually realized because human beings have tested *all* available resources and put to use those that reveal, harmonize with and employ the truth.

The book is set in Pala (suggesting Pali, the language of many Buddhist scriptures), a Pacific island whose culture is now about a century old. Modern Pala has from the beginning synthesized East and West, as Huxley felt the actual world must do; it was "invented" by the "Raja of the Reform" and a Victorian visitor named Dr. Andrew MacPhail. It all started with MacPhail removing a ghastly tumor from the Raja's face, in his nose, one eye and a large part of his throat. Without chloroform or antiseptic, MacPhail performed not the impossible, but—and this is the point—the possible. In 1845 James Esdaile had used hypnosis for hundreds of major operations in India, only to be later ridiculed by his English colleagues.[64] Using the same technique, MacPhail induces a trance and successfully removes the Raja's tumor. Although the operation is not described until the middle of the book, it epitomizes the spirit and strategy of the whole. Such an operation has actually been performed; so may other seeming miracles if we will liberate ourselves from conventional techniques and ideas. The two men, after the Raja fully recovered, could not actually "make the best of *all* the worlds," but "they made the best of many more worlds than any merely prudent or sensible person would have dreamed of being able to reconcile and combine."[65] Huxley would have us forego our prudence, question our assumptions, be willing to follow the truth when it leads us away from the crowd. Each part of his synthesis needs to be taken seriously; but more important to apprehend is the independent spirit of the whole.

Palanese government, as we might expect from the earlier work, is a decentralized federation of various self-governing units. There are half-a-dozen parties and political interests, each of which is allotted a certain amount of space in the newspaper. The economic system, not explained in any detail, limits the wealth of any one person to four or five times the average. There are industries, though no industrial captains. Superphosphates are produced, for example, and copper, paper, and cement. The controlling principle, however, is not "mechanical efficiency" but "human satisfaction." Robert MacPhail, descendant of the Victorian surgeon, has worked in a smelter and been to sea in a fishing boat, to learn "about things and skills and organizations, about all kinds of people and their ways of thinking," more important matters than maximum and most efficient production. MacPhail objects to modern Western "abstract" materialism, which "worship[s] the word and abhor[s] matter." The Palanese have "understanding" as well as "knowledge." They are true materialists, "on the wordless levels of seeing and touching and smelling, of tensed muscles and dirty hands."[66]

Their concrete materialism, however, is only the "raw stuff of a fully human life." Like the Buddhism from which it is primarily derived, and in keeping with the emphasis of much of Huxley's later work, Palanese culture deliberately mixes metaphysics and psychology. Buddhism developed out of Hinduism as Christianity did from Judaism. The Buddha found Hinduism, as Jesus did Judaism, too legalistic and inflexible. But the Buddha's break with orthodoxy was the sharper. Jesus preached the great Commandments of the distant past; the Buddha seems to have made his own discoveries, first by observing the suffering of the world, then by private contemplation and enlightenment. Though the two men are humanity's greatest representatives of compassion, they differ in that the Buddha did not assume, did not even believe in, a personal God, and depended instead on a formidable intellect. The Buddha's findings, growing out of his contact with the world he actually knew, were originally psychological and existential. As Edwin Burtt points out, "Buddhism is the only one of the great religions of the world that is consciously and frankly based on a systematic rational analysis of the problem of life, and of the way to its solution."[67] Hence the appeal of Buddhism to Huxley and other intellectual people—and Huxley's claim in *Island* that understanding oneself will mean understanding the cosmos, and that such understanding will lead to virtuous acts.

The Old Raja's *Notes on What's What,* Huxley's favorite didactic vehicle in *Island,* claims that we are *already,* if we only will realize it, in harmony with ultimate reality. "Nobody needs to go anywhere else. We are all, if we only knew it, already there." What we are, however, Huxley seems to see in various ways. In the Old Raja's psycho-metaphysical notes, which suggest the explanation of Nirvana in the *Lankavatara Sutra*: I am "the reconciliation of yes and no lived out in total acceptance and the blessed experience of Not-Two." I think I am a Manichee, split between opposites, and I want to perpetuate only the "yes." I want to maintain my dualism by abstract thinking with my mind, or by my body in an ascetic or hedonistic act. But if I accept apparent conflict and live the acceptance it is reconciled in the larger harmony. Such acceptance, not a matter of theory or even belief, is rather a continuous moment-to-moment awareness, first of what we are not, then of what we are. It is directed more characteristically outward than inward, toward something or somebody else, and involves all experiences, every imaginable context.[68]

Elsewhere in *Island* the Raja's *Notes* are reinforced. The Palanese completely reject the idea of a wholly other God; they chew their grace at meals, by paying attention to the flavor, the consistency and the temperature of their food, and to the feelings and pressures in their mouths. To remind them of the need for awareness, mynah birds fly about the island, regularly crying "attention" and "here and now"—one of the imaginative motifs in *Island* that really works.

This awareness will both justify and be justified by faith, which is sharply contrasted with mere verbalized belief. It is based on the understanding that reality is universal mind, argued in the Buddhist *Surangara Sutra* and called in *The Doors of Perception* "Mind at Large." Here it is frequently referred to as the Buddhist *tathata,* or "suchness," and sometimes as "the Clear Light of the Void," the ultimate reality Eustace Barnack sees at death. Now the emphasis of the metaphor is on reality stripped of the ideas we superimpose,[69] particularly if we are as prone to verbalize as Aldous Huxley. Our conditioning as Westerners, rationalistic and dualistic, leads us to interpret sense experience as soon as it happens; we are unable to distinguish the sense datum from a category. To the Oriental, because sense experience can be pure, the priceless possibility of reaching suchness, reality such as it is, is opened up.[70] We are as far as we can be from Cartesian dualism, where reality is found in the thinking acts of the mind. To the Old Raja, "The more a man knows about individual objects, the more he knows about God,"[71] a statement which any Zen Buddhist could fully accept, assuming we are to take "knows" as "understands." Huxley is too much the rationalist to suggest the immanent with real power. But at one point a snow-white bull stands "motionless except for his ruminating jaws, . . . godlike in his serene and mindless beauty." Later, during the early evening, brown-skinned natives step briefly "into brilliant existence, then back into nothingness." Nearby, the "good gross odors" of onions and peppers, boiling rice and frying fish, drift "like a reminder from the Other Shore." When Robert MacPhail, in tears because of the impending loss of his wife, sits at the edge of a lotus pool by a Buddha, dragonflies and bees and beetles cluster around the symbolic buds. A moment of awareness of suchness, of enlightenment, helps him to accept the loss he soon will feel. Similarly, Will Farnaby must abandon his Western categories of ugliness and beauty. He thinks of his father as an enormous turd, but with the proper awareness, he learns, even turds can be seen as gentians.

The premises of Pala are by no means entirely Oriental. Huxley's discoveries in Western psychology and science play their part. The human being who is Mind is also physiology, both "the Clear Light of the Void and the vegetative nervous system." A fledgling Palanese nurse is taught a poem in which "I" is a crowd, "obeying as many laws/As it has members"; again the individual is not only psychological, but has a physiology, an anatomy, and a biochemistry as well. Oriental psychology with its metaphysical base is supplemented by Sheldon's empirical system in a check of the child's nervous system, muscles, and gut. Besides Hindu yogas and Buddhist ways, Pala makes use of the exercises of Alexander, along with some that Huxley learned from Laura, his second wife.[72] Palanese pragmatism knows that we amphibians need many aids to live in our various worlds. According to the *Notes*:

> Science is not enough, religion is not enough, art is not enough, politics and economics are not enough, nor is love, nor is duty, nor is action however disinterested, nor, however sublime, is contemplation. Nothing short of everything will really do.[73]

The Buddhism at the root of Pala's metaphysics came to Pala about twelve hundred years before from Bengal, and later through Bengal from Tibet. Hence the Palanese are Mahayana Buddhists, more concerned about the unity and salvation of all than the Hinayana or Theravada Buddhists, who are more monastic, more devoted to the purification of the individual self. As their emphasis on the dangers of language and their "concrete materialism" suggests, they are also under the influence of Zen. "Anybody who gets eloquent about Buddha, or God, or Christ" say the *Notes,* "ought to have his mouth washed out with carbolic soap."[74] A class at school considers the story of Mahakasyapa, who smiled (and therefore understood)—when the Buddha merely held up a single flower instead of trying to put his sermon into words. Traditional Buddhist structures and symbols often appear—a statue, a lotus pool, an impresive ancient temple. But these Buddhists in one crucial respect are hardly even respectable. Their Buddhism is "shot through and through with Tantra."

185]

To the *Encyclopaedia of Religion and Ethics,* this obscure religion is "a kind of degraded *yoga,* which, with the aid of mental concentration, muttered prayers, spells, and other magical expedients, sought to secure all kinds of material advantages and supernatural powers."[75] Ranga Karakuran agrees that "most of it . . . is just silliness and superstition—not worth bothering about. But," he adds, "there's a hard core of sense. If you're a Tantrik, you don't renounce the world or deny its value . . . you make use of it; you make use of everything you do, of everything that happens to you, of all the things you see and hear and taste and touch, as so many means to your liberation from the prison of yourself." The Tantrik principle the Palanese stress is *maithuna,* or sexual intercourse seen as the "yoga of love." As Ranga explains it, it has a Western equivalent in the Male Continence of the Oneida Community, which Huxley had analyzed in *Adonis and the Alphabet.* But besides the principle of intercourse without ejaculation, a non-frustrating method of restraining the egoistic self, *maithuna* allegedly teaches—through the body—understanding of one's essential Buddha Nature. It demonstrates Huxley's first Perennial principle, "thou art That." Started on Pala by the Tantrik original Raja, who saw to the necessary instruction of Dr. MacPhail and his wife, it is an essential part of the training of adolescents, who learn it along with trigonometry and advanced biology, before they have reached the age of fifteen and a half![76]

The surprisingly elaborate details of ancient practice have been explored in an Indian scholar's *Introduction to Tāntric Buddhism.* A man who wished to learn "the sexo-yogic Sādhanā of the Tāntrikas"—to transform his sensual pleasure "into a realisation of infinite bliss in which the self and the world around are lost in an all-pervading oneness"[77]—had to select a guru; then a suitable woman; then, with her propitiate the guru with hymns and worship; then go through a ceremony of initiation into the cult. The aim of intercourse, in Buddhist terminology, was to produce "Bodhicitta"—a "*citta* or mind firmly bent on attaining *bodhi* (enlightenment) and becoming a Buddha thereby." The tendency of the Bodhicitta to "flow," however, had to be checked in the region of the navel. Here a six-part "hatha-yoga" was employed, involving "abstraction," "meditation," "restraint of the breath," "attention," "remembrance," and "final absorption." With proper technique, particularly in the control of the breath, "the flow of semen can be checked at any stage under any condition." To the Tantrik Buddhists there was "no greater sin than discharge"; assuming that sensuality was the aim was "practically adopting the path to hell." But "If the mental resolution . . . be pure, everything will be beneficial not only to the self, but also to the whole world."[78] In the language of Ranga's explanation to Will, *maithuna* makes possible "awareness of one's sensations and awareness of the not-sensation in every sensation." It is actually "dhyana," a form of contemplation.[79] Tantrism is thus Huxley's final solution to the problem of sex. It enabled Huxley, as it had enabled Yeats,[80] to see the sexual act as another approach to the divine.

Palanese psychology and metaphysics determine and are reinforced by Palanese education. With the help of Sheldon's system children are classified, not handled as if they were all the same. In order that they may learn to tolerate those who are physically and temperamentally different, they are sorted out after testing into homogeneous groups. Gradually a few of another type are introduced and a few months later acceptance of differences is achieved. *Ends and Means* on religion and temperament is applied. "Sheep people" and "guinea-pig people," lovers of ritual, are "directed into the Way of Devotion"; "cat people" follow the "Way of Self Knowledge," and the drivingly aggressive "marten people" can go the "Way of Disinterested Action." The Palanese also spot young Wordsworths and Trahernes, distinguish between visualizers and more verbal types, and watch carefully for the easily hypnotized, who may do wonders in deep trance by distortion of time. Alexanderism is introduced early for correct use of the "mind-body" with maximum awareness and minimum strain. Vijaya Bhattacharya, a Muscle Man who does some of the lecturing, explains the best way of putting on one's clothes. Following the Huxley of *Adonis and the Alphabet,* Mr. Menon criticizes Western culture for not educating "the whole mind-body along with the symbol-using intellect." " 'Your cure for too much scientific specialization,' " he tells Will, " 'is a few more courses in the humanities' "—an "excellent" idea, but deceptive, because the humanities, by themselves, " 'don't humanize. They're simply another form of specialization on the symbolic level.' "[81]

Formal education stresses the sciences of life, and employs, at first, the technique of childish games. Scientific thinking today is not a matter of unchangeable laws, but rather a question of probability. Hence, Palanese teachers spin coins, draw lots, and play roulette, or get out the boards and dice for "evolutionary Snakes and Ladders" or "Mendelian Happy Families." Ecology begins as early as multiplication and division, with the "science of relationship" taught along with "the ethics of relationship." After training in compassion and intelligence toward nature—with the help of the "cosmic moral" of soil erosion—the students are ready for "elementary Buddhism," and the metaphysical basis for the "Good Being" they have already learned to seek.

Some Palanese institutions are contrasting analogs to institutions of *Brave New World.* Susila MacPhail sounds no less hyperbolic than Mustapha Mond in her attitude toward Western family life. The average home, she seems to believe, includes "one sexually inept wage slave, . . . one dissatisfied female, two or (if preferred) three small television addicts; marinate[d] in a mixture of Freudism and dilute Christianity . . . bottle [d] up tightly in a four-room flat and stew[ed] for fifteen years in their own juice." The antidote to the tensions of the family is not a parent-less barracks or isolated apartment, but a "Mutual Adoption Club" of about two dozen couples, all of whom adopt each other and all the children. Free to circulate to other parents if they wish, the children grow up not in "telephone booths" run by "predestined jailers," but "in a world that's a working model of society at large, a small scale but accurate version of the environment in which they're going to have to live when they're grown up."[82] Propagation is not controlled by the state. Instead married couples, conscious as Huxley had long been of the dangers of overpopulation, deliberately restrict themselves to no more than three children. The emphasis on freedom of action in Pala and the recognition of human sexuality permit without prejudice homosexual love, and allow for extramarital attachment where husband and wife are necessarily apart. The poems are not doggerel capsules of superimposed morality, but lyrical or reflective expressions of the Buddha Nature. Pavlovian conditioning instills "friendliness and trust and compassion," rather than the *Brave New World* horror of books and flowers. A full humanity and "Good Being" are the aims, not a restrictive morality, or unquestioning service to the state.

In a sense the "savage" of Pala, the critic of its culture, is Murugan, by heredity its future ruler, a sly, vain, power-hungry homosexual boy. Like John in *Brave New World,* he has been virtually ruined by his mother; together, they are supposed to parody contemporary culture in the West. Murugan, when he isn't being admired by Pala's leading enemy, Colonel Dipa, indulges his materialistic dreams in a battered copy of the Sears Roebuck catalog, the *Island* parallel for the complete Shakespeare which provided values for John the Savage. His mother, the Rani, keeps lecturing on the "Crusade of the Spirit," a "World Movement to save Humanity," a "Force for Good, a force that will ultimately Save the World." The capital letters, unfortunately, are not the only example of Huxley's tendency to over-protest. Tantrism is only repulsive; to her, "Purity is the *sine qua non*" of all the "Moral and Spiritual Values." When her associate, Mr. Bahu, claims that Pala makes "every man, woman, and child . . . as perfectly free and happy as it's possible to be," she calls it "a False Happiness, . . . a freedom that's only for the Lower Self."[83]

But the main character of Huxley's fable, Will Farnaby, is a closer parallel to John the Savage. As *Island* opens, Will, shipwrecked and injured on the Palanese coast, is given psychological first aid by two of Pala's children. The Savage, nurtured on Shakespeare, primitive Christianity, and totemism, hates the brave new world and through one of its females is eventually destroyed. Farnaby, a child of contemporary Western culture, learns with the help of a woman to prefer the culture of Pala, though just as it is about to see its end. Since he needs medical care and seems sincerely interested, he is allowed to stay long enough to tour the island and study its institutions. Until his conversion he leads a double life, for unbeknownst to the Palanese he is an agent for Lord Aldehyde, an English oil baron. While he admires and voices praise for Pala's ways, he tries to make an under-the-table deal for Pala's oil. When he isn't touring Pala with recently widowed Susila MacPhail, he negotiates with Murugan's mother, who is all for Westernizing Pala and merging it with Rendang, its power-hungry neighbor. The clash of values in Will parallels the drama of the modern world; the alternatives, a Palanese Utopia or a totalitarian Greater Rendang, were ours—and still can be, if we have the will to change.

Will's past loudly echoes the world of earlier novels of Aldous Huxley, the seamier, more grotesque elements of *Point Counter Point* and *Time Must Have a Stop*. Like Sebastian Barnack, he had found another woman's body much more of an attraction than the spiritual qualities of his own virtuous wife. Mrs.

Farnaby was really, "by temperament," another Marjorie Carling, a "Sister of Mercy" who joined him in "the drama of a love incapable of sensuality self-committed to a sensuality incapable of love." The result—Will's addiction to "alienating frenzies," on a bed bathed in a Porter Gin sign's ghastly light, with a "mindless," demanding, "vulgar" siren, Babs; and severe guilt feelings over the accident that eventually killed his wife.

But Will's Walter Bidlake-like troubles with Molly and Babs stem from heredity and early childhood experience. He was sired, he claims, "By Bully Boozer out of Christian Martyr." After fourteen years of "family servitude," he was able to associate with his aunt Mary, the "only person I ever loved." But a breast cancer, then a liver cancer killed her off in two years, and his education in "Pure and Applied Pointlessness," in the Pascalian abyss was the result. Aunt Mary (probably based on Huxley's mother) was a woman who, after being widowed, devoted herself to helping the aged. When the cancer struck, and "the body broke down, the soul began to lose its virtue, its very identity." She became "almost indistinguishable from the worst and weakest of the old people she had once befriended and been a tower of strength to." Eventually, like Mark Staithes— and presumably, at one stage in his life, like Aldous Huxley— he began to see human beings as maggots and to become himself an entomologist. He is a cynic who has nevertheless "passionately" longed to believe in human decency.[84]

There are times when Will makes points about the culture of his England, but most of this the Palanese already know. He impresses them most with his ugly laugh, his outward appearance. He is not without appeal; his face as Susila puts it is "emphatic and yet sensitive, the quivering, more than naked face ... of a man who has been flayed and left to suffer." He is also "too clever to believe in God ... His muscles would like to act and his feelings would like to believe; but his nerve endings and his cleverness won't allow it."[85] The potential he shows and the interest he declares, however, lead both him and them to think he may be helped. The parallel with Huxley's own life now is clear.

As Will becomes more and more familiar with Palanese culture, his deviousness and cynicism begin rapidly to disappear. In this novel there is no easy, wishful ending, like Anthony Beavis' confident thoughts of his Gandhi-like resistance to hecklers, or the romantic escape in *Ape and Essence* of Loola and Dr. Poole. At the end of the novel, though Will is convinced that the Palanese have found the answers, Murugan and Colonel Dipa have taken over, to wreck Pala and transfer it into a nationalistic state. Mr. Bahu has, earlier in the book, already given reasons: "Pala was completely viable," he says, "until about 1905. Then, in less than a single generation, the world completely changed. Movies, cars, airplanes, radio. Mass production, mass slaughter, mass communication and, above all, plain mass—more and more people in bigger and bigger slums or suburbs." As he predicts, the outside world, in the form of Murugan's lust for power, closes in on this "intolerable" oasis of "freedom and happiness," to force it to conform to the compulsive, "modern" way.[86] Though this pessimistic ending has elicited the charge of a "cry of despair,"[87] it is rather Huxley's acknowledgment of the stubborn refusal of modern man to change his ways. Defensive action is less important to the Palanese than understanding. If we enlarge our understanding more than our provincialisms now allow, the need for violent defense can be made to disappear.

Before the curtain falls Will has a chance to see the Essential Horror yield to a full, rich, comprehensive view of life. For Will to be reoriented and retrained, he must experience both death and revelation. Early in the novel, the death motif is emphasized. Huxley had lost Maria in 1955; Susila MacPhail has just lost her husband Dugald, a "Muscle Man" killed in a mountain-climbing disaster. Her reaction is quite the opposite of Will's anguished guilt toward Molly. Though Dugald's sence is "so constantly present," she realizes, as Laura Huxley tells us Aldous did in his bereavement,[88] that she "must love for two, live for two, take thought for two, must perceive and understand not merely with her own eyes and mind but with the mind and eyes that had been his and, before the catastrophe, hers too in a communion of delight and intelligence."[89] Another death Will is actually called upon to witness—that of Lakshmi, Susila's mother-in-law, another victim of cancer. Like Will's Aunt Mary, she has "parchment-covered bones," "claw-like hands," and "a dark emaciated face." Yet though hypodermics have been used during the periods of most excruciating pain, when death is certain she wants to be kept awake, and is. Unlike Eustace Barnack, who fought with all the strength of his selfish ego, Lakshmi welcomes the Light that accompanies bodily death. As Will recalls his bitterly struggling and protesting aunt, Lakshmi, in contrast, smiles as she feels the Light "along with the pain, in spite of the pain." While screaming peacocks suggest the need for the yoga of love, Lakshmi dramatizes the corresponding yoga of death.[90] Huxley again borrows from *The Tibetan Book of the Dead*, this time for a service administered to a person leaving the world we know. His point is that our insistence on easing pain at death is accomplished with considerable spiritual cost. If this seems to be too easy an answer to accept, let it be known that Huxley administered the *Island* service to Maria, and was given it by Laura when he died, courageously, himself.[91]

After this incident, under the influence of Pala's equivalent of mescaline or LSD, Will has a supremely blissful vision. The "*moksha*-medicine" (moksha = liberation) he takes is a most important substance in Pala, essential to religious education and understanding, and an answering parallel to the deadening soma of *Brave New World*. Though Huxley was far too optimistic about hallucinogens, even in *Island* they are subject to probable development and change. Huxley handles one anti-*moksha* argument through Murugan. Conditioned to believe that true vision comes only with meditation and ascetic discipline, Murugan is sure that "All it gives you is a lot of illusions." He is a Puritan, says Vijaya, "outraged by the fact that . . . even beginners . . . can catch a glimpse of the world as it looks to someone who has been liberated from his bondage to the ego." Dr. MacPhail argues consistently with *The Doors of Perception* and *Heaven and Hell,* claiming that the drug allows more of Mind to flow into the mind of the imbiber. The soundest part of Huxley's case is his allegiance to experimental science. The Palanese are trying to discover what actually happens with hallucinogens and are "just beginning to understand . . . the neurological correlate" of their experience. MacPhail also introduces a metaphysical hedge, by granting that the experience may be only private, producing knowledge only of "one's own physiology." Huxley's faith in the value of the drug remains unshaken: "The fact remains that the experience can open one's eyes and make one blessed and transforms one's whole life."[92]

Shortly after the conversation, Will observes the use of *moksha* in a ceremony of Palanese religion. Immediately after a pre-arranged ordeal, a mountain climbing exercise that teaches them "the omnipresence of death, the essential precariousness of all existence," a group of young people gather in the ancient, mountain-top temple. An old priest chants Sanskrit, then an English poem of Shiva, the divine creator-destroyer:

> You Suchness and Illusion, the Void and All Things,
> You are the lord of life, and therefore I have brought
> you flowers;
> You are the lord of death, and therefore I have
> brought you my heart—
> This heart that is now your burning ground.

Ignorance there and self shall be consumed with fire.
That you may dance, Bhairava, among the ashes.
That you may dance, Lord Shiva, in a place of flowers,
And I dance with you.

"Shivayanama" is chanted; Vijaya speaks briefly of "beauty
made one with horror" and the "yoga of complete and total re-
ceptiveness." Will, instructed about Shiva-Nataraja, the Lord
of the Dance, learns the Palanese attitude toward suffering. In
this manifestation the god Shiva is the Order of Things, at play
like a child. "His toys are galaxies, his playground is infinite
space and between finger and finger every interval is a thousand
million lightyears"; his dance is of "endless becoming and
passing away." He is completely impartial toward death and toward life, toward happiness and desolation, toward evil and
good. His play is *his* eternal bliss, though obviously not ours,
who have to live somewhere between these opposites. In the
dance, however, he steps on Muyalaka, a bestial creature who
represents ignorance and the attachments of egoism. Liberation,
in other words, is possible through understanding. Moreover,
suffering is not the only manifestation of Shiva. After the dance
the ceremony elucidates infinite beauty and compassion. In the
faces of the worshippers appear "the dawning illuminations
of delight, recognition, understanding, the signs of worshipping
wonder that quivered on the brinks of ecstasy or terror," and
soon "the hardly perceptible, ecstatic smile that welcomes a
sudden insight, a revelation of truth or of beauty."[93]

Will's own experience, at the end of the book, is an amplifica-
tion of Huxley's mescaline vision of *The Doors of Perception*
and a development of the thesis of *Heaven and Hell*. Like many
other sections of *Island,* it is apparently based on Huxley's own
experience.[94] The first effect of *moksha* is a feeling of "luminous
bliss," of "one with oneness," a wordless understanding "without knowledge." This is Eckhart's God, Susila indicates, " 'Fe-

licity so ravishing, so inconceivably intense that no one can describe it' "—and hence, "an enormous temptation," the "only temptation that God could succumb to," appropriate as a permanent state of affairs only *before* the knowledge of good and evil. To bring Will out of his greedy Nirvana-indulgence, Susila plays Bach's Fourth Brandenburg Concerto, and "for the first time, his awareness of a piece of music was completely unobstructed." The concerto is not only "uncorrupted by personal history"; it is also "a Present Event . . . without duration," the obverse of the selfish quartet of *Point Counter Point,* where each instrument wanted to be taken as the center of the revolving world. But though Will is able to see what he hears, hear what he sees, and actually to *be* the essence of the music, his vision is still very far from complete. After the room and its objects present themselves as paradise, and a suggestion of words, the fruit of man's knowledge, begins to appear, the point has come for Will to reconcile himself with the Essential Horror. The *moksha*-Heaven must change into *moksha*-Hell. It is symbolized in Huxley's most gruesomely vivid fashion by a "bloodsucker" lizard and two copulating, cannibalistic praying mantices. The sight—a "real" one—is even grislier than Helen's abortion nightmare in *Eyeless in Gaza,* and matches the transformation of the lizards in Dante's *Inferno.* The female mantis chews out an eye, then half the face of the male, even keeps chewing the "oozing stump" when the rest of the head has fallen to the ground—all the while during copulation. As the lizard enters the act and devours both the insects, and the concerto seems transformed into "a rococo death march," the insects become an "endless column of soldiers." Will's memories of Hitler flash across his mind, and soon other kinds of troublemakers appear in a vision reminiscent of Eustace Barnack's at death:

> Huge idiot faces, blankly receptive. Faces of wide-eyed sleepwalkers. Faces of young Nordic angels rapt in the Beatific

Vision. Faces of baroque saints going into ecstasy. Faces of lovers on the brink of orgasm. . . . Onward Nazi soldiers. Onward Marxists. Onward Christian soldiers, and Moslems. Onward every chosen people, every Crusader and Holy War maker. Onward into misery, into all wickedness, into death.

It is all "union with the unity of an insect swarm," experienced with "Knowledgeless understanding of nonsense and diabolism." Soon, "depth below depth of malignant vulgarity, hell beyond hell of utterly pointless suffering."

But as the cocks begin to crow, in another answering echo of *Eyeless in Gaza,* as the mynah birds chime in with their call of "Attention," as Susila presses his cheekbones with her palms, and digs her nails into his forehead, Will begins to learn how to reconcile Heaven with Hell. The Clear Light is not to be greedily indulged in; the Void is light, but it also is compassion. The truer vision that now passes before Will's eyes is a "paradox of opposites indissolubly wedded, of light shining out of darkness, of darkness at the very heart of light." Tears of gratitude cross the former cynic's face, of "Thankfulness for the privilege of being alive and a witness to this miracle, of being indeed more than a witness—a partner in it, an aspect of it." As the selfish, power-hungry outside world descends on Pala, Will, within the limits of humanity, has known what it means to understand.[95] The destruction of Pala and the horrors that may come can be seen as part of Shiva-Nataraja's dance. It should not be forgotten, however, that the Buddha recognized sorrow more fully, perhaps, than anyone else. But he also taught that, no matter how intense, it had an end; that it was mitigated by compassion and amenable to human understanding.

Will's vision surely had its parallel in Huxley's life. *Island,* a projection of harmony after almost a lifetime of inner conflict, represents a final resolution of Huxley's problems, an end of his life-long odyssey. It comprises his answers to all the questions raised in his earlier works, with greater consistency and unity than ever before. Yet though it is already a book of the receding past, *Island* explores themes of developing prominence in the present. It shares the emphasis of a growing philosophical movement, contemporary phenomenology. It embodies the experimental behaviorist approach of B. F. Skinner, even though its final view is hardly the same. Again and again it glosses the work of Herbert Marcuse, particularly his principle of the "logic of gratification." *Island,* however, is no product of academic rigor, no Marcusian dialectic or controlled experiment. Huxley left Balliol without formal academic training in logic, philosophy, comparative religion and science, all of which are essential to his final view. He had instead the complementary attribute, a willingness to speak what he believed without the restraints of academic caution. His achievement in *Island* and in the whole extensive corpus is more important than his weaknesses and obvious shortcomings. He was not a great modern writer, though in 1960 he was nominated for the Nobel Prize.[96] Yet he symbolizes better than anyone else the intricate mental consciousness of modern man. His complexities, his conflicts are both the product and the symptom of our age, and we benefit by his willingness and his compulsion to project them and their resolution, in words. Other writers are finer artists, more rigorous thinkers, warmer toward their fellow human beings. But none reflects and deals with so many modern problems, and none makes clearer both the need for solutions and the difficulty of finding them.

Huxley grapples with the basic questions the reflective person has to ask. In *Island* and elsewhere he deals with ultimate reality, good and evil, suffering and death, the good society, sex and love. On any one of these themes he can be less profound than someone else, but nobody in our culture at least has tried to grapple so tenaciously with them all. Driven at times to a Cartesian complete and radical doubt, Huxley focused his eye on the disheartening contours of our age and defined our problems in large and objective terms. The science which most interested him late in life was human ecology, because it deals, as he put it, with "the problem of Man on Earth."[97] The detachment reinforced by Huxley's early loss of sight may have led to the unappealing traveller's-eye view, but it gave Huxley a perspective denied to those closer to the mass of men. Hence Robert Hutchins, who on specific issues would surely disagree, could call Huxley "one of the great teachers of our time."[98]

It is important to remember, however, the basic assumption behind all of Huxley's later work. To one school of ontology the world as a whole is unintelligible, whatever order we may discern in its parts. It has been said that there is no evidence that "all the systems and structures which we discover . . . are parts of a single system."[99] From *Eyeless in Gaza* on, Huxley assumes the opposite. He takes it on faith that there is a Nature, an Order of Things, which we must both assume and within our limits try to grasp. We can confirm this immanence in our day-to-day existence if we are willing to use all our available resources, and subject all but the basic assumption to a pragmatic, existential test. *Island* is Huxley's equivalent to Yeats' *Vision*. Both writers began as divided men, and poets; both were alert to contraries for most of their lives; both were ultimately reconciled to them; both were able to make final assertions of joy. *A Vision,* however, is a more symbolic work, *Island* a far more literal one. Both symbolize a belief in ultimate order, but *Island* offers a human order here and now. Contraries are resolved on the plane of the divine, yet the divine resolution can be—it really is—immanent in our lives. Even the least appealing heterodoxies urge us to examine cultural pressures and to withstand the destructive ones, however strong. Mankind may not be able to withstand them, but *Island* claims that if it has the will, it can. It denies that one thinker or one method can provide complete or final answers. It prophetically suggests "new psychophysical sciences"[100] and affirms that answers are available if men will use a responsible intelligence, and look. Huxley's ideas, his whole adventure should become not a subject for dismissal on logical grounds, but instead what Whitehead calls a "lure for feeling." They should incite us to use our critical faculties toward greater usefulness and a larger understanding.

In Huxley's last book, *Literature and Science* (1963) and last essay, "Shakespeare and Religion" (1965), there are signs that his pluralism might have found more unified form. He sees both scientists and writers as purifiers of language, one for public and the other for essentially private truth. The scientist can learn from the artist's intuition while the artist should recognize the increasing accuracy of scientists who study aspects of the destiny of man.[101] But theoretically a total unity is involved, since scientific observation is now recognized as a dialogue with nature, no longer involving a subject-object division. If we pursue the analysis of public experience, we will share the conclusion of the contemplative, the one who has experienced the Zen Buddhist's *satori*.[102] Similarly, Shakespeare presents the universe as a "pluralistic mystery," but if we analyze crucial passages in the plays, we will be "well on the way to an existential religion of mysticism."[103] Huxley never could have engaged in the analysis he mentions, or worked out the philosophy for an existential religion. Driven even more by personal need than by his inquiring mind, he was little interested in Whitehead's speculations about God, or even in those of Julian's friend, Teilhard de Chardin. He could never emulate the scholarship of a Northrop, a Toynbee, or a Tillich. He knew, however, at least as well as they, that the West must be alive to the ways and riches of the East, that man cannot live without both science and art, that knowledge must serve a lived acceptance, or faith.

N O T E S

THE COLLECTED EDITION OF THE WORK OF ALDOUS HUXLEY, published in England by Chatto & Windus, is in most cases the one used in this study. For the short stories and novels, place, publisher, and date of the first edition are included in the text at the point where the primary discussion begins, unless (as in two cases) they have been cited before. No further notes are supplied for stories. References to the novels, supplied for the longer and more important quotations, are by chapter, except in the cases of *The Genius and the Goddess* (which has no chapter divisions) and *Ape and Essence* (which has only two, the second extremely long.) In these two cases page numbers are cited.

For non-fiction only the date of the first edition is indicated in the text, with complete publication information in the notes at the point where the work itself actually enters the argument. All page numbers are included. For individual poems, volume titles are furnished, ordinarily in both the text and (with further bibliographical information) in the notes.

Preface

[1] Julian Huxley, ed., *Aldous Huxley: A Memorial Volume* (London: Chatto & Windus, 1965), hereafter referred to as *Memorial Volume*.

[2] *Letters of Aldous Huxley,* ed. Grover Smith (London: Chatto & Windus, 1969), pp. 277-278. Hereafter referred to as *Letters*.

[3] Ibid., p. 740.

[4] Ibid., p. 83.

[5] Laura Archera Huxley, *This Timeless Moment* (New York: Farrar, Straus & Giroux, 1968).

[6] *The Huxleys* (New York and Toronto: McGraw-Hill Book Co., 1968), p. 215.

[7] *Letters*, p. 306.

[8] *Memorial Volume,* pp. 96, 157.

[9] *Letters*, p. 888.

[10] Ibid., pp. 646-650.

[11] Ibid., p. 242.

[12] Ibid., p. 390.

I. Struggles with Style and Form: From the Early Verse to *Crome Yellow*

[1] *The Palatine Review,* IV (October, 1916), 5-13. Reprinted in *Limbo* (London: Chatto & Windus, 1920) and *Collected Short Stories* (London: Chatto & Windus, 1957).

[2] *The Journal of Arnold Bennett* (New York: The Viking Press, 1933), p. 932. The three adjectives were Huxley's own favorites, Bennett writes on February 14, 1927, in one of several entries referring to Huxley and his wife.

[3] *Laughter in the Next Room* (Boston: Little, Brown and Company, 1948), p. 45. Sir Osbert sketches a similar portrait in the *Memorial Volume,* p. 33.

[4] *Memorial Volume,* p. 25.

[5] Some years later Huxley said to an interviewer: "My chief motive in writing has been the desire to express a point of view. Or, rather, the desire to clarify a point of view to myself. I do not write for my readers; in fact I don't like thinking about my readers. . . . I am chiefly interested

in making clear a certain outlook on life." Quoted in *The Huxleys,* pp. 215-216.

[6] *Letters,* p. 63.

[7] Aldous Huxley, *The Art of Seeing* (New York and London: Harper & Brothers, 1942), p. vii. Huxley goes on to tell how in 1939, when his eyesight began seriously to fail, he learned to read without glasses from the method of Dr. W. H. Bates. The bulk of *The Art of Seeing* explains exercises Huxley found helpful. A letter to Lawrence Clark Powell of September 18, 1943, illustrates Huxley's continuing interest in visual education. He has learned that archery can be used to improve vision, and he hopes therefore that visual education can be introduced into archery as it is taught at UCLA. *Aldous Huxley at UCLA,* ed. George Wickes (Los Angeles: University of California Library, 1964), pp. 31, 33.

[8] Interview in *New York Times,* May 6, 1933, p. 14, col. 1.

[9] This account follows Huxley's, in Stanley Kunitz and Howard Haycraft, eds., *Twentieth Century Authors* (New York: H. W. Wilson Co., 1942, p. 698). Other details may be found in the *Letters,* the *Memorial Volume,* and in the letters or reminiscences of D. H. Lawrence, Edith Sitwell, Frank Swinnerton and others. The authorized biography is now being written by Sybille Bedford.

[10] *Twentieth Century Authors,* p. 699.

[11] *Letters,* p. 861.

[12] Ibid., p. 373.

[13] Harold Monro, *Some Contemporary Poets* (London: Leonard Parsons, 1920), p. 124.

[14] *The Burning Wheel* (Oxford: B. H. Blackwell, 1916).

[15] *Jonah* (Oxford: Holywell Press, 1917).

[16] Huxley's preface to *This Way to Paradise* (London: Chatto & Windus, 1930), Campbell Dixon's dramatization of *Point Counter Point,* p. [iv].

[17] *Letters,* p. 26.

[18] Ibid., p. 33.

[19] *Oxford Poetry,* ed. G.[eorge] D.[ouglas] H.[oward] C.[ole] and T.[homas] W.[ade] E.[arp] (Oxford: B. H. Blackwell, 1915). Huxley helped to edit the 1916 volume.

[20] *Letters,* p. 112.

[21] David Daiches, *The Novel and the Modern World* (Chicago: University of Chicago Press, 1939), p. 192. Daiches's chapter on Huxley,

eliminated in the revised version of his book (1960), remains one of the most provocative essays on Huxley's work.

[22] Chapter II. In Chapter XXII he writes an "elegant quatrain" on "brooding love."

[23] Sir Steven Runciman, a student of young Huxley at Eton, remembers that he "often used words that were unknown to us and that we tried thenceforward to add to our vocabulary." *Memorial Volume*, p. 28.

[24] *Wheels: A Second Cycle* (Oxford: B. H. Blackwell, 1917).

[25] Denis Stone, in Chapter X of *Crome Yellow,* envies Gombauld his "face of brass—one of those old, brazen rams. . . ."

[26] "Sincerity in Art," *Essays New and Old* (London: Chatto & Windus, 1926), pp. 303-304.

[27] Two of the other poems in French display a furtive concern for sex and a strange ambivalence toward religion that would probably shock Emberlin's reasonable friend. In "Sonnet À L'Ingénue" the poet, from his "mouldy books," evokes only with difficulty "the dewy and mystic mind of Saint Alacocque." Though the "Sacred Heart bleeds lifelessly" for him, the artless girl speaks and her voice is "like a Seraph, barebottomed like a cloud, praising God," but with its "infinitely mocking psalm." In "Dix-Huitième Siècle" the poet comments on the discreet altar of the love-temple of that age, where "Watteau's beautiful women . . . undid their naughty belts and circumspectly tasted paradise." But after noting the present neglect of the temple, he ends with an image of the "cold Alcove," where "great formless phalluses dangerously grow." Huxley wrote to Juliette Baillot, not yet married to his brother Julian: "I regret to say that I rarely write in French—and then only when I want to be *un peu scabreux:* it certainly is the best language for indecency ever invented. . . ." *Memorial Volume*, p. 43.

[28] *Letters,* p. 81.

[29] Ibid., p. 137.

[30] *Wheels: A Third Cycle* (Oxford: B. H. Blackwell, 1918). See Ruth Temple's analysis, "Aldous Huxley et la littérature française," *Revue de littérature comparée,* XIX (January-March, 1939), esp. 66-89 passim. She cites (p. 87) a letter from Huxley of October 9, 1937, recalling his "imitations de Rimbaud dans sa poésie de jeunesse."

[31] *The Defeat of Youth, and Other Poems* (Oxford: B. H. Blackwell, 1918).

[32] *Memorial Volume,* p. 48.

[33] *Leda* (London: Chatto & Windus, 1920).

[34] *Wheels,* 1919 (Oxford: B. H. Blackwell, 1919). "Frascati's" and "Verrey's," the two new poems in this volume, were reprinted in *Leda.*

[35] "Male and Female Created He Them," in *Leda.* All of *Leda* and selected other poems are reprinted in the Collected Edition volume *Verses & a Comedy* (London: Chatto & Windus, 1946).

[36] For example, Douglas Bush, *Mythology and the Romantic Tradition* (New York: W.W. Norton and Company, Inc., 1963), p. 478: "*Leda* is hardly an important work, yet it is an original combination of conventional mythological romanticism with animal and tropical heat and exotic color." Not so T.S. Eliot, who was "unable to show any enthusiasm" when Huxley asked for his opinion of the book. *Memorial Volume,* p. 30. Giorgio Melchiori notes the "striking similarities in diction" between Yeats's "Leda and the Swan" and Huxley's "ambitious youthful poem, *Leda.*" *The Whole Mystery of Art* (New York: The Macmillan Company, 1969), p. 150.

[37] *Letters,* p. 185.

[38] Ibid., p. 157.

[39] Ibid., p. 168.

[40] In *Coterie* (Easter, 1920), pp. 68-93. Reprinted in *Mortal Coils* (London: Chatto & Windus, 1922).

[41] Frank Swinnerton, *The Georgian Literary Scene* (London: William Heinemann Ltd., 1935). Revised edition (London: Hutchinson & Co., Ltd., 1950), p. 348.

[42] George Wickes and Ray Frazer, "Aldous Huxley," *Paris Review,* XXIII (Spring, 1960), 64.

[43] T. S. Eliot, marking up a family copy of *Crome Yellow,* indicated that Scogan was Bertrand Russell; Gombauld, Mark Gertler, painter and friend of Huxley and Lawrence; that Henry Wimbush was Philip Morrell, husband of Lady Ottoline; and that Priscilla may be a portrait of Lady Ida Sitwell. The volume is in Harvard's Houghton Library, along with a group of photographs taken between 1921 and 1926 at Garsington—of the house and grounds, the Morrells, Gertler, and Leonard and Virginia Woolf. Priscilla's appearance, at least, was more probably drawn from Ottoline. Siegfried Sassoon first saw her descending a ladder, in "voluminous pale-pink Turkish trousers," with Priscilla-like "paint and powder and purple hair." *Siegfried's Journey* (London: Faber & Faber, 1945), p. 8. Alan Pryce-Jones in a retrospective essay referred to *Crome Yellow* as "a private joke shared with the rest of us." "Aldous Huxley—A Modern Prophet," *Listener,* XXXVIII (October 16,

1947), 678. Huxley himself later said "there is something of Norman Douglas in old Scogan of *Crome Yellow*." Wickes and Frazer, p. 76. *The Memorial Volume* is rich in Garsington reminiscences.

[44] *Memorial Volume,* pp. 40-41.

[45] Chapter I.

[46] Chapter V.

[47] The picture Huxley describes here in Chapter XII is actually Caravaggio's "Conversion of St. Paul." See Sir Kenneth Clark, *Memorial Volume,* p. 16 and below, p. 44.

[48] See especially the *Memorial Volume,* passim.

[49] Chapter XIV.

2. Repaintings of the Mask: From Gumbril to Archimedes

[1] *Ends and Means* (London: Chatto & Windus, 1937). Collected Edition (London: Chatto & Windus, 1957), p. 273.

[2] "The Modern Spirit and a Family Party," *Vanity Fair,* XVIII (August, 1922), 98.

[3] "Conxolus," *Along the Road* (London: Chatto & Windus, 1925). Collected Edition (London: Chatto & Windus, 1948), p. 174.

[4] *Letters,* p. 224.

[5] Chapter XIX.

[6] Sir Steven Runciman describes Huxley as a teacher, *Memorial Volume,* pp. 27-28, and Juliette Huxley quotes a letter from Aldous about his teaching, ibid., p. 45.

[7] Jocelyn Brooke, for example, claims that the composer Philip Heseltine ("Peter Warlock") is "easily recognizable in the character of Coleman." *Aldous Huxley* (London: Longmans, Green & Co., 1954), p. 15.

[8] *Letters,* p. 106.

[9] Ibid., p. 83.

[10] Huxley's cousin Gervas indicates that young Aldous was "deeply devoted" to his mother, and himself remembers "the warmth of her understanding of young people." *Memorial Volume,* p. 58.

[11] "My men like satyrs grazing on the lawns/Shall with their goatfeet dance the antic hay." *Edward the Second,* I, 59-60.

[12] Chapter XII.

[13] Chapter XVII.

[14] Chapter XXI.

[15] *Letters,* p. 224.

[16] Ibid., p. 218.

[17] "Mr. Huxley Discusses His Thrice-Told Tale," *New York Times,* October 1, 1950, Section II, p. 1.

[18] See Charles M. Holmes, "Aldous Huxley's Struggle with Art," *Western Humanities Review,* XV (Spring, 1961), 149-156.

[19] Y. Maraini, "A Talk with Aldous Huxley," *The Bermondsey Book,* III (June, 1926), 76-77.

3. The Plight of Discontinuity: Toward *Point Counter Point*

[1] *The Huxleys,* p. 212.

[2] Wickes and Frazer, p. 64.

[3] *Letters,* pp. 208-209.

[4] "Democratic Art," *On the Margin* (London: Chatto & Windus, 1923). Collected Edition (London: Chatto & Windus, 1956), p. 67.

[5] "A Wordsworth Anthology," p. 155.

[6] "Centenaries," p. 8.

[7] "The Author of Eminent Victorians," p. 141.

[8] "The Subject Matter of Poetry," pp. 33, 34. A posthumous work, *Literature and Science* (New York: Harper and Row, 1964) explores the matter further, See below, p. 200.

[9] "Why Not Stay at Home?", *Along the Road,* p. 4.

[10] Ibid., p. 13.

[11] "Books for the Journey," pp. 70-71.

[12] "Wander-Birds," pp. 17-21.

[13] "The Traveller's-Eye View," pp. 27-28.

[14] "Marginalia," December 10, 1920, p. 812.

[15] "Montesenario," *Along the Road,* p. 76.

[16] Ibid., p. 80.

[17] *Memorial Volume,* p. 21.

[18] Ibid., p. 137.

[19] Ibid., p. 40.

[20] "Sabbioneta," *Along the Road,* p. 121.

[21] "Views of Holland," pp. 105-107.

[22] Ibid., p. 104.

[23] Ibid., p. 108.

[24] Ibid., pp. 108-110.

[25] Ibid., pp. 110-112.

[26] *Memorial Volume,* p. 15.

[27] The claim of Jacob Zeitlin, *Aldous Huxley 1944-1963* (Los Angeles: University of California, 1964), p. 8, in one of three addresses at a memorial meeting for Huxley held in the UCLA School of Library Service. Reprinted in *Memorial Volume,* pp. 129-134.

[28] *Memorial Volume,* p. 16.

[29] "Breughel," *Along the Road,* p. 140.

[30] "Patinir's River," pp. 81-83.

[31] "The Palio at Siena," pp. 89-91.

[32] Ibid., p. 97.

[33] Humbert Wolfe, "Along the Road," *The Spectator,* CXXXV (October 17, 1925), 663.

[34] "The Best Picture," *Along the Road,* p. 181.

[35] Ibid., p. 180.

[36] Ibid., pp. 187, 181.

[37] Ibid., p. 183.

[38] Ibid., pp. 181-182.

[39] "A Night at Pietramala," pp. 223-225.

[40] "Montesenario," p. 79.

[41] *Jesting Pilate* (London: Chatto & Windus, 1926). Collected Edition (London: Chatto & Windus, 1948), pp. 40-41.

[42] P. 162.

[43] P. 138.

[44] Pp. 225-227.

[45] P. 109.

[46] P. 110.

[47] P. 192.

[48] P. 194.

[49] P. 290.

[50] P. 192.

[51] P. 291.

[52] *Proper Studies* (London: Chatto & Windus, 1927). Collected Edition (London: Chatto & Windus, 1957), p. ix.

[53] P. viii.

[54] P. xviii.

[55] Ibid.

[56] P. 14.

[57] P. xix.

[58] P. 152.

[59] Vilfredo Pareto, *A Treatise on General Sociology,* IV, trans. Andrew

Bongiorno and Arthur Livingston (New York: Harcourt, Brace and Company, 1963), p. 1916.

60 *Proper Studies,* p. xvii.

61 P. 9.

62 Pp. xii-xiv.

63 P. 3.

64 Pp. 7-13.

65 P. 42.

66 P. xi.

67 P. 78.

68 P. 99.

69 P. 115.

70 P. 136.

71 Pp. 142-143.

72 Pp. 162-163.

73 Pp. 167, 157.

74 Pp. 178-179.

75 P. xvii.

76 P. 157.

77 Pp. 204-206. Huxley rejects Whitehead again in *Time Must Have a Stop,* Chapter VIII, through Paul De Vries, but follows him in *Ends and Means* (see below, p. 115).

78 *Proper Studies,* pp. 208, 215-216.

79 Pp. 218-228.

80 Pp. 240, 237.

81 P. 243.

82 Pp. 231-232.

83 P. 244.

84 P. 248.

85 *Letters,* p. 202.

86 Ibid.

87 Chapter XX.

88 *Letters,* p. 228.

89 Chapter III. Huxley's tone changes completely in *Eyeless in Gaza,* Chapter LIV, where Anthony Beavis's strikingly similar revelation is presented with complete seriousness.

90 *Letters,* p. 235.

91 Ibid., pp. 274-275, where he outlines for his father a more elaborate conception.

[92] "The World of Books," *The Nation & the Athenaeum*, XXXVI (January 24, 1925), 584.

[93] C. C., "The English Morand," *The New Statesman*, XXXII (October 20, 1928), 56.

[94] "Aldous Huxley Again," *The Nation*, CXXVII (October 31, 1928), 456.

[95] Ibid.

[96] "The World of Books," p. 584.

[97] "New Novels," *The New Statesman*, XXIV (January 24, 1925), 448.

[98] Chapter XX.

[99] "The Huxley Heritage," *American Review*, *VIII* (February, 1937), 486-487.

[100] Chapter I.

[101] Murry claimed that the portrait "doesn't seem to touch me personally," and that he did not have the admiration for Huxley that he had for Lawrence. F.H. Lea, *John Middleton Murry* (London: Methuen & Co., Ltd., 1959), p. 159. In 1946 Huxley wrote Murry that he was "sorry for some of the things" he had done. *Letters*, p. 544. Still later, however, to Mrs. Mary Murry, Huxley referred to the "gap between the conceptual and the constitutional in JMM" (ibid., p. 888); and in 1962 called him "an emotionally underendowed (but intellectually highly gifted play actor. . . ." Ibid., p. 930.

[102] Chapter XIII.

[103] "The Rest is Silence," *Music at Night and Other Essays* (Garden City, N. Y.: Doubleday, Doran and Company, Inc., 1931), p. 19.

[104] " 'And Wanton Optics Roll the Melting Eye,' " ibid., pp. 37-38.

[105] *Letters*, pp. 274-275.

[106] Chapter II.

[107] Chapter XXXVII.

[108] " 'And Wanton Optics . . . ,' " pp. 37-38.

[109] Part V, Chapter I.

[110] "Caligula," "Nero and Sporus," and "Nero and Sporus: II," in *The Cicadas, and Other Poems* (London: Chatto & Windus, 1931), are Chelifer's.

[111] Part II, Chapter I.

[112] Part II, Chapter V.

[113] Part II, Chapter I.

[114] *Letters*, p. 234.

[115] Part III, Chapter V.

[116] "Conxolus," *Along the Road*, p. 167.

[117] Part I, Chapter V.

[118] See above, p. 2.

[119] *New York Times*, May 6, 1933, p. 14, col. 1. His sister-in-law points out that "Aldous, in the persons of Philip Quarles and Walter Bidlake, reveals some facets of his own character." *Memorial Volume*, p. 43.

[120] Chapter VI.

[121] See above, pp. 98, 102.

[122] Chapter XXIX.

[123] Chapter XXXIV.

[124] Chapter XIV.

[125] Chapter XXII.

[126] Chapter XIV.

[127] Chapter X.

[128] Chapter XXXIV.

[129] *The Collected Letters of D. H. Lawrence*, II, ed. Harry T. Moore (New York: The Viking Press, 1962), p. 1049.

[130] Chapter XXVI.

[131] *Letters*, p. 324.

[132] "The Rest is Silence," pp. 19-20.

[133] *Rococo to Cubism in Art and Literature* (New York: Random House, Inc., 1963), pp. 296-299.

[134] Ibid., p. 298.

4. Life-Worshipper and Pyrrhonist: *Do What You Will* and *Brave New World*

[1] "Vanity Fair Up-to-Date," *The New Republic*, LVII (December 5, 1928), 75-76.

[2] *D. H. Lawrence* (New York: Duell, Sloan and Pearce, 1950), p. 371.

[3] *Letters*, p. 187.

[4] Ibid., p. 332.

[5] Reprinted in *The Collected Letters of D. H. Lawrence*, II, p. 1248.

[6] Ibid., p. 1264.

[7] Ibid., p. 1252.

[8] "Fashions in Love," *Vanity Fair*, XXIII (September, 1924), 32, 92, reprinted in *Do What You Will* (London: Chatto & Windus, 1929). Collected Edition (London: Chatto & Windus, 1956), p. 139.

[9] Ibid., pp. 134, 139-140.

[10] Ibid., pp. 140-141.

[11] "Pascal," pp. 276-279.

[12] *Letters,* p. 61.

[13] "Pascal," pp. 282-283.

[14] "One and Many," p. 1.

[15] Ibid., pp. 11-14.

[16] Ibid., p. 50.

[17] Ibid., pp. 41-45.

[18] Ibid., pp. 15-18. In a particularly disturbing passage (p. 18), Huxley invites us to wish that the Jews had remained "not forty, but four thousand years in their repulsive wilderness."

[19] *History of the People of Israel,* I, trans. C. B. Pitman (London: Chapman & Hall, 1888), p. xi.

[20] "Wordsworth in the Tropics," p. 119.

[21] Ibid., pp. 113-114.

[22] Ibid., pp. 119-120.

[23] "Swift," p. 99.

[24] "Baudelaire," p. 193.

[25] Ibid., pp. 199-202.

[26] Ibid., p. 198.

[27] "Pascal," pp. 235, 237.

[28] Ibid., pp. 241-243.

[29] Ibid., pp. 260-261.

[30] Ibid., p. 271.

[31] Ibid., pp. 250-254.

[32] Ibid., p. 234.

[33] Ibid., p. 235.

[34] *Collected Letters,* II, p. 1125.

[35] Ibid., p. 1127.

[36] Ibid., p. 1125.

[37] Ibid., p. 1209.

[38] Ibid., p. 1096.

[39] Ibid., p. 1123.

[40] Though Lawrence in one letter prefers the "pagan many gods" to the "Jewish monotheistic string," (ibid., p. 796) he urges the same correspondent "to find a centre, a focal point within . . . of real at-one-ness." Ibid., p. 1031. Lawrence admits conflict in the form of polarities (see, for example, Graham Hough, *The Dark Sun* (New York: G. P. Putnam's Sons, 1959), pp. 222-230, but does not believe in being different selves "by turns."

[41] Right after Lawrence's death, Huxley thought of Lawrence as a "queer devil," with "many charming and beautiful things" about him, along with much that "wasn't sympathetic." *Letters,* p. 335.

[42] Though Huxley did not totally abandon the form, *The Collected Short Stories* contains nothing after *Brief Candles.*

[43] *The World of Light* (London: Chatto & Windus, 1931). Reprinted in *Verses & a Comedy.*

[44] Ross Parmenter, "Huxley at Forty-Three," *Saturday Review of Literature,* XVII (March 19, 1938), 10.

[45] In spite of the fact that in the *Letters,* p. 338, Huxley indicates that he based the story on an incident recorded by Chateaubriand, and admits only envy and fascination.

[46] *Vulgarity in Literature* (London: Chatto & Windus, 1930). Reprinted in *Music at Night,* p. 248.

[47] Ibid., p. 270.

[48] Ibid., pp. 294-298.

[49] Ibid., pp. 260-265.

[50] Ibid., pp. 265-267.

[51] Ibid., p. 288.

[52] Ibid., p. 286.

[53] Ibid., p. 287.

[54] Ibid., p. 293.

[55] "Beliefs and Actions," pp. 104-105.

[56] " 'And Wanton Optics . . . ,' " p. 38.

[57] "Belief and Actions," p. 98.

[58] "Meditation on the Moon," p. 70.

[59] "On the Charms of History and the Future of the Past," p. 131.

[60] "To the Puritan All Things Are Impure," pp. 159-160.

[61] "Selected Snobberies," p. 199.

[62] "Foreheads Villainous Low," pp. 185-186.

[63] Foreword to *Brave New World.* Collected Edition (London: Chatto & Windus, 1950), p. viii.

[64] Chapter XVI.

[65] Chapter XVII.

[66] Sir Julian Huxley says that Aldous did not go to him for the "biological facts and ideas" of the novel, but got them from his own reading and "occasional discussions with me and a few other biologists, from which we profited as much as he." *Memorial Volume,* p. 22.

[67] The Huxley of 1946 has already published *The Perennial Philosophy* and suggests its ideas as a third alternative to the "insanity" of the super-

civilized world and the "lunacy" embodied in the primitive religion of the Savage's Indian village. Foreword to *Brave New World*, pp. vii-viii.

[68] *Letters*, p. 348.

[69] William Spanos, to whom I am indebted for this idea, hints at the analogy between Mustapha Mond and the Grand Inquisitor, with *Brave New World* an existentialist retelling of Dostoyevsky's tale. *A Casebook on Existentialism* (New York: Thomas Y. Crowell Co., 1966), pp. 4, 13.

[70] *Man in the Modern Age* (Garden City, N. Y.: Doubleday & Company, Inc., 1957), p. 3.

[71] Ibid., p. 160.

[72] Ibid., p. 194.

5. Existence, Essence and Pacifism: *Texts and Pretexts* to *Eyeless in Gaza*

[1] *New York Times*, November 28, 1936, p. 3, col. 4.

[2] Ibid. See also Sybil Morrison, *I Renounce War* (London: Sheppard Press, 1962), pp. 10-11.

[3] Julian Huxley says that Aldous "first overcame his resistance to speaking in public in 1935 . . . in a lecture on Peace and Internationalism. . . ." *Memorial Volume*, p. 23.

[4] "Shakespeare and Religion," ibid., p. 175.

[5] *Texts and Pretexts* (London: Chatto & Windus, 1932). Collected Edition (London: Chatto & Windus, 1959), pp. 1-3.

[6] *Letters*, p. 365.

[7] *Texts and Pretexts*, p. 15.

[8] P. 40.

[9] P. 68.

[10] Pp. 33-34.

[11] P. 168.

[12] P. 39.

[13] "Primitive Peoples," *The New Republic*, LXXIX (June 20, 1934), 160.

[14] "Huxley in the Tropics," *The Nation*, CXXXVIII (May 16, 1934), 568-569.

[15] *Beyond the Mexique Bay* (London: Chatto & Windus, 1934). Collected Edition (London: Chatto & Windus, 1950), p. 245.

[16] P. 292.

[17] P. 74.

[18] Pp. 85-86.

[19] P. 207.

[20] P. 83.

[21] Pp. 314-315.

[22] "Justifications," *The Olive Tree, and Other Essays* (London: Chatto & Windus, 1936). Collected Edition (London: Chatto & Windus, 1960), p. 155.

[23] "Writers and Readers," pp. 14-15.

[24] "Words and Behaviour," pp. 83-84.

[25] R. Ellis Roberts, *H. R. L. Sheppard* (London: John Murray, 1942), pp. 89-90.

[26] Ibid., p. 277 and Morrison, p. 36.

[27] Morrison, pp. 1 and 10.

[28] *New York Times,* November 28, 1936, p. 3, col. 4.

[29] *An Encyclopaedia of Pacifism,* ed. Aldous Huxley (London: Chatto & Windus, 1937), p. 46.

[30] Pp. 12, 25.

[31] P. 72.

[32] P. 4.

[33] Pp. 80-81.

[34] *We're Not Going to Do Nothing* (London: Left Review, 1936). Huxley then responded to Lewis in a personal letter of January 8, 1937. *Aldous Huxley at UCLA,* p. 13.

[35] D. S. Savage, George Woodcock, Alex Comfort, and George Orwell, "Pacifism and the War," *Partisan Review,* IX (September-October, 1942), 421.

[36] *New York Times,* February 7, 1937, p. 39, col. 6.

[37] A sermon delivered at the Cathedral of St. John the Divine in New York on May 16, 1937, has a contemporary ring: "The church must catch fire again if it is to give any service to this generation. . . . The church has not fulfilled our hopes in the world today." *New York Times,* May 17, 1937, p. 15, col. 2.

[38] *New York Times,* August 22, 1939, p. 10, col. 6.

[39] Morrison, p. 36.

[40] *Letters,* p. 365.

[41] Ibid., p. 371.

[42] Ibid., p. 378.

[43] Ibid., pp. 390, 392.

[44] Ibid., p. 398.

[45] Ibid., p. 376.

[46] Ibid., p. 398.

[47] Like Anthony, Huxley lost his mother when he was young; and both fathers in a short time married again. Like Huxley's brother Trev, Anthony's closest friend commits suicide in his youth. Anthony attends a school modeled after Huxley's Hillside, then also goes to Eton and to Oxford where he too reads, voraciously, everything. Though Thomas Aquinas, Remy de Gourmont and St. John of the Cross are in his Oxford room, a more significant parallel is his arm-chair acceptance of life-worshipping "completeness," along with a knowledge of and critical attitude toward Lawrence. Anthony is not a novelist but a sociologist, much like the next year's Huxley of *Ends and Means*. See *Memorial Volume*, pp. 42, 56, 59, 61.

[48] *Letters*, p. 409.

[49] Ibid., p. 384.

[50] Ibid., p. 390.

[51] William York Tindall, *Forces in Modern British Literature* (New York: Alfred A. Knopf, 1947), p. 210, note. Sheppard appears almost anagrammatically in *Eyeless in Gaza* in a reference to Purchas, a pacifist Christian preacher, in Chapter II.

[52] *An Encyclopaedia of Pacifism*, pp. 81-82.

[53] Chapter II.

[54] *Letters*, p. 400.

[55] F. Matthias Alexander, *The Use of the Self* (London: Methuen & Co., Ltd., n.d.), pp. 6-36.

[56] Alexander's techniques, however, are actively being used in certain schools for the training of actors.

[57] "End-Gaining and Means-Whereby," *The Saturday Review of Literature*, XXIV (October 25, 1941), 5. A review of *The Universal Constant in Living*.

[58] Chapter XXIII.

[59] Chapter XIII.

[60] *Beyond the Mexique Bay*, p. 7.

[61] Chapter X.

[62] Chapter XII.

[63] (1) Chapters I, III, VIII and XII, all dated August 30, 1933, deal with Anthony and Helen Ledwidge on the roof; Chapters XXI, XXVI, XXXI, XXXVII, XLI, XLVII, XLIX, LI, LIII, LIV, with various dates from August 31, 1933, to February 23, 1935, are about Anthony's trip to Mexico, his relationship with Miller, and his part in the pacifist move-

ment. (2) Chapter IV, VI, IX, and XV, from November 6, 1902, to January, 1904, deal primarily with Anthony as a young boy. (3) Chapters V, XI, XIV, XVIII, XX, and XXII, dated December 8, 1926, the day of Mary Amberley's party; and Chapters XXIV, XXXIV, XXXIX, and XLV, from June 23, 1927, to April 14, 1928, deal with various problems of Mary and Helen. (4) Chapters X, XVI, and XIX, dated June 18-July 7, 1912, involve primarily Brian Foxe's relationship with Joan Thursley; and Chapters XXVII, XXX, XXXIII, XXXVI, XLIII, XLVIII, and LII, from May 27, 1914, to July 24, 1914, detail the events leading up to Anthony's seduction of Joan and the resulting suicide of Brian. (5) Chapters XXV (May 20, 1931) and XXIX (May 24, 1931), the first a view of John Beavis with his second wife, the second about Helen Ledwidge just before her phone call from Anthony. The journal chapters, with dates from April 4, 1934, to January 1, 1935, are II, VII, XIII, XVII, XXIII, XXVIII, XXXII, XXXV, XXXVIII, XL, XLII, XLIV, XLVI, and L. Huxley may have evolved his structure from *The Sound and the Fury* (1929). Faulkner, like Huxley, dated his chapters, the final one the earliest by a matter of eighteen years. With four chapters instead of fifty-four, however, he exercises greater control over space and time; and the single, sudden jump backward and the shifts in point of view provide overtones absent in Huxley's novel.

[64] Chapter I.
[65] Chapter III.
[66] Chapters LIV and XLVI.
[67] In his Preface to *The Nigger of the 'Narcissus.'*

6. Reform and Sainthood: From *Ends and Means* to
Time Must Have a Stop

[1] According to Ronald Clark, *The Huxleys,* p. 242, Huxley was "moved partly by a wish to settle his son in an American university, partly by his wife's horror of involvement in another war. . . . Yet it was rather bitterly remarked by his critics that in *What Are You Going to Do About It?* crossing the Atlantic was not among the recommended answers."

[2] *Letters,* p. 410, note.

[3] According to George Wickes it was Jacob Zeitlin who "first induced Huxley to come to Los Angeles," from Taos, where he and Maria were visiting Frieda Lawrence. *Aldous Huxley at UCLA,* p. 6. Huxley's

friend Anita Loos claims that the dry air was "soothing to his lungs" and its clarity (in 1937!) helped his vision. *Memorial Volume,* p. 90.

[4] Letter to Zeitlin of December 10, 1937. With Mr. Zeitlin's help Huxley became a script-writer in Hollywood (*Aldous Huxley at UCLA,* pp. 6-7), but at this point is ready to return if a scenario is not accepted. Ibid., p. 15.

[5] Clark, p. 287.

[6] *New York Times,* April 13, 1937, p. 23, col. 2; and December 12, 1937, Sec. I, p. 45, col. 2.

[7] *Ends and Means* (London: Chatto & Windus, 1937). Collected Edition (London: Chatto & Windus, 1957), pp. 129-137.

[8] P. 151.

[9] P. 159.

[10] P. 9.

[11] P. 59.

[12] "Mirage in the Waste Land," *The New Republic,* XCIII (December 8, 1937), 152.

[13] *Ends and Means,* p. 56.

[14] P. 50.

[15] P. 39.

[16] P. 175.

[17] Translated as *A Chance for Everybody* (London: Chatto & Windus, 1939), with a foreword by Huxley.

[18] *Ends and Means,* pp. 74-75.

[19] P. 14.

[20] "Mr. Huxley's New Jerusalem," *The New Republic,* XCIII (January 19, 1938), 315.

[21] *Memorial Volume,* p. 23.

[22] Ibid., p. 107.

[23] *American Sociological Review,* III (April, 1938), 260.

[24] *The American Journal of Sociology,* XLIII (March, 1938), 832.

[25] *Ends and Means,* pp. 3-5.

[26] Thomas Barensfeld, "Aldous Huxley's Seven Years in America," *New York Times,* June 27, 1943, Sec. 7, p. 2, col. 1.

[27] In, for example, Richard Chase, "The Huxley-Heard Paradise," *Partisan Review,* X (March-April, 1943), 143-158.

[28] *Letters,* p. 408.

[29] Ibid., p. 322.

[30] Gerald Heard, *Pain, Sex and Time* (New York and London: Harper & Brothers, 1939), pp. 258-285.

[31] *Ends and Means,* pp. 1-3.

[32] P. 3.

[33] P. 267.

[34] Pp. 267-277.

[35] Pp. 253-256.

[36] Pp. 270-274.

[37] P. 262.

[38] P. 265.

[39] P. 275.

[40] Pp. 280-282.

[41] Pp. 286-289.

[42] John A. T. Robinson, *Honest to God* (Philadelphia: The Westminster Press, 1963).

[43] *Letters,* p. 158.

[44] *Ends and Means,* p. 240.

[45] Ibid.

[46] P. 245.

[47] Pp. 298-301.

[48] Pp. 259-260.

[49] *Letters,* p. 428.

[50] William H. Sheldon, "Constitutional Factors in Personality," in *Personality and the Behavior Disorders,* I, ed. J. McV. Hunt (New York: Ronald Press, 1944), 526-549. A useful table of the three groups of personality traits appears on p. 543.

[51] See, for example, David C. McClelland, *Personality* (New York: William Sloan Associates, 1951), pp. 121-130; Philip E. Vernon, *Personality Tests and Assessments* (London: Methuen & Co., Ltd.) p. 37; Donald W. Fiske, "A Study of Relationships to Somatotype," *Journal of Applied Psychology,* XXVIII (December, 1944), 517; Henry Clay Smith, "Psychometric Checks on Hypotheses Derived from Sheldon's Work on Physique and Temperament," *Journal of Personality,* XVII, 320. In a letter to Edmund Sidney Pollock Haynes of March 25, 1945, Huxley said that he himself was "the wrong shape for a story teller and sympathetic delineator of character within a broad social canvas. The fertile inventors and narrators and genre painters have all been rather burly genial fellows. . . . what chance has an emaciated fellow on stilts?" *Aldous Huxley at UCLA,* p. 35. Sheldon told Humphry Osmond that Huxley "was one of the very few people who really understood what he was getting at." *Memorial Volume,* p. 119.

[52] *Ends and Means,* p. 232.

[53] Pp. 232-240.

[54] Pp. 307-310.

[55] Pp. 319-320.

[56] Pp. 321-328.

[57] *Letters,* p. 440.

[58] Ibid., p. 441.

[59] Barensfeld, p. 2, col. 1.

[60] Part I, Chapter XII.

[61] Part I, Chapter X.

[62] Gerald Heard says that Huxley got the longevity idea from Julian, who told him of carp more than one hundred years old in a Scots Duke's pond. "The Poignant Prophet," *Kenyon Review,* XXVII (Winter, 1965), 59.

[63] Part II, Chapter II.

[64] Part I, Chapters VIII and IX.

[65] Part I, Chapter IX.

[66] Part II, Chapter VII. As Heard sees it, men can bring about their own mutation, achieve a true revolution in the psyche. Somehow, they must bring "the constant pressure of attention up to the limit of awareness" by a vigilant, alert contemplation, where the "self-consciousness becomes aware of being exposed to and radiated by an intensity and range of consciousness completely beyond any physical experience of the self and, therefore, because of its very vividness, beyond words." *Pain, Sex and Time,* pp. 198-199.

[67] Part I, Chapter XII.

[68] Part I, Chapter VIII.

[69] Ibid.

[70] "Huxley's Pantheon," *Catholic World,* CLII (November, 1940), 208.

[71] Part I, Chapter XII.

[72] Part II, Chapter V.

[73] I am indebted to John MacQueen for alerting me to the allegorical elements of the novel.

[74] Part I, Chapter IV.

[75] *Grey Eminence* (London: Chatto & Windus, 1941). Collected Edition (London: Chatto & Windus, 1956), p. 210.

[76] *Letters,* p. 462.

[77] *Grey Eminence,* p. 296.

[78] Pp. 73-77.

[79] Pp. 79-87.

[80] P. 87.

[81] P. 226.

[82] P. 135.

[83] P. 168.

[84] P. 312.

[85] "Joseph, Father," *The Columbia Encyclopedia,* 2nd ed. (New York: Columbia University Press, 1956), p. 1023.

[86] *Grey Eminence,* p. 17.

[87] P. 98.

[88] P. 281.

[89] Pp. 285-286.

[90] P. 81.

[91] P. 287.

[92] Pp. 300-304.

[93] In his Introduction to Danilo Dolci, *Report from Palermo* (New York: The Orion Press, 1959), p. ix. Huxley sees Dolci as "one of these modern Franciscans-with-a-degree."

[94] In a letter to Cass Canfield of Harper and Row of January 5, 1958, Hugh Trevor-Roper says: "As history, I do not think *Grey Eminence* should be condemned . . . although there are rash and random generalizations in it, and some very questionable judgments." He finds the philosophical argument "thoroughly perverse and erroneous," but for that reason very readable.

[95] *Grey Eminence,* p. 265.

[96] Pp. 235-241.

[97] Wickes and Frazer, p. 70.

[98] In a letter of September, 1943 to Victoria Ocampo, Huxley indicated clearly his own belief in this principle. *Memorial Volume,* p. 80.

[99] Chapter XII.

[100] Chapter XIII.

[101] Chapter XV.

[102] In, for example, *The Perennial Philosophy,* Chapter I.

[103] Chapters XXV and XXVIII.

[104] See *The Tibetan Book of the Dead,* ed. W. Y. Evans-Wentz (London: Oxford University Press, 1957). This edition is equipped with three prefaces, two forewords, and a "Psychological Commentary" by Carl Jung.

[105] Lāma Anagarika Govinda, "Introductory Foreword," *Ibid.,* p. lxiii.

[106] Ibid., p. lix.

[107] Chapter **XXX**.

[108] Chapter **XXVII**.

[109] *Letters,* pp. 498-499.

7. THE PERENNIAL PHILOSOPHY

[1] A three-page typescript carbon entitled "Trabuco," here quoted passim, is in the UCLA collection. See *Aldous Huxley at UCLA,* pp. 16-17.

[2] See especially *What Vedanta Means to Me,* ed. John Yale (New York: Doubleday & Company, Inc., 1960), passim.

[3] Brochure, "About the Vedanta Society of Southern California." Published and distributed by the Society.

[4] Wendell Thomas, *Hinduism Invades America* (New York: The Beacon Press, 1930), pp. 73-78.

[5] Christopher Isherwood ed., *Vedanta for the Western World* (London: George Allen & Unwin Ltd., 1948), p. 1.

[6] So Wendell Thomas grants, p. 252, but elsewhere his book points out inconsistencies and weaknesses in the Vedantist view.

[7] Conversation with Huston Smith, January 24, 1963.

[8] *Time Must Have a Stop,* Chapter XXX.

[9] *The Perennial Philosophy* (New York and London: Harper & Brothers, 1945), p. 2.

[10] Pp. 2-8.

[11] "Trabuco" prospectus, p. [1].

[12] *The Perennial Philosophy,* p. 25.

[13] Pp. 21-22.

[14] P. 51.

[15] P. 23.

[16] Pp. 40, 38.

[17] P. 96.

[18] P. 101.

[19] "God's Greatest Mistake," *The Christian Century,* LXII (December 12, 1945), 1384.

[20] *The Perennial Philosophy,* p. 249.

[21] Ibid.

[22] In *An Encyclopaedia of Pacifism,* however, it is grouped with Taoism and Buddhism under the heading "China, Pacifism In," p. 17.

[23] Quoted from *The Dark Night of the Soul,* in Walter T. Stace, *The*

Teachings of the Mystics (New York: The New American Library, 1960), pp. 187-189.

24 Ernest Wood, *Vedanta Dictionary* (New York: Philosophical Library, 1964), p. v.

25 Heinrich Zimmer, *Philosophies of India* (New York: Pantheon Books Inc., 1951), p. 427.

26 R. C. Zaehner, *Hindu and Muslim Mysticism* (London: University of London, 1960), p. 15.

27 *Letters*, p. [660].

28 *The Perennial Philosophy*, p. 82.

29 Pp. 93-94.

30 Pp. 121, 133.

31 P. 136.

32 Chase, "The Huxley-Heard Paradise," p. 158.

33 *The Perennial Philosophy*, p. 65.

34 Pp. 65, 299-300.

35 Wood, p. 31.

36 Ibid., p. 33.

37 *The Perennial Philosophy*, p. 1.

38 Mary Bracegirdle's comic fear of repression in *Crome Yellow* becomes caustic irony four years later in *Those Barren Leaves,* where Filippo Lippi, once seen phrenologically as having a "bump of art," is now "an incestuous homosexualist with a bent towards anal eroticism." Part IV, Chapter 2. And though Freud is again a joke in most of *Brave New World,* Huxley referred to him scornfully as late as "A Case of Voluntary Ignorance," *Esquire,* XLVI (October, 1956), 128. Huxley objected to Freudian psychology because "it is based exclusively on a study of the sick," and because it "is only concerned with the past." Wickes and Frazer, p. 65. See also above, p. 147.

39 The most elaborate attempt at psychological analysis of Huxley through his work is, so far as I know, James Hull's Zurich dissertation, *Aldous Huxley* [:] *The Growth of a Personality,* published in part (Zurich, 1955). See also Edwin B. Burgum's *The Novel and the World's Dilemma* (New York: Oxford University Press, 1947), pp. 140-156, and D. S. Savage, "Aldous Huxley and the Dissociation of Personality," *Sewanee Review,* LV (Autumn, 1947), 537-568. All have been useful in the preparation of this study.

40 *The Nature and Destiny of Man,* I, (New York: Charles Scribner's Sons, 1953), pp. 14-15 and 265 ff. Huxley attacks Niebuhr's *Faith and History* in his essay on Maine de Biran in *Themes and Variations.*

[41] *The Courage to Be* (New Haven and London: Yale University Press, 1962), pp. 157-160.

[42] *The Perennial Philosophy,* p. 187.

[43] P. 167.

[44] *Memorial Volume,* p. 49.

[45] "After Ten Years," *The New Yorker,* XXIII (October 25, 1947), 27. Huxley reiterated the common claim that since novelists can no longer assume a "stable background" for their characters it is "extraordinarily difficult to write a novel today."

[46] *The Gioconda Smile* (New York: Harper & Brothers, 1948), pp. 196, 198.

[47] *New York Times,* October 9, 1950, p. 21, col. 2, and October 15, 1950, Sec. II, p. 1, col. 1.

[48] *Letters,* p. 545.

[49] Foreword to *Brave New World,* p. viii.

[50] Ibid., p. ix.

[51] Ibid., p. xii.

[52] For example, the executive of a state has "an almost miraculously efficient machine of coercion," combining secret police with modern destructive weapons. *Science, Liberty and Peace* (London: Chatto & Windus, 1950), p. 6. Mass production and technological unemployment increase the dependence of the masses upon the leaders (pp. 12 ff.), presumably of any country one might name.

[53] *Ape and Essence,* Collected Edition (London: Chatto & Windus, 1951), pp. 93-94.

[54] P. 138.

[55] II:ii, 117-122.

[56] *Ape and Essence,* p. 99.

[57] P. 68.

[58] Pp. 71-72.

[59] P. 111.

[60] P. 106.

[61] The UCLA Library has two typescripts, differing versions, in binders "as submitted for motion picture consideration." *Aldous Huxley at UCLA,* p. 22.

[62] Christopher Isherwood makes some amusing comments on the Huxley's desert house, *Memorial Volume,* p. 156.

[63] *Ape and Essence,* pp. 148-149.

[64] Philip P. Hallie, *Maine de Biran* (Cambridge, Mass.: Harvard University Press, 1959), pp. 32-33.

65 Ibid., p. 37.

66 Ibid., p. 16.

67 "Variations on a Philosopher," *Themes and Variations* (London: Chatto & Windus, 1950). Collected Edition (London: Chatto & Windus, 1954), pp. 1-2.

68 Ibid., p. 15.

69 Ibid., p. 23.

70 Ibid., pp. 24-25.

71 Ibid., p. 30.

72 Ibid., p. 15.

73 Ibid., pp. 16-19.

74 *Letters,* p. 524.

75 "Variations on a Philosopher," pp. 113-122.

76 Wickes and Frazer, p. 79.

77 Heard, "The Poignant Prophet," p. 63.

78 "Variations on a Philosopher," p. 142.

79 "Art and Religion," p. 155.

80 Ibid., pp. 153-154.

81 "Variations on a Baroque Tomb," pp. 165-170.

82 "Variations on *The Prisons*," p. 197.

83 Ibid., p. 208.

84 A letter of July 24, 1941, asks Jake Zeitlin to locate some rare French books he needs. *Aldous Huxley at UCLA,* p. 16.

85 *Letters,* p. 624.

86 *The Devils of Loudun* (London: Chatto & Windus, 1952). Collected Edition (London: Chatto & Windus, 1961), p. 10.

87 P. 31.

88 P. 121.

89 Pp. 132-133.

90 Pp. 324-326.

91 Pp. 232-256.

92 *Aldous Huxley at UCLA,* p. 17.

93 *The Devils of Loudun,* pp. 354-355.

94 Pp. 331, 357-358.

95 P. 330.

96 P. 349.

8. THE PRIVILEGE OF BEING: *Island*

[1] *The Devils of Loudun*, p. 104.

[2] P. 80.

[3] P. 349.

[4] *The Genius and the Goddess*, p. 11.

[5] P. 9.

[6] P. 58.

[7] P. 119.

[8] By W.Y. Tindall.

[9] *The Genius and the Goddess*, pp. 120-121.

[10] Pp. 131, 151.

[11] P. 14.

[12] P. 60.

[13] *Letters*, p. 782.

[14] *The Doors of Perception* (London: Chatto & Windus, 1954). Collected Edition, with *Heaven and Hell* (London: Chatto & Windus, 1960), pp. 12-13.

[15] P. 58.

[16] P. 16.

[17] P. 58.

[18] P. 27.

[19] Pp. 31-34.

[20] "Mescalin and Mr. Aldous Huxley," LV (April 26, 1956), 507.

[21] *Mysticism: Sacred and Profane* (Oxford: Oxford University Press, 1957).

[22] "The Author's Experience with Mescalin," ibid., pp. 212-226.

[23] Ibid., p. xiv.

[24] Ibid., pp. 21-22.

[25] Ibid., p. 29.

[26] Ibid., p. 213.

[27] *The Doors of Perception*, pp. 62-63.

[28] *Memorial Volume*, p. 118.

[29] "A Drugstore for the Soul?" *Encounter*, II (May, 1954), 76-77.

[30] *The Doors of Perception*, p. 53.

[31] *Heaven and Hell* (London: Chatto & Windus, 1956). Collected Edition, with *The Doors of Perception* (London: Chatto & Windus, 1960), p. 116.

[32] Pp. 123-129.

[33] *The Perennial Philosophy,* p. 38; *Heaven and Hell,* p. 128.

[34] P. 74.

[35] *Memorial Volume,* p. 105.

[36] *Heaven and Hell,* pp. 83-85.

[37] Pp. 89-93.

[38] P. 98.

[39] P. 116.

[40] "History of Tension," *The Scientific Monthly,* LXXXV (July, 1957), 9.

[41] Quoted in Laura Huxley's *This Timeless Moment,* pp. 138-139. Maria Huxley died in 1955; Huxley married Laura Archera in 1956.

[42] Ibid., p. 131.

[43] *Letters,* p. 863.

[44] *The Doors of Perception,* pp. 21, 25.

[45] Pp. 60-62.

[46] "Knowledge and Understanding," *Adonis and the Alphabet* (London: Chatto & Windus, 1956), p. 39. Published in America as *Tomorrow and Tomorrow and Tomorrow* (New York: Harper & Brothers, 1956).

[47] Ibid., pp. 51-52.

[48] Ibid., p. 68.

[49] As early as *Texts and Pretexts* (1932), for example, p. 40.

[50] "The Education of an Amphibian," pp. 17-18.

[51] Ibid., pp. 19-35.

[52] *Poets of Reality* (Cambridge, Mass.: Harvard University Press, 1965), p. 3. Miller goes on to discuss at length Conrad, Dylan Thomas, and William Carlos Williams, besides Yeats, Eliot, and Stevens.

[53] "The Education of an Amphibian," p. 36.

[54] "The Desert," pp. 77-78.

[55] "Mother," pp. 172-173.

[56] Hubert Benoit, *The Supreme Doctrine* (London: Routledge & Kegan Paul, 1955), pp. vii-viii.

[57] Letter from William J. Woestendiek to Charles M. Holmes, October 24, 1963.

[58] *Brave New World Revisited* (New York: Harper & Brothers, 1958), p. 4.

[59] Pp. 15, 13.

[60] Pp. 33, 36.

[61] Pp. 129-141.

[62] So, of course, the island of *Brave New World* suggests. Huxley apparently talked to Christopher Isherwood about the subject matter of

Island as early as January, 1940. *Memorial Volume*, p. 160. Correspondence in the Harper and Row files makes clear the sense of urgency which attended the composition of the book, which was slow and frustrating.

[63] Julian Huxley, ed., *The Humanist Frame* (London: George Allen & Unwin Ltd., 1961), pp. 415-432.

[64] See Milton H. Erickson, Seymour Hershman, and Irving I. Secter, *The Practical Application of Medical and Dental Hypnosis* (New York: The Julian Press, Inc., 1961), pp. 6-7.

[65] Chapter VIII.

[66] Chapter IX.

[67] *The Teachings of the Compassionate Buddha* (New York: The New American Library, 1961), pp. 22-23.

[68] Chapter V.

[69] See James B. Pratt, *The Pilgrimage of Buddhism* (New York: The Macmillan Company, 1928), pp. 240-241 and 256; and Edward Conze, *Buddhism* (Oxford: Bruno Cassirer, 1957), p. 167.

[70] See F. Harold Smith, *The Buddhist Way of Life* (London: Hutchinson's University Library, 1951), pp. 89-90.

[71] Chapter V.

[72] As he indicates in his Foreword to Laura Archera Huxley's *You Are Not the Target* (Greenwich, Conn.: Fawcett Publications Inc., 1965), pp. vii-viii.

[73] Chapter IX.

[74] Chapter V.

[75] VII, p. 211.

[76] Chapter VI.

[77] Shashi Bhushan Dasgupta, *An Introduction to Tāntric-Buddhism*, 2nd ed. (Calcutta: University of Calcutta, 1958), pp. 145-146.

[78] Ibid., pp. 159-192.

[79] Chapter VI.

[80] See "The Mandukya Upanishad," *Essays and Introductions* (London: Macmillan & Co. Ltd., 1961), p. 484.

[81] Chapters IX, XIII.

[82] Chapter VII.

[83] Chapter V.

[84] Chapters VII, XIV.

[85] Chapter IV.

[86] Chapter V.

[87] Patrick O'Donovan, "Aldous Huxley's Island Paradise," *New Republic*, CXLVI (April 30, 1962), 17.

[88] *This Timeless Moment,* p. 27. Mrs. Huxley also quotes Huxley's extended account of Maria's death, pp. 20-25. In this "touching document of human love," as she quite properly calls it (p. 20), Huxley makes clear how he told his dying wife that he "was with her and would always be with her in that light which was the central reality of our beings." P. 24.

[89] Chapter IV.

[90] Chapter XIV.

[91] Heard, "The Poignant Prophet," p. 69, *Memorial Volume,* pp. 123-124, *This Timeless Moment,* pp. 306-308, and note 88, above.

[92] Chapter IX.

[93] Chapter X.

[94] *This Timeless Moment,* p. 146. Mrs. Huxley was surprised "to find much of our lives in *Island.*"

[95] Chapter XV.

[96] A copy of the nomination is in the files of Harper and Row.

[97] See his foreword to S.P.R. Charter, *Man on Earth: A Preliminary Evaluation of the Ecology of Man* (Sausalito, California: Angel Island Publications, Inc., 1962), pp. vii-xv.

[98] *Memorial Volume,* p. 100.

[99] Herbert W. Schneider, *Ways of Being* (New York and London: Columbia University Press, 1962), p. 102.

[100] It is worth mentioning here that some "eminent biochemists" share Huxley's optimism about mind-improving drugs (*Memorial Volume,* p. 71); and that Sir Isaiah Berlin believes that Huxley "stood on the edge of, and peered beyond, the present frontiers of our self-knowledge." Ibid., p. 149.

[101] *Literature and Science,* pp. 39 ff.

[102] Ibid., p. 76.

[103] "Shakespeare and Religion," *Memorial Volume,* pp. 172, 175.

INDEX

Adler, Alfred, 47
AE. *See* Russell, George William
Aldington, Richard. 71
Aldous Huxley: A Memorial Volume, ix-xii
Alexander. F. Matthias, 99-100, 119, 176, 185, 188
Anthony, Joseph, 167
Aristophanes, 26
Arnold, Matthew, 4
Athenaeum, The, 39, 41, 62
Atkinson, Brooks, 149
Augustine, 117

Bach, Johann Sebastian, 60, 196
Balzac, Honoré de, 26, 41, 62, 79, 80, 138
Bardo Thödol. See *Tibetan Book of the Dead, The*
Barth, Karl, 117
Bates, W. H., 176, 203
Baudelaire, Charles, 65, 73-75, 80, 91

Bedford, Sybille, ix, 203
Beerbohm, Max, 95
Beethoven, Ludwig van, 60, 68-69, 114
Benet of Canfield, Father, 130-132
Bennett, Arnold, 202
Berlin, Isaiah, ix, 229
Berulle, Cardinal Pierre de, 124-125, 131, 132
Bhagavad Gita, 140
Blake, William, 168
Bloomsbury, 21
Blunden, Edmund, 90, 95
Bonhoeffer, Dietrich, 117
Bradley, F. H., 84-85, 98
Breughel, Pieter, 44
Broad, C. D., 168, 171
Broch, Hermann, 158
Brown, Harrison, 112
Buber, Martin, 145
Buddha, 46, 78, 121, 127, 168
Buddhism, 107, 127, 141, 143, 144, 147, 158, 169, 180, 185.

Index